I0125826

CONSTITUTIONAL POWERS AND POLITICS

CONSTITUTIONALISM
AND DEMOCRACY

Gregg Ivers and
Kevin T. McGuire,
Editors

Constitutional Powers and Politics

HOW CITIZENS THINK ABOUT AUTHORITY AND INSTITUTIONAL CHANGE

Eileen Braman

University of Virginia Press | Charlottesville and London

University of Virginia Press
© 2023 by the Rector and Visitors of the University of Virginia
All rights reserved
Printed in the United States of America on acid-free paper

First published 2023

9 8 7 6 5 4 3 2 1

Library of Congress Cataloging-in-Publication Data

Names: Braman, Eileen, author.
Title: Constitutional powers and politics : how citizens think about authority and
    institutional change / Eileen Braman, University of Virginia Press.
Description: Charlottesville : University of Virginia Press, 2023. | Series:
    Constitutionalism and democracy / Gregg Ivers and Kevin T. McGuire, editors |
    Includes bibliographical references and index.
Identifiers: LCCN 2023024503 (print) | LCCN 2023024504 (ebook) |
    ISBN 9780813950198 (hardcover : acid-free paper) | ISBN 9780813950204
    (paperback : acid-free paper) | ISBN 9780813950211 (ebook)
Subjects: LCSH: Federal government—United States. | Legislative bodies—United
    States. | Constitutional law—United States. | Election law—United States. |
    Constitutional amendments—United States. | United States. Supreme Court. |
    Political questions and judicial power—United States.
Classification: LCC KF4600 .B73 2023 (print) | LCC KF4600 (ebook) |
    DDC 342.73/042—dc23/eng/20230615
LC record available at https://lccn.loc.gov/2023024503
LC ebook record available at https://lccn.loc.gov/2023024504

For Brad, for listening . . .
and for students of government powers everywhere,
the next steps are yours

CONTENTS

I am a believer in interdisciplinary work. It is how I think, and how I aspire to contribute to important conversations on matters that affect us all. I hope researchers across disciplinary lines who care about government authority will find the research and approach in this book useful. Beyond a political science audience, I hope that those in psychology, law—and anyone who cares about government powers—will engage with the ideas and evidence presented here.

Every fall when I teach constitutional law, I tell my students about the sense of awe that I feel whenever I am near Independence Hall in Philadelphia, knowing that it is where the framers accomplished their important task in the summer of 1787. One of the things that strikes me in teaching that class as part of a political science curriculum is that instructors usually talk about legal theory, constitutional doctrine, and historical assertions of authority in particular circumstances without saying (or, indeed, knowing) much about how ordinary citizens think about the novel exercise of government authority. I hope the findings reported in this book help address that gap.

Another lesson I have learned is how important it is to help students see that the framers were exceptionally creative, well-informed, but imperfect humans who built an exceptional but imperfect system of government. As time goes on, that system has required, and will yet require, modification by mere mortals like themselves. Evidence here suggests citizens are open to having a conversation about constitutional change and that they can be convinced to embrace institutional change to improve their prospects. I hope that readers are inspired rather than daunted by this challenge.

This book is much closer to the dissertation I thought I would write when I entered the Political Science Department at Ohio State University than the one I ultimately produced. After all, my adviser, Greg Caldeira, whose work with collaborator James Gibson is frequently cited here, was and remains one of the foremost authorities on the legitimacy of judicial institutions. For better or worse, it became the dissertation not written because understanding how various factors influence legal decision-making caught and retained my scholarly attention. In some respects, it is fortuitous that my interest in how citizens think about the appropriate exercise of authority and institutions took a back seat for a while. This project began in earnest about ten years ago with a twin set of experiments administered to undergraduates at Indiana University. The time it has taken this work to evolve has resulted in the replication of some of its central findings and, perhaps more important, a changing political environment that has enabled certain aspects of this inquiry in ways that I quite honestly did not envision.

The first time I thought about applying prospect theory to the study of institutional change was in a Political Psychology in International Relations class jointly taught by Richard Herrmann and Phil Tetlock. I designed an experiment to see whether telling European citizens about the rights they derived from decisions of the European Court of Justice would make them resistant to attempts to curb the burgeoning authority of the transnational institution. I never dreamed I would have the opportunity to apply this thinking domestically to an established institution like the US Supreme Court. How times change . . .

So, in thinking about my academic mentors, I inevitably go back to these influences from graduate school. Along with my committee members, Lawrence Baum, Tom Nelson, and the other professors I was lucky to encounter during my time there, these scholars have powerfully shaped the approach and thinking outlined in this and all my research endeavors. I am extremely grateful to all of them.

Of course, I must also acknowledge my past and current colleagues at Indiana University, including my friend and current department chair, Lauren MacLean. Ted Carmines has been instrumental in enabling our annual team module on the Cooperative Congressional Elections Survey (CCES) for several years running. This book would not have been possible without that support and a 2016 Time-Sharing Experiments for the Social Sciences (TESS) award in 2016 for a survey project titled "Exploring the Role of Constitutional Considerations, Public Support and Personal Preferences in Citizen Assessments of Proposed Congressional Action on Immigration and Gun Control." Thanks to the principal investigators of that project for enabling this important scholarly resource. The publication of this book was also supported by a grant-in-aid from Indiana University.

Special thanks to past and current Indiana colleagues, including Bill Bianco, Vanessa Cruz-Nichols, Christopher DeSante, Mike Ensley, Barnard Fraga, Matthew Hayes, Margie Hershey, Yana Krupnakov, Abdulkader Sinno, Regina Smyth, Steven Webster, and Jerry Wright, for invaluable input at various stages of this project. I am also grateful to my colleagues at Mauer Law, including Charles Geyh, Victor Quintanilla, and Susan Williams.

Thanks to Beth Easter and Alex Badas, who both have shaped my thinking about measuring legitimacy and public reactions to judicial outputs in innumerable ways. Alex's insights and deep knowledge of the literature were especially important in reviewing some of the theoretical arguments raised here. Thanks again to Larry Baum on this count as well. A recent Indiana University graduate, Rachel Lipofsky, did the lion's share of the coding of open-ended justifications for survey participants' assessments of legislative authority that are analyzed in chapter 4. We had many coding meetings over Zoom during the course of the pandemic. I am hugely appreciative of her excellent work under less than ideal circumstances.

I would also like to take the opportunity to acknowledge the contributions of colleagues outside the department, particularly Brandon Bartels, Ryan Black, Paul Collins, Jamie Druckman, Morgan Hazelton, Lisa Holmes, Tim Johnson, Chris Krewson, Wendy Martinek, Michael Nelson, Sarah Pashak, Jeff Rachlinski, Jeff Segal, Logan Strother, Justin Wedeking, and Chris Zorn, who have specifically commented on this work or given much-valued advice at various stages of this project.

Some of the language and empirical analyses here have been published as free-standing articles in the *American Journal of Political Science* ("Thinking about Government Authority: Constitutional Considerations and Political Context in Citizens' Assessments of Judicial, Legislative, and Executive Action," 65(2): 389–404), the *Journal of Law and Courts* ("Assessing the Credibility of Constitutional Experts," 11(1): 86–103), and *Political Psychology* ("Institutional Prospects: Exploring Perceptions of Past Benefits and Future Risks from Supreme Court Decisions and Support for Institutional Change," 44(1): 21–41). I thank those journals, their editors, and anonymous reviewers for the journals for their important input to the work as it is presented here.

I am thrilled to have the chance to pull this work together, fully develop its theoretical underpinnings, and explore the implications of this research in a more comprehensive manner. I hope (and believe) the finished product is more than the sum of the individual pieces that have been published. I am especially happy to have the opportunity to present the quantitative and qualitative evidence on perceptions of government authority and expertise in one place to demonstrate the usefulness of employing experimental methods to study these phenomena. Moreover, the level of cumulative support for institutional change reported in chapters 6 and 7 reveals more than either would in isolation.

Thanks to Gregg Ivers and Kevin McGuire, Constitutionalism and Democracy series editors at the University of Virginia Press, for their help in bringing this work to the attention of the press. I cannot imagine a better outlet for this project. I appreciate the thoughtful comments of both anonymous readers who took the time to review the ideas and research presented in this book. It is much better for their input. Thanks also to Fernando Campos, senior project editor Wren Morgan Myers, and history and politics editor Nadine Zimmerli for their help in shepherding this book through the publication process.

On a personal level, I would like to thank my friends in Indianapolis and beyond for their support over the last several years, including Miki Bird, Kevin Collins, Sara Dunlap Gwiasda, Greg Gwiasda, Bonnie and Jay Payne, Tara and Daniel Simon, Jeff Hilton, Dale Hinkle, Todd Bakke, Michelle Merrill, James (Sherlock) Becktel, Christen Foege Rees, and Mark Stratton, and some of my oldest and dearest friends, Leena Raichur Bhatia, Nehal Parikh Dandamundi, Karen Jacobs, Nagu Gupta Kent, Donna Vitale Savoretti, and Lorraine Katt. You are just the best!

Thanks also to Stormy, Perkins, and Scribbles (yes, they are cats) for emotional support I could never adequately describe. To George Spelman, Janet, Andrew, Steven, Evelyn, Jared, and especially Marlene Braman (my awesome mom): thank you for everything!

Brad and Dallas Spelman, I could not have completed this book without your constant love and support. Thanks so much for putting up with me.

I

Setting Up the Inquiry

That the people have an original right to establish, for their future government, such principles as, in their opinion, shall most conduce to their own happiness, is the basis on which the whole American fabric has been erected. The exercise of this original right is a very great exertion; nor can it, nor ought it to be frequently repeated. The principles, therefore, so established, are deemed fundamental.

—John Marshall, Chief Justice of the Supreme Court, *Marbury v. Madison* (1803)

Introduction

O N JUNE 24, 2022, the US Supreme Court released its opinion in *Dobbs v. Jackson Women's Health Organization* (2022), prompting important discussions about government overreach and constitutional design at the root of our democratic system. The decision overturned *Roe v. Wade* (1973), the controversial precedent declaring that women had the constitutional right to choose to have an abortion and that states could not entirely prohibit the procedure until fetal viability, defined as the point at which a fetus can survive outside the mother's womb. A generation of citizens who came of age with the capacity to make such decisions were faced with a new reality. State legislatures could now prevent their children from having the same choice. Following the court's announcement, competing conceptions of the proper role of government were starkly on view in the evening news. Christian groups celebrated the decision as a moral victory that allowed states to prioritize the sanctity of potential life over other interests; opponents bemoaned the judgment as a fundamental intrusion into the physical autonomy of citizens and the fundamental right of women to determine their own life trajectories.

The political circumstances surrounding the court's legal decision loomed large, compounding the debate over the proper extent of governmental authority in the lives of its citizens. Today, as when *Dobbs* was announced, a clear majority of Americans support women's right to choose to have an abortion.[1] This in itself was not particularly problematic; the Supreme Court, as the protector of minority rights, often issues unpopular decisions in our democratic system. The way in which the particular constellation of justices issuing the majority opinion in *Dobbs* ascended to the bench, however, raised concerns about the legitimacy of democratic practices across all three branches of government. A combination of calculated actions and happenstance created the equivalent of the "perfect storm," giving rise not only to the *Dobbs* majority but also to important questions about the appropriate operation of institutions in our government system.

The chain of events started in the spring of 2016 when the Senate failed to take up the nomination of Merrick Garland to the Supreme Court. Republican officials argued that because it was President Obama's last year in office, it would be better to wait until after the 2016 election to allow the incoming president to select the next justice. This left citizens wondering whether the Senate was improperly neglecting its role in providing advice and consent for vacancies on the court. Numerous legal experts pointed out that the refusal to consider a nominee to the nation's top court because it was a presidential election year was unprecedented, and that nothing in the Constitution demanded this result. They argued that members of Congress were essentially depriving President Obama of his constitutionally designated authority to nominate Supreme Court justices because Senate leadership sought to gain an unfair advantage in a hotly contested election year.

This was closely followed by a presidential contest in which Donald Trump, the winner of the Electoral College, failed to obtain a majority of the popular vote. Thus for the second time in less than twenty years Americans were faced with the consequences of utilizing an electoral procedure to select the nation's chief executive that could contradict the will of the majority. Once more citizens were left to question whether the American democratic system *should* function this way, while political pundits openly questioned the legitimacy of the policy mandate given to a particularly divisive president who did not receive a majority of the popular vote.

The clearest example of how political circumstances influenced thinking about government authority and institutions, however, came at the end of the Trump administration. As a result, in part, of Justice Ruth Bader Ginsburg's unexpected death, President Trump was able to successfully appoint three conservative justices to the Supreme Court during his term. Each of these appointments was the subject of a good deal of controversy. This led to public officials, including former attorney general Eric Holder, to suggest substantial changes to the Supreme Court itself. During the 2020 Democratic primaries several candidates argued that a heavily weighted conservative court was grossly out of step with society. They advocated for changes to the institution, including adding judges to the court above its current nine-person membership and doing away with life tenure for its justices. As I demonstrate in chapter 7, contrary to portrayals of the public as unwilling to consider fundamental change to our governing bodies, these proposals garnered a good deal of democratic support.

In this book I ask two questions relevant to institutional outputs like *Dobbs*. First, what makes individuals see such pronouncements as a *legitimate* (or *illegitimate*) exercise of official authority in our constitutional system? To what extent do people's attitudes about political issues come into play? Their perceptions of the influence of appropriate versus inappropriate considerations in officials' decision-making? Their understandings of public opinion about controversial policy matters? Second, assuming that citizens understand both that the Supreme Court plays an important role in arbitrating between representative government and the rights of individuals in our democracy *and* that they will not always agree with the court's decisions, how do individuals balance the benefits and harms they see as emanating from that institution? Specifically, I explore how citizens value democratic institutions like the Supreme Court, and how such assessments might translate into support for (or opposition to) fundamental government change.

As the circumstances giving rise to the *Dobbs* majority so clearly demonstrate, concerns about the appropriate exercise of official authority in our constitutional system do not apply just to judicial institutions. I therefore explore assessments of authority and thinking about change across all three branches of government. Much of the thinking and findings about the legitimacy of institutions in political science have disproportionately focused on the courts. In this book, I outline a theory of how people think about government action and constitutional change that can be applied across different kinds of government institutions.

Politics and the Perception of Government Power

For some time, political science researchers have been aware that citizens' behavior is powerfully influenced by their political attitudes. We are motivated to support and defend candidates we like; we are more likely to agree with their policy arguments; and we more willingly accept their interpretation of ambiguous evidence and events. But in a system of limited government, thinking about questions of institutional power could and *arguably should* operate differently. There are constraints, memorialized in the Constitution, that specifically control what government officials can and cannot do; legal experts are regularly employed to help citizens understand how those constraints apply to novel assertions of authority in light of constitutional doctrine and historical precedent. Moreover, the notion that power corrupts applies with equal force to ambitious government officials on both sides of the political aisle. All this implies that citizens should be concerned about officials who seek to extend their authority beyond its rightful bounds, regardless of who is in office.

Indeed, it appears that current politics *is* urgently concerned with matters of government authority but that such concerns are largely imbued with partisan sentiments. Pundits and politicians are often quick to argue that government officials exceed the appropriate bounds of their authority when those officials take actions with which they disagree. Clearly, not all citizens perceived the Supreme Court as in need of fundamental reform or government officials as acting inappropriately under the circumstances that gave rise to the *Dobbs* decision. It seems we are most likely to believe officials are acting improperly when they take actions with which we do not agree; we are more likely to want changes to institutions when we feel we are losing ground. Politics in the new millennium seems to be marked by personalities on both sides of the political spectrum using charges of constitutional overreach to fire up their base.

In this way the interpretation of official authority in the American democratic system is akin to an uncalled penalty in a football game. Consider the infamous 2019 playoff match between the New Orleans Saints and the Los Angeles Rams. Saints fans argued that a significant rule infraction that officials failed to penalize was as clear as day when it occurred in the final minutes of the game. Those rooting for the Rams, on the other hand, did not see any violation, or else argued there was room for interpretation by the referees under the circumstances. The Rams moved on to the big game, but not without hard feelings and demands to change the rules to allow for the electronic review of similarly consequential noncalls in future contests.

These days, constitutional interpretation is a game anyone can follow. Some citizens consider the opinions of expert legal commentators that the media employ to help us understand the action, while others pay more attention to the views of their favorite cable news or radio personality. The prevalence of partisan and anti-intellectual rhetoric makes it increasingly likely that individuals will come to their own understanding of how the rules should apply. Citizens commonly perceive officials whom they like as following procedural requirements relating to the exercise of government authority and officeholders whom they do not support as flouting constitutional dictates to achieve illegitimate ends.

The Inquiry

Concerns about official authority play an important role in our current political environment that can have significant implications for the evolution of our governing system. How ordinary citizens think about government powers is critical because most novel assertions of authority are never the subject of formal judicial review. As such, the appearance of widespread acquiescence can have real consequences for the expansion of institutional powers over time, and public opposition can serve as a significant hurdle for officials trying to stretch the bounds of their authority beyond what the public is willing to accept. Furthermore, there has been a good deal of talk about changing the rules of the game with respect to how government institutions operate. In addition to calls to change the Supreme Court, there have been recent discussions about doing away with the Electoral College and ending the filibuster in the Senate. Some of these changes, such as eliminating life terms for Supreme Court justices, would require a constitutional amendment; others might be accomplished by less arduous means. Still, any major change to governing institutions would likely require widespread democratic support to overcome the twin forces of political inertia and opposition by those who benefit from the way the current system works.

In this book I explore how citizens' political attitudes and perceived interests influence their thinking about official authority, institutions, and fundamental government change. The investigation is informed by theory and research across the social sciences. In chapter 1 I set up the inquiry and develop my theoretical framework by drawing attention to discrepancies in how scholars in law and political science talk about the legitimate exercise of government authority. I suggest an understanding of legitimacy across disciplinary lines that incorporates both normative considerations and popular support for outcomes and institutions. Exploring the oft-cited distinction between "specific" and "diffuse" support (Easton 1965; Caldeira and Gibson 1992), I propose that researchers can benefit from refining our understanding of the concept of legitimacy to better accommodate how people think about individual government outputs, institutional outcomes over time, and institutions themselves. Though these assessments are no doubt related, they are conceptually distinct. I posit that a slight change of focus, from whether individuals support institutions and their outputs to whether they *perceive democratic institutions as working for or against personal and societal interests,* can have significant payoffs for understanding how people think about fundamental government change.

I begin the empirical inquiry in part 2 by exploring how people think about individual government actions. I employ the concepts of procedural justice (Tyler 2006) and motivated reasoning (Kunda 1990) from psychology to investigate how individuals think about the appropriate exercise of power across the three branches of government. Utilizing data collected from a series of similarly designed experiments administered to nationally representative samples, I delve into how institutional rules and political context shape assessments of judicial, legislative, and executive actions. I test the idea that citizens' views of the legitimacy or appropriateness of government action are inexorably related to their opinions about the issues that are the subject of that action and their feelings about prominent officials who are invoking what may be characterized as questionable means to achieve desired outcomes. I specifically explore the limits of such motivated perceptions and discuss the implications of the findings for providing meaningful constraints on government actors in our constitutional system.

Because cited legal authorities are often the first to alert citizens to issues of government power, in part 2 I also investigate how individuals assess the credibility of experts when they are told that the consensus among authorities is consistent or inconsistent with their own policy views on controversial matters. Moreover, by analyzing the open-ended responses of experimental participants who are asked to justify their views of legislative measures relating to immigration and gun control, I delve deeper into how people think about authority by exploring *what citizens have to say* about expertise, government action, and constitutional constraint in the context of contested policy matters.

The perceptions of government action I explore in part 2 are relevant to calls for institutional change because they pertain to concerns about official overreach and the extent to which citizens see governing institutions as serving personal and societal interests. In part 3, I suggest that individuals come to value institutions based on benefits they perceive as deriving from those institutions' outputs. Those who believe officials routinely violate constitutional rules to achieve desired ends are unlikely to see the governing institutions that those officials inhabit as functioning appropriately for the benefit of the citizenry. Similarly, individuals who believe their policy demands are not being adequately addressed in the current system are likely to question the utility of continuing with the business of government-as-usual. I posit that the cumulative effect of perceived overreach and/or frustrated policy expectations will be support for fundamental changes to the system because these perceptions influence whether citizens see institutions as working for or against important interests.

Specifically, I explore the extent to which citizens value the US Supreme Court by prompting them to consider how society and people like themselves have been (and may yet be) influenced by decisions of that institution over distinct periods of time. I then employ a framework known as prospect theory (Tversky and Kahneman 1981, 1987) from behavioral economics to inform expectations about citizens' support for fundamental change to governing institutions. Prospect theory suggests that citizens who think of government in terms of personal or societal losses will be more likely to take risks to try to forestall impending setbacks than those who think of government in terms of gains.

Positing that constitutional change entails a substantial degree of uncertainly, I devise a theoretical framework where constitutional change is the "risky option," compared to the status quo of maintaining how government currently operates. Using intuitions from prospect theory's model of decision-making under risk, I test the idea that citizens who perceive themselves as *facing impending losses* will be more supportive of strategies and measures involving fundamental change to governing structures than individuals who expect policy gains.

Chapter Outline

The inquiry proceeds as follows. In chapter 1, I develop my theoretical framework by considering existing research on how people think about government authority. I also outline my investigative approach and discuss why the methods that I utilize are appropriate to explore how people think about official action, democratic institutions, and fundamental government change.

In part 2 I explore how people think about the use and abuse of government powers. Ultimately, such findings speak to the capacity of institutional rules, which may not always be the subject of formal judicial action, to meaningfully constrain official actors. I discuss the results of experiments testing a hybrid model of legitimacy that considers the relative influence of *decision-making rules* and *aspects of the political environment* on how citizens think about the appropriate exercise of authority. In line with the motivation for the inquiry, I find that both rules and political factors are important to how people think about judicial, legislative, and unilateral executive action but that the relative importance of different aspects of our democratic environment varies across institutions.

Chapter 3 considers how individuals think about constitutional experts. Citing research on the acceptance of scientific and policy expertise, I explore the attitudinal and demographic factors that contribute to citizens' judgments about the credibility of constitutional authorities who express views that are consistent or inconsistent with their own views on issues that are the subject of legislative and executive action. In chapter 4, I analyze how experimental participants justify their assessments of legislative actions through open-ended questions that ask about measures relating to immigration and gun control. This approach leads to a deeper understanding of how feelings about controversial issues can interact with citizens' beliefs about expertise and constitutional design to shape perceptions of government action.

Part 3 moves up a level of aggregation to investigate how citizens think about democratic institutions. In chapter 5, I explore factors that influence citizens' assessments of the personal and societal benefits they have received from decisions of the US Supreme Court. Employing an experimental design, I ask respondents to consider how they have been influenced by decisions of the Supreme Court over different decision-making eras. My goal is to see how participants' partisanship, the time frame they are asked to consider, and the interaction between those factors influence assessments of retrospective benefits from the court. I then describe a second experiment prompting participants to look forward in time and answer questions about the benefits and losses they expect to receive from the courts' pronouncements in the near and more distant future.

Chapter 6 uses insights from prospect theory to explore how citizens think about government change by looking at how electoral expectations influence support for strategies and measures involving fundamental changes to the American democratic system. I test whether individuals who expect to lose ground in the 2020 elections are significantly more likely to endorse political strategies that involve constitutional change than respondents who expect to win elections, controlling for relevant factors such as partisanship. I also investigate how electoral prospects shape support for specific measures that involve changing powers across the three branches of the federal government.

In chapter 7, I test how perceptions of past benefits and future risks from Supreme Court outputs measured in chapter 5 influence citizens' support for change to that institution that were proposed by Democratic candidates in the 2020 presidential primaries. Overall, the findings indicate a good deal of support for fundamental change to the court. Probing the factors that contribute to such support, I explore how citizens' attitudes regarding institutional change are related to their assessments of retrospective benefits and prospective risks emanating from the court's decisions, controlling for relevant attitudinal and demographic variables.

I summarize findings in the conclusion with a discussion of how the inquiry adds to our knowledge of how people think about government action and fundamental institutional change. In the current political climate, it is essential to examine how people think about authority to understand whether institutional rules effectively constrain officials and how constitutional powers can evolve over time. It is also important to consider whether we need to change the rules to better address potential overreach and structural inefficiencies in the current political environment. Admittedly, thinking about changes to our government system can be unsettling for many individuals. As Chief Justice John Marshall cautions in the epigraph to this introduction, establishing constitutional rules "is a very great exertion" that cannot, and ought not, be frequently repeated.

Current events and recent research by political scientists suggest, however, that this might be a particularly opportune time to explore how citizens think about fundamental changes to our governing system. The events involving citizens storming the Capitol building on January 6, 2021, illustrate that even a small group of people unhappy with the way the political system operates can pose a significant threat to democratic governance. Larry M. Bartels (2020) and Matthew Graham and Milan Svolik (2020) have published studies indicating that such feelings may be more widespread. Their research details an alarming increase in the extent to which citizens are willing to endorse antidemocratic sentiments and tolerate the violation of democratic norms. Such tendencies seem to be grounded in a combination of partisan and/or ethnic antipathy, coupled with frustration over how the system is currently working. These authors and others conclude that such findings do not bode well for the future of our democratic political system (Levitsky and Ziblatt 2018).

Meaningful change, however, does not necessarily have to entail tearing everything down. While it is true that we have not instituted the sort of fundamental changes to our government system that would require constitutional amendment in almost thirty years, such change is possible. Various scholars and journalists attribute the reluctance to embrace such change to a failure of the public will. In *Constitutional Faith* (1988), law professor and political scientist Sanford Levinson argues that Americans treat the Constitution and its founders with a sort of religious reverence that prevents citizens from thinking for themselves about how to solve current problems. In a book aimed at popular audiences, *The Frozen Republic: How the Constitution Paralyzes Democracy* *(1996)*, journalist Daniel Lazare largely echoes these sentiments.[2] These are powerful arguments that can certainly promote constitutional inertia, but when these claims were originally put forth, they were largely anecdotal, without a great deal of empirical support. Additionally, the political environment has changed a great deal in the past few decades, suggesting citizens may be more open to altering our governmental system than such thinking presumes.

The findings presented in this book, particularly in chapters 6 and 7, reveal much more support for strategies and measures involving fundamental institutional change than such arguments suggest. As I discuss in the conclusion, government transformation requires political entrepreneurs who know how to navigate the system to put change in motion. The results detailed here suggest that, armed with new ideas about how government institutions could operate more efficiently and arguments that appeal to citizens' willingness to embrace risk, constitutional entrepreneurs may discover that Americans are significantly more willing to consider fundamental alterations to our system than most people expect.

After all, Chief Justice Marshall did not say the great constitutional exertion should never be repeated, only that it should not frequently be repeated. Perhaps now is a good time to have a meaningful discussion about doing just that. This entails acknowledging that it may be worthwhile to rethink how our government institutions operate. Just as important, those advocating for change will need to frame their arguments so that citizens perceive that the benefits accruing to themselves and society from altering the system will operate to improve their prospects sufficiently to justify the substantial risk inherent in the endeavor. Indeed, engaging in this sort of dialogue might be our best chance of maintaining our republic in light of antidemocratic forces pulling in the opposite direction.

1 | Conceptualizing and Studying Perceptions of Appropriate Government Authority and Support for Institutional Change

O UR SYSTEM OF government entails a complex relationship between fundamental constitutional principles and the rough and tumble of everyday politics. Citizens are taught from an early age that the judges who interpret the Constitution must be insulated from politics for several important reasons. Federal judges enjoy life tenure, for instance, so that they can maintain neutrality in judgments that might concern political actors and institutions without fear of reprisal. They are appointed rather than elected so that jurists can protect minority rights from encroachment by majority will and the principles in the document can be interpreted consistently over time, without undue attention to temporary trends in public mood.

Watching current events, however, citizens also come to understand that constitutional interpretation is inexorably immersed in politics. The governing bodies that the Constitution was designed to limit and empower are largely staffed by individuals who have gained their position through popular election and political appointment. Those officials often need, and actively seek to maintain, the support of the people who put them there. Many of the issues that the Constitution speaks to pit basic matters of individual freedom against communal will and conflicting visions of the greater good. Moreover, we know from seventy-five years of research on judicial behavior that judges are not immune to political influences. Notwithstanding years of training in appropriate tools of legal reasoning aimed at curbing personal biases in their decision-making, judges' attitudinal preferences can have a powerful influence on how they interpret legal provisions in particular circumstances (Pritchett 1948; Schubert 1962; Segal and Spaeth 1993, 2002).

As a result, interpretation of the Constitution may be simultaneously conceived of as both *separate from* and *imbued with* politics. How do citizens navigate such terrain? Perhaps at one point, not too far in our past, the answer was to leave constitutional analysis to experts: judges and lawyers trained in the tools of legal decision-making. But as Keith Bybee (2010) observes, people have an increasingly sophisticated understanding of the role personal factors play in judges' interpretations. Under these circumstances, one might wonder whether the constitutional authorities that are so often employed by the media possess any sort of useful proprietary knowledge in the minds of citizens. The prevalence of claims of official overreach, paired with increasing skepticism about the authority of experts in general, suggests that rather than defer to legal authorities, people are likely to make decisions about the propriety of contested government action on their own.

While it can be an interesting academic exercise for law professors and political scientists to think about concepts like "executive power" and "federalism" in the abstract, citizens generally do not. Instead, most people make judgments about the appropriate use of government power and the desirability of specific policy measures in the context of the current political environment, which may include partisan debates, public opinion polls, and news stories featuring officeholders about whom individuals have strong feelings. In this chapter I argue that understanding how people think about the appropriate exercise of authority is important to explore the "conditions under which" institutional powers may expand via widespread acquiescence to novel assertions of authority.

Looking at the way government authority is understood at the intersection of disciplinary fields allows us to think about concepts relating to state power from different perspectives; this can lead to theoretical insights into how social scientists study phenomena related to government and its outputs. I present a conceptualization of legitimacy that is informed by insights from law and political science. I assert we should refine our understanding and measures of the concept to better reflect how people think about outcomes and institutions in politically consequential ways. Finally, I discuss my empirical approach, which employs experimental methods and the analysis of responses on national surveys to explore how people think about authority, institutions, and fundamental change.

Conceptualizing Legitimacy

Citizens' perceptions of the legitimacy of government action is at the center of the relationship between the individual and the state. These perceptions have significant implications for the survival and evolution of government systems. This is especially true in the United States, where there is a history of the expansion of institutional powers for offices such as the presidency through public acquiescence to assertions of authority that were undertaken to address matters of public concern.

People often equate *authority* and *legitimacy* when talking about government power (Gibson and Caldeira 2009). In fact, the terms refer to distinct aspects of state capacity. Authority is the power to make rules and compel others to follow them. Legitimacy, on the other hand, involves a sense of "rightfulness" in the exercise of government authority (Tyler 1990, 2006). Generally, citizens want to be confident that *the people making the rules are the appropriate ones to be doing so* and that they are *following required procedures.*

Authority and legitimacy are, of course, related. Government actors do not necessarily need legitimacy to have authority; people may be compelled to follow the dictates of rulers who threaten them with physical force even if they do not see them as the rightful holders of authority. Although legitimacy is not strictly necessary for governing regimes to exercise authority, it can be very helpful in several respects. Perceptions of legitimacy are an important part of how citizens become positively or negatively oriented toward government institutions and outputs (Hibbing and Theiss-Morse 2002; Gibson and Caldeira 2009). Research shows that individuals are more likely to obey laws and abide by policy decisions that they perceive are the result of the appropriate exercise of authority (Tyler 1990). Legitimacy also helps with the stability of regimes. If the people see leaders as entitled to their official status, through election or by some other means, citizens will be less likely to want to overthrow the government (Hurwitz 1973). Further, if a regime is viewed as legitimate, its people will be more likely to take extraordinary measures to preserve it. Individuals are more likely to fight and die for a system of government they believe in than one they do not (Von Billerbeck and Gippert 2017). Finally, having the support of citizens can help with issues of foreign recognition in the international arena (Murphy 1999).

Despite the centrality of the concept in thinking about government and how citizens relate to the state, there seems to be a discrepancy in how researchers from different fields understand legitimacy as a result of different points of emphasis. Looking closely at how legal scholars and political scientists employ the term reveals that scholars across disciplines think about legitimacy quite differently. When legal scholars talk about legitimacy, they are largely concerned with procedural formalities, that is, whether officials are *following required rules.* For instance, in his 1964 book, *The Morality of Law,* Lon Fuller lists eight specific procedural requirements laws must meet to be considered justly promulgated and moral.[1] As Lawrence Friedman and Grant

Hayden state, "Basically, when people say that laws are 'legitimate,' they mean that there is something rightful about the way the laws came about. In other words, legitimacy is mostly used as a procedural concept—or if you will a legal one" (2017, 227).

In contrast, political scientists discuss and operationalize legitimacy primarily in terms of widespread *public support* for outcomes (Zink, Spriggs, and Scott 2009) and institutions (Caldeira and Gibson 1992; Gibson and Caldeira 2009; Bartels and Johnston 2020; Zilis 2021). Some researchers speak in terms of the public's acceptance of, tolerance for, or acquiescence to the court and its pronouncements (Nicholson and Hansford 2014; Cann and Yates 2016). The main difference is that, generally speaking, for political scientists, public sentiment confers legitimacy, rule following does not.

In isolation, neither conceptualization is satisfactory. Thinking about legitimacy solely in terms of following required procedures disregards the fact that our democratic regime and the rules that govern officials concern complex understandings of the authority of various government actors that must be supported by the citizenry to be sustainable. Viewed in this light, the reason why the media coverage of citizens storming the Capitol on January 6, 2021, was so disturbing to many Americans was because those individuals posed a challenge to widely held understandings of institutional authority and offered a glimpse of what could happen if more citizens openly questioned the right of elected representatives to conduct the nation's democratic business.

Defining legitimacy only in terms of popular support, however, ignores the normative aspect to legitimacy, which entails following decisional requirements necessary to ensure limited government in our constitutional democracy. These requirements are themselves institutions, or widely accepted norms and procedures that help ensure government and its outputs reflect the values and priorities of the people. If public support were the only relevant consideration for determining whether official action was appropriate, then Congress could routinely pass laws that infringed on minority rights as long as most citizens agreed that those laws were desirable. If that were the case, citizens' ability to adhere to their preferred religion or to voice unpopular opinions could be broadly curtailed.

I propose that both normative and popular conceptualizations of legitimacy are necessary to fully understand the concept. Acknowledging that the essence of legitimacy lies somewhere between these two conceptualizations, I employ psychological theory and experimental methods to investigate how rules and political context interact in the minds of citizens to shape basic assessments of government action. I start with the premise that there are two primary sources of legitimate governmental authority in the United States, *institutional rules* and *democratic support,* the latter of which often depends on the political context in which government officials are acting.

Each is reflected in the American constitutional system. Authority in the federal government, for instance, is conferred by constitutional provisions that grant and limit the powers of democratic institutions such as Congress. These provisions include rules that officeholders must follow to ensure they are acting appropriately. Government officials also derive authority from voters through democratic processes, including elections, by means of which specific individuals are chosen to fill institutional roles. As such, rule following and the prevailing political environment should each play a role in how citizens think about the appropriate use of official authority.

Public Opinion and Government Powers

It is important to understand the factors that influence perceptions of legitimate state action because how people view authority can have significant implications for the expansion of government powers in the United States. Legal experts and political scientists have theorized about the role of the public in endorsing measures when officials, such as the president, have taken questionable constitutional action. Bruce Ackerman (1991) posits that ratifying elections, in which the public passes judgment on presidential actions taken in critical "constitutional moments," can validate assertions of authority that may have been questionable at the time they were made. Voting, however, is a rather blunt instrument of assessment that may not reveal how citizens feel about particular assertions of power, especially where other issues are relevant in elections.

As Keith Whittington (1999) points out, not all assertions of authority are the subject of ratifying elections. Shifts in power often occur through the "constitutional constructions" of government officials as they take action that may never be the subject of formal judicial or widespread democratic review. Legal scholars have argued that the institutional capacities of each branch should guide our normative assessments of how constitutional powers evolve regarding complex separation of powers issues in both domestic (Johnson 2004) and foreign policy domains (Zeisberg 2013).

It is not clear that the public attends to such nuance in its assessments of government power, but citizens *are* commonly aware of government officials' claims to authority in response to matters of public concern. Politicians in different branches or across distinct levels of government often attempt to take action to address salient issues as a way to attract the support of certain constituencies that they perceive as important for their political fortunes, even when it is not altogether clear they have the authority to do so. Their ability to take such actions is enabled by the fact that many of the government powers set forth in the Constitution are vague and undefined (Solum 2010; Fallon 2017).

When officials undertake measures that are questionable to address current problems, public acquiescence can appear to ratify their behavior, while widespread opposition can pose a significant obstacle to state officials trying to stretch the boundaries of power beyond what the public is willing to accept. Constitutional scholars, for instance, generally acknowledge the expansion of executive war powers in this regard over our nation's history. Terry Moe and William Howell (1999) have written that ambiguity in the Constitution regarding executive authority is a presidential "resource" that chief executives can use to augment their authority.

American political development scholars who study the presidency have written at length about how executive power tends to expand in times of crisis as presidents act in response to pressing national problems (Skowronek 1996; Whittington and Carpenter 2003). Scott James (2009) effectively argues that this approach contextualizes the "conditions under which" institutional rules meet political context, giving rise to the potential for constitutional change to occur. What the American political development frame cannot explain, however, is *how various considerations act in the minds of citizens* lead them to accept new claims of authority as appropriate. This is significant because when action is not formally challenged, it is up to citizens to decide for themselves whether they think the action is legitimate or whether officials have overstepped the bounds of their authority. Thus, understanding the factors that contribute to citizens' assessments of government action should shed light on the circumstances in which officials are most likely to be successful using the resource of constitutional ambiguity.

Researchers who study the presidency have been quite interested in these issues in the past several years (Christenson and Kriner 2017, 2020; Lowande and Rogowski 2021; Reeves and Rogowski 2022). A study looking at perceptions of presidential action finds that citizens are more likely to support assertions of executive authority when such assertions accord with their own partisan preferences. In an experiment conducted on a nationally representative sample, Christenson and Kriner (2017) find that Democrats are more likely to support presidential action when they are told it was taken by President Obama and Republicans are more likely to support it when they are told it was taken by President George W. Bush. This demonstrates that partisanship is important in assessing government authority—but it leaves unclear several issues that this inquiry is well equipped to investigate.

For example, looking at "support" for action might obscure whether citizens see the policy as desirable as a matter of public policy or whether they see it as an appropriate exercise of power. Tom Tyler (1990) asserts that even if you disagree with a particular action as a matter of policy, you may still recognize the authority of government actors to take that action. In experiments on legislative and executive authority analyzed here, I disaggregate these distinct assessments of official authority. Participants are asked whether they agree that Congress (or the president) "should take this action" as a way to gauge the extent to which participants perceive the measure as *desirable,* and also whether they see it as a *"legitimate, or appropriate,* exercise of legislative (or executive) authority."

Moreover, just looking at partisan identity does not tell us what aspect of that orientation is relevant in assessing government authority. Democrats are more likely to agree with the policy implications of actions taken by President Obama, but they are also more likely to support Obama and approve of his actions generally. In the study on presidential authority, I again disaggregate these distinct concepts to test the relative importance of *policy agreement* and *executive approval* in participants' assessments of unilateral executive action.

In work challenging notions of increased emergency authority for chief executives in the context of the COVID-19 crisis, Kenneth Lowande and Jon Rogowski (2021) show that people are just as likely to support an action that is taken by the president by executive order as they are to support identical measures achieved with congressional input through legislative means. In testing their hypotheses, Lowande and Rogowski assume that procedural concerns dampen citizens' expressed support for measures. Recent studies by law and courts scholars demonstrate, however, that the causal arrow can go in the opposite direction: views of the desirability of action can influence perceptions of appropriateness. Studies by Dan Simon and Nicholas Sturich (2011), Alex Badas (2016), and Strother and Gadarian (2022) all show that people who hear about judicial pronouncements with which they disagree are more likely to see judges as acting politically rather than in accordance with legal doctrine. Again, this indicates we need to be careful to distinguish between assessments of the desirability and assessments of the appropriateness of authority in a manner that looking at expressed support for policy action fails to adequately achieve.

A final reason why it is important to understand how people view the appropriate exercise of government authority is because following rules of procedure serves an important mollifying function for citizens who may be unhappy with the outputs of institutions or the outcomes of elections. Tom Tyler has written at length on how conceptions of "procedural justice," or the idea that outcomes are a result of prescribed rules that ensure fairness and input from interested parties, can influence citizens' perceptions of authority. He writes, "People are found to believe authorities are more legitimate when they view their actions as consistent with fair procedures" (2006, 381). Studies by Tyler and others focus on procedural considerations in the judicial and legislative contexts, such as whether interested parties are treated fairly (Tyler 1990), whether affected constituencies have a "voice" in debate (Tyler 1994), and the deliberative nature of decision-making (Tyler 1994; Gangl 2003; Doherty and Wolack 2012). These studies indicate that one of the primary benefits of positive perceptions of procedural justice is that it leads to the acceptance of results with which citizens do not necessarily agree. This is particularly important in a pluralistic political system.

This aspect of legitimacy was recently tested in the last presidential election cycle. Starting well before the November 2020 election, incumbent president Donald Trump planted seeds of democratic unrest by suggesting the only way he could lose the election would be if it was "rigged" against him. When he ultimately lost the popular vote and the Electoral College, Trump and his surrogates continued to argue that the election was unfair because necessary procedures were not followed. His failure to accept the results conflicted with over two hundred years of historical precedent involving the peaceful transfer of power in the US democratic system. Moreover, his ability to convince others of the "Big Lie" regarding fraudulent electoral procedures resulted in significant discontent, culminating in the January 6, 2021, Capitol riot.

The notion that citizens' support for any individual or outcome could influence their willingness to accept the results of a presidential election so profoundly is an important phenomenon requiring serious investigation. Clearly, it involved a series of complex events that will provide fodder for scholarly research from different perspectives for many years to come. Understanding what makes citizens perceive particular government actions as appropriate so that they are more likely to accept outcomes they do not agree with is a very small, but important, part of this puzzle. I therefore start my empirical inquiry in part 2 by looking at what contributes to citizens' perceptions of the appropriateness of official action, before turning to how people think about democratic institutions and fundamental government change in part 3.

Studying Perceptions of Appropriateness and Support for Institutional Change

Investigating how people think about legitimacy is not a new endeavor. Gregory Caldeira and James Gibson have developed and refined a survey measure commonly referred to as "legitimacy," which many scholars and policymakers view as the gold standard in understanding how citizens think about judicial institutions such as the Supreme Court (Caldeira and Gibson 1992; Gibson, Caldeira, and Spence 2003; Gibson and Caldeira 2009). Specifically, the measure taps "diffuse support" for judicial institutions. Citing Easton (1965), Caldeira and Gibson (1992) characterize diffuse support as a facet of legitimacy, along with "specific support" for institutions and their outputs. Diffuse support is generally defined as an indication of the extent to which citizens are willing to protect legal institutions from external threats that might be posed by other branches of government. Specific support, on the other hand, refers to citizens' "approval of policy outputs in the short-term" (Gibson and Caldeira 2009, 39).

Since Caldeira and Gibson proposed measures to study these aspects of legitimacy with respect to legal institutions, studies of diffuse and specific support have occupied the field of political science studies pertaining to the legitimacy of the courts in the United States. The history of this research is not without controversy. Early debates revolved around how to measure each theorized aspect of legitimacy (Murphy and Tanenhaus 1973; Caldeira and Gibson 1992; Mondak and Smithey 1997; Caldeira, Gibson, and Spence 2003) and how such support is related to perceptions of fairness (Gibson 1989; Tyler and Rasinski 1991). More recently scholars have debated the role of ideological disagreement with decisions in shaping diffuse support for courts (Bartels and Johnston 2013; Christenson and Glick 2015; Gibson and Nelson 2016) and what the relationship between diffuse and specific support should look like (Gibson and Nelson 2015; Bartels and Johnston 2020). These debates have certainly advanced our understanding of how people think about judicial institutions. It is also important to recognize, however, that there is a good deal of path dependence in the way political scientists understand the legitimacy of courts that neglects the normative aspect of the construct and can obscure the relationship between how people think about institutions and their outputs (Braman and Pickerill 2011).

As with the Constitution itself, it might be time to take a hard look at how we are used to doing things, and consider alternative approaches. I suggest we reconsider how we conceptualize and measure legitimacy as it pertains to courts and other democratic institutions. This should help us clarify important aspects of the concept and take advantage of theoretical frameworks that can lead to new insights. Of course, this does not mean we need to jettison the more familiar measures or what we have learned from them, but we should acknowledge that looking at things from a different perspective may serve us better in several respects. For instance, researchers who study legitimacy could certainly differentiate better between how citizens think about (1) individual government action, (2) institutional outputs over time, and (3) institutions themselves. In the next chapter, I consider how people make decisions about the appropriate use of government authority in particular instances. As I pointed out in the introduction, citizens are commonly faced with making these kinds of judgments in our current political environment.

The extant literature is plagued with vague levels of aggregation and imprecise terminology. Both diffuse and specific support involve attitudes toward institutions over time. Political scientists have characterized specific support as involving "a set of attitudes toward an institution based on fulfillment of demands for policy" (Caldeira and Gibson 1992) and as "short-term" support for institutions (Gibson and Caldeira 2009; Zilis 2021), without saying much about what is included in that set of attitudes, which policy demands are relevant, or how long that term extends. As mentioned above, even when researchers ask citizens whether they support particular actions, responses are likely to conflate perceptions of the appropriate use of authority with whether individuals see particular policy measures as desirable.

Moreover, notwithstanding his staunch defense of measures of diffuse support over the years, in an early article Gibson stated, "It is not obvious that legitimacy can be directly measured in survey research" (1989, 487). To be fair, he seems to have been referencing the Supreme Court's ability to convince citizens of the wisdom of contested policy action, in line with Dahl's (1957) "legitimization" hypothesis concerning the role of the court in our democratic system. But this illustrates that researchers' conceptualization of legitimacy has evolved over the years and that the way political scientists employ the term has been removed from its normative roots for some time.

Legitimization is not appropriateness, just as public support for institutions and their outcomes is not appropriateness. Surely we can measure the factors that make citizens see government action as appropriate with survey methods; we can be careful to distinguish those measures from assessments of the desirability of official action. Arguably, doing so should help us better understand why people come to support institutions and their outputs over time, and maybe even how those institutions derive the persuasive authority that Dahl hypothesized so long ago.

Rather than exploring whether citizens support judicial institutions per se, as most of the research on legitimacy in political science does, my aim in part 2 of this book is to see how individuals think about government action across judicial, legislative, and executive branches of government. The inquiry includes judicial decisions, but I am interested in what factors contribute to participants' assessment of a particular decision as an appropriate exercise of authority, rather than how that decision shapes how individuals think about judges or courts. It is a fine distinction but an important one that renders widely used measures of diffuse support for legal institutions inappropriate for this investigation. Of course, it is very likely that perceptions of individual assertions of authority influence overall perceptions of (and support for) democratic institutions cumulatively, in a linear or perhaps more likely a nonlinear manner, such that assessments of particularly salient or personally relevant actions have a disproportionate influence on citizens' thinking about institutions. This contributes to what makes understanding how individuals think about particular claims of authority important: once we have a basic knowledge of how people think about the appropriateness of individual actions, we can explore whether these perceptions combine in simple or complex ways to shape overall assessments of governing bodies.

The approach also posits that we should refine our thinking about legitimacy to better reflect how people think about government in consequential ways. I have already made the case for why understanding perceptions of the appropriateness of government action is important. Here I concentrate on thinking about institutional outputs over time and fundamental government change. A good deal of the discussion about how much specific support is, or should be, related to diffuse support concerns the extent to which researchers expect people's feelings about outputs over time to impinge on loyalty to the institution itself. Citing Gibson and Caldeira's "positivity theory" (2009), Gibson and Nelson (2015) propose that individuals are generally resistant to calls to change the Supreme Court because of loyalty to the institution instilled through early socialization processes and periodically reinforced through symbolic imagery (Gibson, Lodge, and Woodson 2014). As such, they assert that diffuse support is relatively immune from intermittent disagreements with institutional outputs and that researchers who find that ideological disagreement detracts from institutional loyalty to the Supreme Court often conflate specific support with diffuse support by utilizing flawed measures. Some of those researchers have responded that treating ideological opposition to outputs as wholly distinct from diffuse support does not allow for the possibility that one can erode the other (Christenson and Glick 2019; Bartels and Johnston 2020, 36–59).

Somewhat separate from this ongoing debate, I assert here that existing approaches focusing on diffuse and specific support for institutions may not adequately reflect how citizens think about fundamental change to governing bodies. When contemplating alterations to democratic institutions, people are likely to consider whether those bodies serve important interests. Consequently, we should shift our thinking about these matters from whether people support institutions and their outputs over time to whether citizens *perceive institutions as functioning to provide benefits or cause harm to themselves and society.*

To be clear, these concepts are very likely to be connected. People who approve of the outputs of the Supreme Court are more likely to see the court as providing personal and societal benefits than are citizens who do not approve of its outputs. But even if you do not agree with outcomes, you may still see the court as providing benefits to society in that it protects important minority rights and checks the actions of other branches of government. This demonstrates that support for outcomes is theoretically distinct from perceived benefits. Moreover, this shift in thinking from support for institutions and their outcomes to perceived benefits from institutions allows us to make informed predictions about citizens' level of support for change to governing bodies by taking advantage of prospect theory, a theoretical framework developed by Amos Tversky and Daniel Kahneman (1981, 1987).

Prospect theory is a model of "decision under risk." Very briefly, it posits that when faced with risky decisions, people are likely to consider how they are currently faring with respect to the status quo. If individuals see themselves as receiving benefits in the current system, they are characterized as thinking in the "domain of gains" and are likely to resist taking chances that could interfere with those gains. If, on the other hand, they see themselves as losing ground, they are thinking in the "domain of losses" and so are more likely to choose risky options to try to prevent setbacks.

Positing that change to governing institutions is a risky decision because it involves a good deal of uncertainty in terms of (1) what political conditions may be in the future and (2) how changes will actually operate when they are implemented, I suggest that insights from prospect theory can help us predict whether citizens are likely to support changes to democratic institutions depending on how individuals perceive themselves as faring with respect to those bodies. Those who feel that they are benefiting from institutional outputs or think they are likely to benefit in the future will resist change, while those who feel that they are losing ground or facing impending losses should be more likely to support proposals for change.

There are several benefits to using this approach to thinking about support for change to democratic institutions such as the Supreme Court. First, prospect theory is intentionally subjective; it takes account of individual perceptions of how decision-makers see themselves as faring with regard to prevailing conditions. This means researchers do not have to make broad assumptions about what aspects of institutions citizens value most. Gibson and Caldeira's positivity theory implicitly presumes that people continue to support the Supreme Court's institutional integrity because the benefits that individuals understand they receive from the court through early socialization experiences generally outweigh momentary losses they perceive as coming from decisions with which they disagree. But even Gibson and Nelson acknowledge that for some citizens, ideological disagreement can have an impact on diffuse support (2015, 173). Obviously, this makes sense, but the point at which such erosion occurs is likely to be different for everyone. Theoretically one may conceptualize this as an individual "tipping point" at which people no longer believe that the benefits they get from the court as it is currently structured outweigh the losses the institution's outputs are causing themselves and society.

Viewed in this light, support for institutional change may stem from a number of disappointing outcomes over time or from one very impactful pronouncement. As Michael Zilis (2021) demonstrates, for some people it may be prompted by the perception that the court is making decisions that negatively affect relevant group interests. At the same time, just as positivity theory predicts, other individuals will likely deem the role that the court plays in protecting rights and checking other branches as paramount, such that they will always feel that they receive more benefits than losses from the institution. Asking people how they are influenced by decisions of the court, as I do in chapter 5, allows individuals to make that judgment *for themselves* in light of prevailing conditions and considering outputs they deem relevant to making that judgment. Another advantage of this approach is that by directing people's attention to impacts from past and future court eras, we can explore how different political conditions and levels of uncertainty influence their assessments of perceived benefits.

Theorizing about support for fundamental change in this way also allows us to think about support for change across different types of government institutions. Notwithstanding the fact that citizens' thinking about the legitimacy of governing bodies should certainly apply to executive and legislative institutions, conceptions of specific and diffuse support have been disproportionately applied to courts. The well-worn measure of diffuse support in the literature is court specific in that it asks about people's willingness to protect judicial bodies from threats to their institutional integrity. This make some sense as courts are particularly vulnerable in our democratic system. But researchers have been hard-pressed to translate how diffuse support may be expressed for other governing bodies in our constitutional system. Thinking about institutions in terms of perceived benefits can apply broadly to other branches of government, helping to shed light on how people think about fundamental alterations to executive and legislative structures. In chapter 6 I explicitly explore how perceived benefits, derived from electoral expectations, influence citizens' support for institutional change to Congress and the presidency.

A final concern about existing measures of legitimacy involves how well the theoretical construct captures citizens' willingness to entertain concrete proposals to alter government institutions. This is a rather important point because the measure of diffuse support has always been conceptualized as demonstrating citizens' willingness to protect the court from institutional threats posed by other branches. Several of the questions that constitute the diffuse support measure prompt respondents to engage in a kind of thought experiment, asking what the appropriate response should be if certain decision-making patterns were evident on the court.[2]

Badas (2019a) calls into question how well the prevailing measure of diffuse support captures citizens' propensity to back specific suggestions to change the Supreme Court in light of Republican proposals to alter that institution at the start of the last decade. Comparing predictions of the commonly utilized measure of diffuse support for the Supreme Court (Gibson, Caldeira, and Spence 2003) with a scale utilizing questions that ask about citizens' support for strategies to change the court that were similar to changes suggested by Republican politicians, Badas (2019a) finds that diffuse support underestimates people's willingness to support changes to the institution compared to his "applied legitimacy" measure. He concludes that diffuse support undervalues citizens' readiness to "punish" justices for decisions that are ideologically at odds with their preferences.

Ironically, diffuse support itself cannot be used to gauge citizens' support for concrete proposals to change the Supreme Court because the measure was specifically developed to approximate such attitudes. The two concepts are so closely related that in analytical terms they are considered endogenous, and it would be inappropriate to have one predict the other. It is important to acknowledge that thirty years ago, when Caldeira and Gibson (1992) first conceptualized the measure, there was no real credible threat to the institutional integrity of the court. Indeed, it is only quite recently that suggestions to change the court have gained prevalence in political discourse such that they have entered popular awareness. Arguably the last time there was such a threat was during Roosevelt's court-packing plan in 1930s. Thus, under the circumstances, the best measure of the sort of loyalty to the institution Caldeira and Gibson sought to explore was necessarily hypothetical.

Recent developments, however, provide a unique opportunity to realistically investigate what has been an extremely influential, but entirely theoretical, construct over the past thirty years. Like Badas (2019a), in the part of this inquiry that explores citizens' willingness to support proposals to alter the Supreme Court, I am interested in individuals' thinking about concrete proposals to change that institution. In contrast to Badas, the suggestions for institutional change that I investigate were being championed by Democratic politicians during the 2020 primary season rather than the proposals Republicans proffered several years earlier. The survey items I utilize were specifically drafted to take advantage of recent debates about whether and how to change the court, considering those proposals. It is also worth noting that my approach does not necessarily entail citizens wanting to "punish" judges for ideological incongruence; instead, I posit that citizens support change to make institutions work better for themselves and society. In this way, it is more forward- than backward-looking or retributive. Even where retrospective evaluations are relevant to the investigation, my approach conceives of support for change as an effort to improve the future prospects of citizens and society rather than an attempt to discipline past or current officeholders.

A Word about Methods

In light of the various concerns I have raised pertaining to the conceptualization and study of citizens' thinking about government action, institutions, and support for change, I proceed with an empirical investigation aiming to address some of these issues. How we understand complex concepts like legitimacy and conceive of support for fundamental government change is especially important for empirical researchers seeking to explore how people think about political institutions. Once we make the case for understanding why a construct is important, we need to break it down into its component parts to test the relative influence of different factors on how citizens relate to government entities. Experiments provide a powerful way to examine how people understand the political world in which they are embedded.

As with all empirical studies, the research reported in this book involves a choice about how to investigate the way citizens think about government. Critically, the choice of method should be driven most powerfully by the questions we are trying to explore. Here I use a combination of experimental methods and quantitative and qualitative survey analyses to understand how citizens think about authority and institutional change in the context of current political debates. The utilization of experimental techniques in national surveys allows the manipulation of theoretically relevant factors in the context of current political matters that citizens hear and think about in their everyday lives. By exploring the influence of these factors under different counterfactual conditions, we can observe the relative importance of each in citizens' assessments of the appropriateness of official authority. Moreover, analyzing how people justify those responses reveals a great deal about how people use information from cited experts and how they understand specific constitutional provisions that relate to matters of official authority.

Of course, experiments are not the only way to way to explore how individuals think about assertions of state power. Alternative approaches might involve asking individuals about specific measures taken by government actors such as the president, or about legislation passed by Congress, through the use of in-depth interviews or more traditional survey methods. Each of these approaches has its advantages and disadvantages. Interviews would provide a rich understanding of how citizens think about particular assertions of state authority, but good, in-depth interviews are expensive and time-consuming to conduct. As a result, researchers who utilize interview techniques must generally limit themselves to a manageable number of research participants. It is an exceedingly difficult task to make confident generalizations about how citizens in general think about government from a small population of interviewees. Moreover, teasing out commonalities and differences in perceptions and, more important for this sort of investigation, what drives those similarities and discrepancies, critically depends on the skills of the researcher. Although I do not employ them here, for researchers who are well versed in qualitative methods, in-depth interviews would be a powerful tool to conduct this kind of inquiry.

Utilizing survey techniques allows researchers to explore the responses of a larger swath of the population. With modern statistical analyses we can be more confident about generalizations crafted from the responses of survey participants. Surveys, however, can also be expensive—especially those employing nationally representative samples. Moreover, asking people how they feel about government action that has already occurred does not provide the counterfactual leverage that is so important to infer causality about the role of particular aspects of the political environment in shaping assessments of official behavior. For instance, a survey that asks citizens how they feel about President Biden reinstating the DREAMers program, providing undocumented individuals who were born in the United States with a path to citizenship as long as they meet certain requirements, is offered in the context of widespread democratic support for that program.[3] It is difficult to know what role that level of support plays in individual assessments of the policy without some point of comparison. Indeed, to understand the extent to which public support influences assessments of President Biden's decision to reinstate the program, among the many other relevant factors that might influence such assessments, one would have to possess some idea of how survey participants would respond if public opinion were otherwise, such that a majority of citizens opposed the exact same program. Obviously, this is impossible to ascertain using traditional survey techniques because history happens only one way; in our current political climate most Americans support the DREAMers program.

Experimental methods allow researchers to alter theoretically relevant aspects of the decision environment to observe the influence of those factors under various counterfactual conditions. By comparing how individuals assess the same assertion of authority when some experimental participants are told most people support that action and other participants are told most people oppose it, we can compare how people with similar and different views assess that action in each counterfactual circumstance. This allows empirical researchers to isolate and evaluate the impact of public support on citizens' assessments of official action. As long as participants are randomly assigned to counterfactual conditions, we can be confident that differences across experimental groups are the result of manipulations and are not attributable to other factors because any potentially confounding influences should be equally distributed across conditions. Experiments have a good deal of internal validity, which means that when researchers identify significant differences between treatment groups, they can be relatively confident that those differences are attributable to aspects of the decision environment that were varied across conditions.

Further, when experimental methods are combined with the benefits of applying modern survey techniques to national samples, researchers can have a good deal of confidence generalizing findings to larger populations. The ability to infer that findings apply to individuals and situations other than those specifically employed in research scenarios relates to the external validity of research. As a result, studies that involve experiments that are conducted on nationally representative samples randomly assigned to counterfactual conditions have a good deal of internal and external validity (Mutz 2011). The experiments I analyze in this book exploring how individuals assess constitutional expertise and authority across the three branches of government were all conducted using national samples from surveys commonly used in political science research.

Another consideration in evaluating research involves the extent to which results are replicable across research situations. This involves the reliability of findings over time and theoretically relevant circumstances. The replication of results across studies can contribute to the confidence researchers have that they have identified relevant features of the environment that influence the phenomena they are interested in understanding—and that their results are not just a fluke, or limited to the circumstances prevailing in particularized investigations. Part of the reason for testing assessments of authority across the different branches of government in chapter 2 is to observe the general applicability of rules and features of the political environment in assessments of government action. It may be that some aspects of the democratic context are important for judging the appropriateness of actions of some government officials but not others. Looking at whether findings replicate across scenarios involving different institutions helps reveal these patterns.

Moreover, the experiments testing assessments of judicial authority and unilateral executive authority were purposefully designed to be quite like those in previous studies looking at assessments of the authority of those officials that were conducted using different issues and different types of experimental populations (Braman and Easter 2014; Braman 2016). That studies were conducted across time, issues, and (in the case of executive authority) presidential administrations allows greater confidence in results when the findings are similar. As one might expect, there are also differences across samples and with respect to distinct democratic institutions. I am careful to note these differences as well, particularly where they are theoretically relevant.

The experiments detailed in part 2 also provide a window for exploring how people think about constitutional expertise and justify their assessments of government authority. I take up these issues in chapters 3 and 4, respectively. In chapter 3, I explore why participants assigned to different conditions choose to credit or discredit the experts cited in experimental scenarios. In chapter 4, I consider responses to open-ended questions that ask individuals to justify why they think legislative action on immigration and gun control is or is not desirable and/or appropriate. The examination provides additional insight into how people think about expertise and government authority in the context of contested policy matters where we have some control over the information given to participants.

Turning to how people think about institutions and fundamental government change in part 3, I argue that people come to value institutions such as the Supreme Court in terms of benefits they perceive themselves and society to be receiving from the court's outputs. In chapter 5, I again use experimental methods to test how past decision-making legacies, and different levels of uncertainty about the future, can influence citizens' assessment of retrospective benefits and prospective risks from Supreme Court decisions.

Chapter 6 details how insights from prospect theory can help us think about support for institutional change. I test the intuition by using citizens' expectations for national contests in the November 2020 election. By asking survey respondents whether they expect their party to win the presidency and majorities in each house of Congress just prior to that election, I obtain a realistic approximation of their "electoral prospects" in those contests. I test whether those who expect to lose elections are more likely to support "risky" strategies involving fundamental government change, such as amending the Constitution and holding a national constitutional convention, than those who expect to win elections, while controlling for relevant factors such as partisanship and current support for national institutions. I also test whether electoral prospects influence support for changes to the institutional powers of the president, Congress, and the Supreme Court. Chapter 7 uses an alternative conceptualization of citizens' risk domain, namely, the valuations of the Supreme Court from chapter 5, to explore how individuals' assessments of retrospective benefits and prospective risks influence their support for specific changes to the Supreme Court that were proposed during the 2020 election cycle.

The combination of experimental methods, statistical survey analysis, and qualitative techniques that I use in the inquiry are intended to help us understand how citizens think about official authority, institutions, and fundamental government change across all three branches of government. In the chapters that follow, I go into more detail, describing the theoretical motivation, hypotheses, and specific operationalization of concepts for each of the studies that contribute to our understanding of important questions about how people relate to the American system of government in the context of current policy debates.

II

Thinking about Government Action

There are more instances of the abridgment of the freedom of the people by gradual and silent encroachments of those in power than by violent and sudden usurpations.

—James Madison, "Address at Virginia Ratifying Convention," June 1788

2 | Exploring How People Think about Government Action

IN CHAPTER 1, I proposed that perceptions of legitimacy are best understood as a combination of how citizens think about rules and the political context surrounding official action. This means I need to isolate and measure the role of each of these factors in how people think about government action to test the relative influence of each in individuals' assessments. According to Donald Kinder and Thomas Palfrey, the disaggregation of complex phenomena is one of the most important contributions of experimental methods to the study of political science (1993, 23). I take advantage of this benefit in exploring how people think about the appropriate exercise of authority.

In this chapter I explain my logic in designing the inquiry into how people think about official authority. I outline the specifics of the three experiments fielded on national samples that I analyze in this section of the book. Two of the three experiments had the advantage of being informed by previous research testing hypotheses with convenience samples of undergraduates and workers on Amazon's Mechanical Turk, or MTurk, platform, a crowdsourcing marketplace (Braman and Easter 2014; Braman 2016). In those studies, different issues were utilized in the scenarios that were given to experimental participants. Looking at whether results replicate over time and across issues can help us judge the reliability of findings within particularized institutional contexts. Therefore, I refer to findings from those studies when discussing experiments involving citizens' perceptions of both judicial and unilateral executive authority.[1]

For the most part, findings from the previous studies are quite similar to findings from the national samples that I discuss here, but there are some differences. I am particularly mindful of how results involving the same kind of government officials may vary because of differences across samples, issues, and, in the case of executive authority, presidential administrations. But I also believe that some of the differences across experimental administrations are theoretically relevant. I emphasize that further testing is necessary to unpack what is driving observed differences where alternative explanations are plausible.

Disaggregating Legitimacy: Rules and Politics

There is good reason to believe both rules and politics are important in public assessments of state action. As referenced in chapter 1, there has been a great deal of research on "procedural justice" demonstrating that if citizens believe that government outcomes are the product of fair procedures, they are more likely to abide by those laws and to accept decisions with which they disagree. While such studies have done a great deal to highlight the importance of procedure in assessments of government outputs and institutions, most do not consider how individuals think about action in the context of *specific constitutional provisions* that empower and limit the authority of government officials and national institutions. These kinds of procedural considerations may come in several forms; I test three in the context of this inquiry.

First, institutional rules can involve appropriate versus inappropriate grounds for judgment. For instance, when judges exercise the "judicial power" assigned to them by Article III of the Constitution, legal text, intent, and precedent are viewed as appropriate grounds for decisions; bribes, which call to mind a tit-for-tat exchange that serves judges' individual self-interest, are not. Other influences, such as political contributions and ideology, may fall between these extremes, so that some deviations from judicial neutrality are seen as a more serious threat to legitimacy than others.[2] To account for this variability, I conceptualize legitimacy as a continuum for the purposes of studying perceptions of the appropriate exercise of authority in my investigation of how citizens think about the legitimacy of court outputs. One advantage of this approach is that it enables me to test how citizens view alternative motivations in relation to one another.[3]

A second procedural factor involves what the Constitution says about the relative power of national actors, such as the president, and institutions, such as Congress. Formally speaking, it is the job of Congress to enact law and the president's job to enforce it, but sometimes the line between the two can be blurred with respect to particular policy measures. Courts are commonly called on to intervene when one branch charges that another is infringing on its authority. I employ this sort of institutional conflict in this study to see what factors are relevant in citizens' assessments of unilateral executive authority when there is a question as to whether the chief executive should be acting in the absence of legislative approval.

A third institutional consideration involves what level of government should act to address matters of public concern. In our federal system questions of state versus federal capacity often come into play, especially involving salient matters such as immigration and gun control. Constitutional considerations may again be relevant here, as well as attitudes about the relative efficiency of national versus state government officials. In the study of legislative authority, I explore how people think about congressional action in the context of legislation where national measures could be infringing on state prerogatives.

It is also important to note that judgments about official authority are not made in a vacuum. We know from research on motivated decision-making (Kunda 1990) that policy preferences and feelings about government actors often influence political judgments (Lodge and Taber 2013). Indeed, a growing body of research tends to show that political factors are important in public support for institutions and outputs. Bartels and Johnston (2013) and Christenson and Glick (2015) find, for instance, that agreement with the policy implications of decisions can affect diffuse support for the Supreme Court. As referenced earlier, Christenson and Kriner (2017) find people are more likely to support the actions of prominent government officials, including the president, if those officials share their partisan identity.

Of course, merely saying that the democratic environment is important does not tell us what aspects of the larger political environment matter or when they will matter to citizens in thinking about government authority. In this book I specifically identify several aspects of the political environment that should be relevant to citizens in considering the appropriate use of authority: (1) the level of public support for the proposed action, (2) participants' views on the problem being addressed, (3) their feelings about the officials taking the action, and (4) citizens' preferences about the distribution of power between state and national institutions. I also specify alternative hypotheses regarding the conditions under which these variables might play a significant role in the assessment of appropriate executive authority. In the following section I set forth the general contours of my expectations derived from the theories and findings on procedural justice and motivated reasoning from psychology and political science.

General Expectations about Assessments of Government Authority

The logic set forth above leads to several testable hypotheses about how people think about the appropriate exercise of government authority. First, both rules and political factors are likely to matter in how individuals assess government action. To explore this idea, my approach is to give experimental participants a hypothetical article in which I alter the information they are given about official action. I also ask them questions about their attitudes about the issue the action involves and about relevant government actors to explore the role their personal preferences play in such judgments.

To test the influence of *institutional rules* in each experiment, I manipulate what participants are told about whether government officials are following required rules of decision-making. For judicial actors, this involves altering the motivation for judgments that lead to particular policy outputs. For the experiments involving legislative and executive action, I use legal experts often employed by the media to explain how constitutional provisions and past precedent relate to novel assertions of authority. In the experiments on unilateral presidential authority, for instance, one-third of experimental participants are told that experts agree that the president has clear authority to act, one-third are told that expert consensus is that the president does not have constitutional authority to take the same action, and one-third are told that expert opinion on the matter is mixed. If rules matter, participants who are told that officials are following rules should be more likely to say the government action is appropriate than participants who are told that government officials are not following the rules. This should be the case across institutions for judges, Congress, and the president.

Each experiment also employs a manipulation to test the importance of *democratic support* on assessments of legitimacy. This aspect of political context seems particularly important in judgments about the appropriateness of official action. Majoritarian conceptions of democracy suggest state authority is most appropriate when most people agree with what officials are doing (Lipset 1983). For experiments across all three branches, I alter what individuals are told about popular support for the policy implications of the action that is the subject of the hypothetical article. Half of the participants in all experiments are told 85 percent of the population support the action and half are told that only 15 percent of citizens support the action. If majority support matters, participants should be significantly more likely to say official action is appropriate when a substantial majority of individuals are in favor of what officials are doing.

The other political variables I consider as part of the democratic environment recognize that people bring their own political values and preferences to assessments of appropriate authority. Research shows that personal preferences often make a difference in how individuals assess evidence (MacCoun 1998) and form opinions about policy and candidates (Taber and Lodge 2013). Citizens tend to make more positive assessments about the performance of candidates whom they admire (Lau and Redlawsk 2006) and assess research that supports their opinions as more skillfully executed than research that does not (Lord, Ross, and Lepper 1979). This is often referred to as "motivated reasoning" because psychologists have speculated that these tendencies are driven by a motivation to believe we are correct. Making assessments that support our prior beliefs is a directional goal that serves esteem in complex ways. Indeed, this sort of motivated decision-making can happen even when people have no obvious reason for doing so.

It makes sense that these tendencies could also come into play in making judgments about the legitimacy of government authority. I measure participants' *political preferences* about the policy issue that is the subject of official action across scenarios involving each branch of government. The intuition from motivated reasoning is that individuals will be more likely to perceive actions they agree with as the result of the appropriate exercise of authority than actions that result in policies they do not support.

How individuals feel about the official taking particular action is also likely to matter in thinking about authority. This should be especially true for assertions of executive authority, as the president is a highly visible figure whom most citizens have strong feelings about (Tyler 1982; Rudolph 2003; Malhorta 2008). Thus, in the experiment concerning perceptions of executive power, I measure *presidential approval* among experimental participants. The intuition is that those who approve of the president should be more likely to give him the benefit of the doubt in judging the appropriateness of unilateral executive authority than those who do not approve of his job performance.

Finally, how people feel about the distribution between state and national authority could influence how they feel about the legitimacy of proposed congressional action when it arguably impinges on state prerogatives. Because the study of legislative authority involves state powers, I measure participants' *views about federal authority* in the experiment on perceptions of congressional action. Political science research reveals that people tend to view state and local governments more favorably than the federal government and see them as more "efficient" in terms of spending tax dollars (Cole and Kincaid 2000). We also know that, in the abstract, citizens prefer states to "take the lead" on such issues as education and crime, but they envision the federal government doing more with respect to immigration and health care (Schneider, Jacoby, and Lewis 2010). We know much less about how these general preferences translate to thinking about specific policy measures. As such, I measure participants' preferences on the division of power between state and federal authority to see whether it matters in assessments of national legislative action that is the subject of experimental scenarios.

I purposely look at perceptions of authority *across* the branches to determine whether what citizens are told about rules and the aspects of political context that I investigate are relevant across the board or are more important for some institutional contexts than others. To be clear, in all three experiments I test the importance of *rules, public support,* and *individuals' policy preferences* in assessments of authority. Participants' feelings about the president are examined only in the experiment on unilateral executive authority; opinions about federalism are considered only in the context of legislative action that may infringe on state powers.

How Might Rules and Politics Interact?

I am interested not only in which of the identified political factors are significant in citizens' thinking about government authority across institutional outputs but also in when they matter. Abstract questions about what we want from our representatives may be different from how we think about specific assertions of authority in the context of real-world problems citizens care deeply about. Looking at the interplay between rules and political context in how people understand government authority should reveal whether, consistent with conventional wisdom, citizens' personal preferences are predominant in assessments of official power or whether institutional rules may temper the influence of attitudinal factors.

Research on motivated reasoning suggests one manner in which rules and politics could interact in the perception of government authority. Psychological studies tell us motivated biases are most powerful where criteria for assessment are ambiguous (Hodson, Dividio, and Gaertner 2002); when people have a desire to be accurate, they will use the most appropriate criteria available, but where criteria are indeterminate, directional goals and context can affect judgments in systematic ways (Kunda 1990; Braman 2009). The most appropriate criterion by which to judge the legitimacy of authority is the information participants are provided about compliance with decision-making or constitutional rules. Thus, when participants are told experts agree that action is either consistent or inconsistent with constitutional requirements, we should not expect political factors to influence assessments about the legitimacy of proposed action.

Instead, research on motivated reasoning suggests that political factors should play more of a role when constitutional cues regarding authority are unclear. This pattern of results would be consistent with the idea that rules can constrain the role of political considerations in how people think about governmental authority. I refer to this as the *constraint hypothesis*. Alternatively, it is entirely possible that constitutional considerations do not constrain the role of the political variables in a manner consistent with motivated reasoning. Political factors might be important in assessments of legitimacy regardless of rules pertaining to authority. Employing experimental methods should allow us to observe which of these alternative processes is going on in the minds of citizens as they think about actions across the three branches of government.

In the next section I discuss the specific design of and findings from the experiments administered by national surveys to test how citizens perceive authority across the branches of government. As we will see, the findings are largely consistent with the idea that rules and politics are both important in citizens' assessments, but certain aspects of the political environment are more important for some democratic outputs than others. There is also evidence that rules are less important than perhaps they should be for government actors to be meaningfully constrained by constitutional considerations in the minds of citizens. Finally, the findings suggest that political considerations are increasingly important exactly where some may expect them to be, in assessing the appropriateness of unilateral executive authority of a particularly polarizing president.

The Experimental Scenarios

In designing each of the scenarios to test this hybrid conception of legitimacy, my goal was to make the experimental stimuli that participants are asked to respond to similar to information they would encounter outside the study involving assertions of government authority. People commonly learn about novel assertions of official authority through reports in the media. Current debates about immigration and gun control provide fertile ground for this kind of investigation. Political officials in different branches often try to attract the support of different constituencies by enacting measures to deal with these issues.

Questions about which branch or level of government is best suited to act with respect to particular problems can be challenging for individuals because constitutional provisions regarding institutional powers are often unclear. Citizens can find it difficult to navigate this territory, which involves complex legal doctrine and esoteric constitutional provisions. Still, people seem to understand the stakes can be substantial with respect to issues on the nation's policy agenda. How they come to evaluate the appropriateness of particular measures can have implications for current policy debates and understandings of government powers for years to come.

Table 1 summarizes the experiments conducted with national samples for this inquiry. The design of each study is purposely quite similar, though not identical. One difference is in how I operationalize the appropriateness of decision rules as a result of how individuals consume information and think about government action across the branches. In the judicial experiment, the motive for the decision (bribe, contribution, ideology, or legal considerations) stands as the operationalization of appropriateness; for the other branches I invoke the opinions of constitutional experts in manipulating compliance with constitutional rules. The logic is that citizens can directly judge for themselves what is appropriate for judges in a way they cannot when evaluating the appropriateness of the actions of legislative and executive actors as arcane provisions and historical precedents can be involved in determining the propriety of novel assertions of presidential and congressional authority. I also manipulate the direction of a reported decision in the judicial context to see how it interacts with participants' preferences in assessments of the appropriateness of authority across judicial motivations.

Each of the experiments involves scenarios touching on immigration policy. In the study on legislative authority, however, half of the participants were given an alternative scenario describing proposed congressional legislation regarding gun control in order to vary the ideological implications of the policy at issue.

All of the experiments involve a hypothetical article. Participants were not given a source for the article, but each scenario started with a date and "AP" to simulate the style used by the Associated Press news service. The Time-Sharing Experiments for the Social Sciences (TESS) study of congressional authority took place in September 2016. The experiments involving judicial and executive authority were included in the same 2017 CCES administration a year later (participants got one or the other scenario). Prior to reading the hypothetical article in each administration, participants were asked a series of questions, including the relevant policy question for the scenario provided.

TABLE 1. Experimental design for perceptions of government action

Type of action	Sample	Independent variables		Measures
		Experimental manipulations		
Judicial (judicial authority) Stimulus: hypothetical article describing state judge's decision on the constitutionality of law prohibiting in-state tuition benefits for undocumented students	National sample from CESS (Fall 2017), *n* = 508	1. Grounds for decision by state judge (law, ideology, contribution, bribe) 2. Public support for policy (15% vs. 85%) 3. Direction of decision		Policy support
Executive (unilateral executive action) Stimulus: hypothetical article describing proposed executive action by President Trump taking away federal funds from sanctuary cities	National sample from CCES (Fall 2017), *n* = 490	1. Expert legal consensus on constitutional authority (clear authority, divided, clearly no authority) 2. Public support for action (15% vs. 85%)		Policy support, Presidential approval
Legislative (national vs. state authority) Immigration stimulus: hypothetical article describing proposed congressional action restricting in-state tuition benefits for undocumented students. Gun control stimulus: hypothetical article describing proposed congressional action requiring universal background checks for buyers and limiting ammunition purchases	National sample from TESS (Fall 2016), *n* = 801	1. Issue (immigration vs. gun control) 2. Expert legal consensus on constitutional authority (clear authority, divided, clearly no authority) 3. Public support for action (15% vs. 85%)		Policy support, Support for federal authority

The main *dependent variable* I analyze in this chapter asks participants whether they believe the action that is the subject of the scenario is "a legitimate, or appropriate, exercise" of government authority. In the studies of executive and legislative authority participants were also asked whether they thought the legal experts cited in the article were "credible" regarding this question of government authority; I analyze responses to this credibility question in the next chapter. In those studies individuals were also asked whether they thought officials *should* take the action described in the article, to distinguish participants' assessments of desirability from their views of the appropriateness of the action. In the experiment on legislative authority, the questions about the desirability and appropriateness of the action were followed by open-ended prompts asking participants to briefly describe their reasoning for each response. I analyze the open-ended justifications participants gave for their assessments of the desirability and appropriateness of legislative action in chapter 4.

The appendix to chapter 2 provides the specific scenarios and question wording used in each study. In the sections that follow I describe the thinking surrounding specific aspects of the design and analysis of results across judgments of judicial, legislative, and unilateral executive authority.

Assessments of Judicial Authority

Federal judges are not supposed to decide cases based on their personal biases or feelings about litigants who may appear before them. Their authority comes from their expert knowledge of law and their ability to remain relatively neutral between adversarial parties. We abide the power these unelected officials have in our representative democracy because we need them to say how legal rules should apply in particularized circumstances when there is a dispute between litigants. The exercise of legal expertise ensures important democratic values are upheld in our judicial system, including fairness and equality before the law. The consistent application of rules across circumstances also allows individual to predict the consequences of behavior based on previous judicial pronouncements. As such, it is the role judges play as expert arbiters of the law that legitimates the distributive decisions they make between citizens. To the extent judges deviate from neutrality or the appropriate tools of legal decision-making, they overstep the bounds of their authority in our constitutional system.

Of course, to some this may seem like an overly formalistic characterization of what judges do. As I mentioned in the introduction to this book, many years of research on judicial behavior indicate that jurists often fall short of this ideal. Judges are unavoidably human. Their personal and ideological preferences can certainly shade their reasoning in conscious and perhaps unconscious ways, even when they believe they are using appropriate legal criteria (Braman 2009). Moreover, as Bybee (2010) reports, scholars who study judicial behavior are not the only ones who understand this; citizens have an increasingly complex and often conflicted understanding of the exercise of judicial authority in our democracy. Sometimes, as a result of early socialization processes, individuals see judges as fair and motivated by legal considerations; at other times they perceive them as interested policy-oriented decision-makers driven by partisan loyalties. Bybee posits that most individuals do not actively attempt to reconcile this contradiction in their own thinking about judicial motivations. He attributes the reluctance to address the conflict to norms of civility, or the notion that it is fundamentally impolitic to challenge the idea that judges, who purport to be using appropriate tools of decision-making in their judgments, may be subject to alternative influences.

Democratic theory, however, has not caught up with the more complex understandings of judicial behavior that scholars and citizens may now have. It still requires judges to act as neutral experts in their adjudication of disputes for their judgments to be legitimate. This is true not only of federal judges, who are not elected but appointed by the president and confirmed by the Senate, but also of state judges, who are often elected. Consider that even elected judges act improperly by failing to recuse themselves when they have a conflict of interest that prevents them from acting impartially between parties. Additionally, states do not generally allow officials who have not been trained in the tools of legal analysis to preside over complex civil litigation or criminal matters involving defendants who have been accused of felonies under state criminal codes.

Moreover, judges foster this conception of their own authority by writing legal opinions to justify their decisions; *all judges, regardless of how they are selected, cite legal authority to justify their decisions in individual cases.* In those decisions they never say they are deciding a case because of which litigant they prefer or because of their political ideology, or even because the decision is what they believe their constituents most prefer. It is their expert application of legal rules that legitimates the decisions all judges make. To the extent they stray from appropriate norms of legal reasoning, their authority can justifiably be called into question.

The fact that citizens hold alternative conceptions of judicial motivations, coupled with the democratic obligation of judges to adhere to the law, provides an opportunity for individuals seeking to call into question pronouncements with which they disagree. Over the past few decades, charges of "judicial activism" accusing judges of overstepping the bounds of their appropriate authority have become quite common. Badas (2016) demonstrates that citizens are more likely to see judgments they agree with as the result of appropriate legal considerations and those they disagree with as driven by more dubious ideological considerations. The clear implication is that individuals are likely to perceive judges who make decisions they favor as acting appropriately and those who make decisions they do not agree with as acting inappropriately. Research on motivated reasoning suggests, however, that there can be limits to this kind of biased perception (Kunda 1990).

Braman and Easter (2014) find that decision-making rules have a significant impact on assessments of judicial authority, but that political factors are also important. They provide evidence that political factors matter in assessing the appropriateness of some, but not all, pronouncements that undergraduate participants were told resulted from different kinds of judicial motivations. In two experiments conducted in 2012 employing hypothetical articles describing state court decisions about (1) gay marriage and (2) tort reform, the authors find that participants rated decisions motivated by legal considerations as more appropriate than decisions motivated by ideology, political contributions, or bribes. Across both experiments the relative ratings of appropriateness were as predicted; participants were most likely to see decisions they were told were a result of legal considerations as appropriate and least likely to see decisions they were told were driven by political contributions or bribes as appropriate; decisions that were characterized as being a result of the judge's personal political preferences fell between these extremes in both experiments.

Additionally, for salient issues (gay marriage in 2012), undergraduate participants were more likely to see decisions consistent with their policy preferences on gay marriage as appropriate; for less salient issues (tort reform), significant democratic support for outcomes tended to boost assessments. These patterns emerged for decisions that participants were told were motivated by ideology and legal considerations, but not for decisions that participants were told were the result of bribes or political contributions. Regardless of preferences or democratic support, participants tended to assess decisions motivated by bribes and political contributions as similarly suspect.

Although there is not much reason to believe that undergraduate participants think about judicial authority in ways that are systemically different from how most citizens think about judicial outputs, testing hypotheses with a national sample of participants, as I do here, should help determine whether these findings replicate over time and across issues. Moreover, in the previous study, participants' assessments of decisions driven by bribes and political contributions were included in distinct experimental scenarios. Including them as alternative manipulations in the same scenario involving a state court judgment about immigration benefits enables more direct comparisons of these alternative motivations.

Judicial Authority Experiment

The investigation of assessments of judicial authority entails a 4 × 2 × 2 experimental design. I manipulate what people are told about officials following appropriate rules in the judicial context by manipulating the motivation of a state judge (bribe versus political contribution versus ideology versus law) for a decision on whether undocumented students are entitled to in-state tuition benefits. I also manipulate the direction of the decision (for immigration rights versus against immigration rights) to see how it interacts with participants' expressed preferences on the issue. Finally, I manipulate the level of public support for such benefits (15 percent versus 85 percent) to see how this influences judgments about the legitimacy of judicial action driven by more versus less appropriate motivations.

For the analysis of the CCES data, I conduct a four-way ANOVA of all assessments using (1) judicial motivation, (2) direction of the decision, (3) level of public support, and (4) participants' expressed opinion about in-state tuition benefits as factors.[4] The analysis is fully specified so that all possible interactions between variables are also included. Then, because I am interested in the role of political factors (public support and preferences) across motivations, I disaggregate the data to conduct a fully specified three-way ANOVA for each decision scenario (bribe, contribution, ideology, and law) to investigate the conditions under which political factors are relevant in judgments.

Results of Assessments of Judicial Authority

In the main ANOVA, judicial motivation is clearly significant in the assessment of the legitimacy of judicial authority (F (3, 504) = 5.86, p < .001; effect size = .036). Moreover, the relative order of motivations is as predicted. As figure 2 demonstrates, participants judged decisions driven by legal motivations as most appropriate (marginal mean of 4.35) and decisions that participants were told were tainted by bribes as least appropriate (3.52). Decisions suspected of being driven by ideology fell between these two extremes (4.06). Participants saw decisions tainted by political contributions as just slightly more appropriate than those motivated by bribes (3.54); the difference between the two is not significant, although both were deemed significantly less appropriate than decisions motivated by ideology ($p < .02$ and $p < .03$, respectively) and law ($p < .001$).

The level of public support for the outcome of the decision is not significant in the main ANOVA ($F_{(1, 506)} = 1.03$, n.s.). Theoretically, there is no reason to expect that the direction of the decision or the policy preferences of participants, in and of themselves, should be significant. And indeed, neither the direction of the decision ($F_{(1, 506)} = 1.07$, n.s.) nor participants' preferences on the restriction of tuition benefits ($F_{(1, 506)} = .03$, n.s.) are significant in assessments. Moreover, the interaction between the direction of the judge's decision and the level of popular support for the outcome is not significant in the main ANOVA ($F_{(2, 505)} = .50$, n.s.).

We do observe, however, that the *interaction between participant's preferences and the direction of the decision is significant*: participants are more likely to see decisions that are consistent with their policy preferences as more appropriate than decisions that go against those preferences ($F_{(2, 506)} = 38.12$), $p < .001$; effect size = .074). In light of the high saliency of immigration issues in 2017, this finding is not surprising.[5] Disaggregated analyses indicate that the

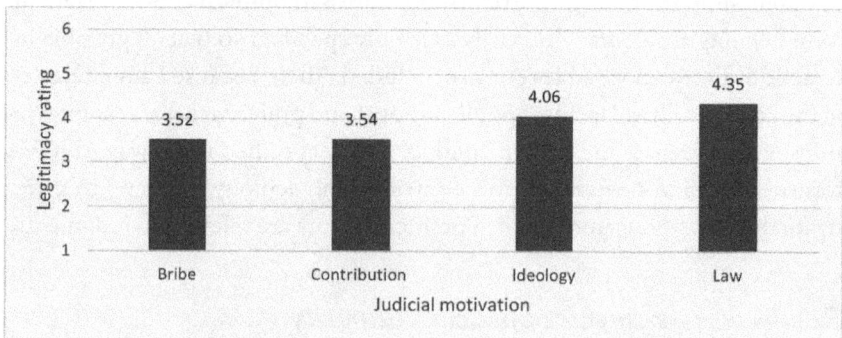

FIGURE 1. Marginal means for legitimacy assessments by judicial motivation

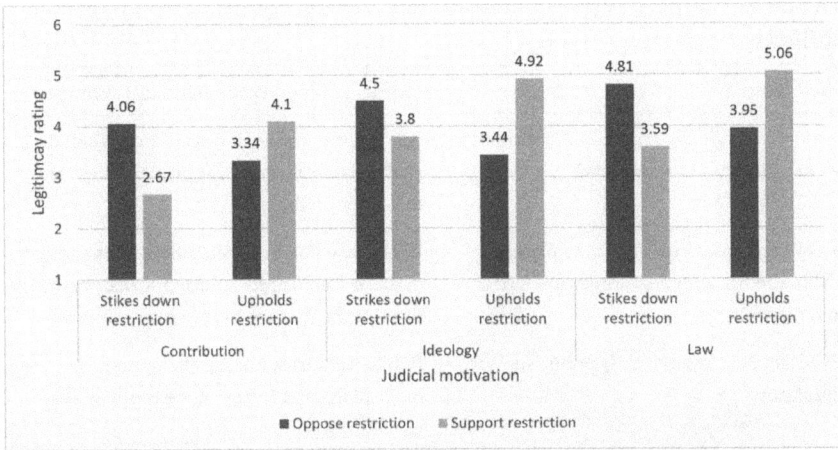

FIGURE 2. Significant interactions for legitimacy assessments in disaggregated analyses

interaction does not reach conventional levels of significance when partici-pants are led to believe the decision is the result of a bribe (F (1, 129) = 2.87, n.s.). The interaction is significant, however, in all the other decision contexts.

Figure 2 illustrates that when participants are led to believe the decision is driven by legal considerations, those who do not support tuition restric-tions are more likely to see the decision as appropriate when it supports im-migration rights than when it goes against those rights; the opposite pattern emerges for those who support the restriction of in-state tuition benefits (F (1, 126) = 11.62, p < .001; effect size = .092). This is also true where participants are told the decision is the result of judicial ideology (F (1, 131) = 16.94, p < .000; effect size = .12) and where they are told the decision could be tainted by a political contribution (F (1, 118) = 11.28, p < .001; effect size = .089). The level of public agreement for the judicial outcome is not significant for any decision category, and neither is its interaction with the direction of the decision.

Discussion of Results of Assessments of Judicial Authority

Table 2 summarizes the results of relevant hypotheses tests in the experiment on assessments of the legitimacy of judicial outputs. Not surprisingly, the re-sults demonstrate that rules matter in citizens' assessments of judicial author-ity. Of the political factors investigated, political preferences clearly mattered more than public support for outcomes in assessments of decisions involving

TABLE 2. Results of experimental hypotheses for assessments of judicial authority

Hypothesis	Results of experiment on judicial authority
Institutional rule hypothesis: Do rules matter in legitimacy assessments?	The judicial motivation condition is significant; relative ratings of appropriateness are in the order predicted.
Policy preferences hypothesis: Do preferences interact with decision to influence judgments?	The interaction between preferences and judgments is significant in the main analysis and in three of the four motivational conditions.
Public support hypothesis: Is public support significant?	Public support is not significant in the main analysis or in any of the motivational conditions.
Constraint hypothesis: Do rules constrain the role of political factors?	The constraint hypothesis receives partial support. Political factors are not significant for decisions characterized as driven by bribes, but for all other categories, preferences are significant in assessments.

the salient issue of immigration reform. Participants' feelings about in-state tuition benefits interacted with the direction of the decision as anticipated. Moreover, preferences could not boost the assessment of decisions citizens judged to be inherently suspect, those driven by bribes in this instance.

Contrary to the experimental hypotheses, participants did not judge decisions driven by legal considerations as clearly legitimate regardless of preferences. Thus the constraint hypothesis proved half right for assessments of judicial authority: although preferences did not matter when decision criteria were clearly inappropriate, they did matter when participants were told that decisions were the result of appropriate legal criteria. Although the average rating of decisions driven by law was higher than the average rating in the other decision categories, it was a mere 4.35 on the seven-point scale. Thus it seems there is still plenty of room for preferences to influence judgments of appropriateness in this category. Indeed, although decisions motivated by law were seen, on average, as more legitimate than those driven by ideology, the difference was not significant. This result is likely because of a general skepticism that citizens have about the motivations of judges even when they are told that decision-makers are using legally appropriate criteria.

Assessments of Legislative Authority in the Context of Federalism

The federal structure of the United States is often touted as one of the great accomplishments of our constitutional system. It allows state and federal officials to address matters of public concern based on the relative capacities of each level of government. Within this structure there is a division of power that is grounded in part in constitutional provisions and common law understandings of the appropriate exercise of government authority. One significant factor that can limit the authority of Congress is the distribution of power in our federal system. States have general "police powers" to enact regulations for the health, safety, and morals of their citizens. Federal authority is, in theory, limited by the specific dictates of the Constitution, but where the federal government acts pursuant to its legitimate authority, its power to do so is supreme.[6]

Notwithstanding this legalistic division of labor, most matters of public concern are complex, inviting cooperative efforts by state and federal officials. As a result, the line between state and federal power in particular policy domains is not always clear. Questions about congressional authority are most definitively answered through the interplay of legislative action and Supreme Court decisions as to the constitutionality of particular legislation. Often, however, Congress may take action that is constitutionally suspect but never formally litigated in a case that makes its way to the Supreme Court. Over time, such unchallenged action may take on an "air of validity" that has real consequences for state power (Marshall 2008). For instance, if Congress does something of dubious constitutional validity that is immediately challenged and struck down by the court, it may be widely perceived as illegitimate; but if it does something that is not challenged, the action can take on an appearance of validity that augments authority over time.

In a series of annual surveys starting in 1999, Richard L. Cole, John Kincaid and their co-authors (see, e.g., Cole and Kincaid 2000; Kincaid and Cole 2001, 2008; Cole et al. 2004) measured citizen attitudes about general issues relating to federalism. Among the most important findings from these data is that citizens have relatively stable attitudes about how much they trust different levels of government and which levels of government act most efficiently in terms of utilization of tax dollars (Cole and Kincaid 2000; Cole, Kincaid, and Rodriguez 2004). Perhaps unsurprisingly, the findings generally indicate that people have a more positive view of state and local government than they do of national authority. A study by Schneider, Jacoby, and Lewis (2010) that uses 2006 CCES data echoes these findings and demonstrates that citizens have different opinions about which level of government should "take the lead" in nineteen policy domains. The authors report that citizens prefer state and local government to be the primary actors in such areas as providing public transportation and reducing crime, but they want the federal government to play a more active role on issues concerning immigration and health care (2010, 9–10).

One thing these studies do not address is how citizens feel about the appropriate exercise of government authority in particular policy domains in light of constitutional provisions that actually grant and limit the authority of government actors. Indeed, as Schneider and his co-authors acknowledge, "People are often unclear about respective roles and responsibilities [of key political leaders] . . . [and might have] difficulties with respect to technical questions about the government institutions most capable of dealing with specific problems and issues" (2010, 4–5). They suggest this lack of information may manifest as "random noise" in survey data.

It is not at all clear, however, that understandings of intergovernmental power are randomly distributed in the population. Moreover, controlling for demographics like ideology does not entirely solve the problem because such measures can conflate the influence of distinct factors, such as support for specific policy measures and support for federal authority more generally. Rather than omit such information, it is better to *control for* it in an experimental setting. That is what I do here. In a realistic article discussing proposed national action, experimental conditions provide information to participants about (1) constitutional provisions that might provide authority for the exercise of national versus state authority and (2) what consensus there is among legal scholars about the claim of federal authority under those provisions. Specifically, participants are told that legal experts either agree that Congress has *clear authority to act,* or that congressional authority is *unclear,* or that experts agree Congress *does not have authority to act.*

The level of expert consensus is specifically manipulated to test the influence of understandings of constitutional norms on participants' assessments of legitimacy. It is important to note, however, that in this age of academic skepticism and hyperpartisanship, it is not at all clear that citizens will defer to legal experts in what they are told about the appropriate exercise of national congressional authority. Indeed, some might think that citizens' personal views about the desirability of legislation, rather than what they are told about institutional powers, would drive their interpretations of appropriate government action. This is part of the dynamic that I investigate here.

Legislative Authority Experiment

The experiment on assessments of legislative authority employs a 2 × 3 × 2 design. I present participants with a mock newspaper article that raises the question of congressional authority to take particular legislative measures pertaining to gun control or immigration. Because I am interested in seeing how these variables operate despite the ideological implications of the type of policy being proposed, I specifically vary the ideological direction of policy in each article. In the gun regulation scenario, participants are told that Congress is considering passing legislation to require background checks of those who acquire firearms from private sellers and to limit the number of rounds in magazines for guns sold in interstate commerce. In the immigration reform scenario, the article describes proposed legislative action that would take away federal funding from schools that allow undocumented students to receive in-state tuition benefits. Thus, on average, conservatives should be against proposed measures in the gun control article and in favor of the congressional measures described in the immigration reform scenario. The opposite pattern should emerge for liberals.

Each participant was exposed to a hypothetical article stating that Congress was considering acting pursuant to its authority to regulate interstate commerce in Article I (for the gun control scenario) or its authority to enact legislation regarding immigration and to control the expenditure of national funds (for the immigration reform scenario). In both scenarios, measures were pitted against states' authority under the Tenth Amendment to regulate for the health, safety, and welfare of their citizens (gun control) or to dictate how state education resources were allocated as independent sovereign entities (tuition benefit scenario).

Participants were explicitly told that the Supreme Court had not yet considered the issue, but constitutional experts were weighing in on the matter. One-third of participants were told legal experts agreed it was clear Congress had the constitutional authority to take the proposed action, one-third were informed that opinion among legal experts was divided and that it was unclear how the Supreme Court would rule on the issue, and one-third were informed that legal experts agreed Congress lacked the authority to take the proposed action because it infringed on state prerogatives. The level of democratic support for each measure was also manipulated. Half of the participants were told a recent poll indicated that over 85 percent of Americans agreed Congress should take the measures described and half were told that fewer than 15 percent of Americans agreed with the proposed action.

A total of 801 participants took part in the national sample as part of the TESS program in August 2016. There were 396 participants in the gun regulation conditions and 404 in the immigration conditions. Results from the immigration conditions were previously reported (Braman 2021). Results for the gun control scenario have not been previously published. Findings here include pooled analyses for both experimental scenarios.[7]

First, experimental participants were asked to answer several policy questions relating to their views on political issues of the day. Among these questions were some pertaining to the two policy measures that are particularly relevant for the analyses. Specifically, participants were asked a series of balanced questions, including the extent to which they thought guns should be regulated by the government and whether they agreed that government benefits such as health care and public education should be limited to citizens and those legally in the United States. The initial battery of questions also asked participants about (1) their level of satisfaction with certain state and national actors and institutions and (2) whether they thought the national government was taking away "too much" authority from the states in dealing with pressing political issues.

After these questions, each participant read one of the hypothetical articles containing the experimental manipulations involving either the gun control or tuition benefit legislation. Because each scenario involved relying on constitutional experts, participants were also asked whether or not they thought the experts cited in the article were "credible experts" on the issue. Responses of all participants were analyzed regardless of their response to this question to reflect the fact that this sort of variance no doubt exists among the general public.[8] Participants then answered questions about the desirability and legitimacy of the proposed congressional action. Finally, at the end of the experiment participants were asked demographic questions and debriefed as to the nature of the study.

Results of Assessments of Legislative Authority

As a preliminary matter, as one might expect, there was a significant positive correlation between participants' desirability ratings and their assessments of the appropriateness of congressional action, but the relationship was not perfect. The correlation between the two assessments was .81 for the gun control scenario and .64 for the scenario on the restriction of tuition benefits.[9] This seems to confirm Tyler's (1990) assertion that you do not necessarily have to agree with a policy to see it as legitimate; it also helps justify the decision to disaggregate these two distinct concepts.

To test the experimental hypotheses, I analyze appropriateness responses in two distinct phases. First, to observe how the manipulated variables influenced participants thinking about the legislative authority that was the subject of each scenario, I conduct ANOVAs of legitimacy responses. Specifically, I conduct a three-way ANOVA of legitimacy ratings. The same factors are used in each analysis: (1) issue (gun control versus immigration), (2) level of public support (majority support versus opposition), and (3) the degree of expert consensus as to congressional authority (clear authority, unclear, clearly no authority). Each model is "fully saturated" so that I also test for all two- and three-way interactions in the analysis.

Then, to test hypotheses about the role of policy preferences and participants' views of the appropriate distribution of power in such judgments, I specify a series of ordered probit models analyzing legitimacy judgments. Those models include preference measures, the manipulated variables (with relevant interactions), and a number of additional controls. I undertake both types of analysis because I am critically interested in the main effect of manipulated variables. The substantive importance of those variables is much easier to understand through the presentation of simple marginal mean differences in ANOVA than by trying to account for interactive effects in an ordered probit model—particularly where one of the variables (expert consensus) takes on three distinct values. To specifically test the moderation hypothesis, I conduct four ordered probit regressions, one for the entire sample and three disaggregated analyses for each constitutional consensus condition to see how political variables operate when consensus is clear, unclear, and there is a consensus that Congress does not have authority to act.

ANOVA Results

Legitimacy ratings were not significantly different across issue area ($F(1, 795)$ = 2.45, n.s.), although participants were somewhat more likely to see the proposed national legislative authority on immigration as more appropriate than the proposed legislation on gun control. The majority support variable acts

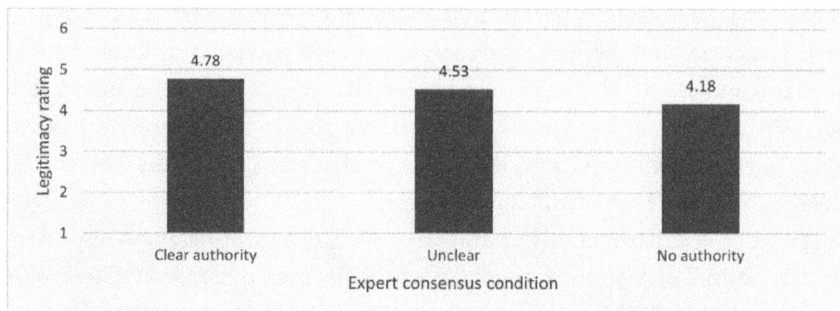

FIGURE 3. Marginal means for expert consensus conditions in legislative authority experiment

as anticipated, in that participants were more likely to say congressional action was legitimate when they were informed that there was majority support for that action (marginal mean = 4.60) than when they were told there was majority opposition (marginal mean = 4.39), but the variable does not reach conventional levels of significance ($F (1, 795) = 2.50$, n.s.).

There is a significant difference, however, in legitimacy judgments, depending on the level of consensus among constitutional scholars about congressional authority to act ($F (2, 794) = 6.65, p < .001$). As the marginal means in figure 3 demonstrate, participants in the national TESS sample were most likely to say legislation was legitimate if the consensus among experts was that Congress had authority to act and least likely to say the action was legitimate when experts agreed Congress did not have authority to act. This result is consistent with the institutional rule hypotheses.

None of the higher-level interactions are significant in the ANOVA. As the issue variable does not reach conventional levels of statistical significance and does not significantly interact with other manipulated variables, I aggregate data across issues but include controls for the variable and all interactions in the ordered probit regression analyses.[10]

Ordered Probit Regression Results

Ordered probit regression allows us to test for the influence of participants' policy views and their feelings about federalism on assessments of appropriateness of the proposed congressional action. Specifically, policy preferences are measured on a 1–7 scale, where higher numbers reflect support for gun control measures and restriction of tuition benefits to citizens and those in the country legally. Views on federalism are measured on a 1–6 scale, with higher numbers representing more support for state authority.

I also control for participants' ideology (measured on a 1–5 scale, with higher numbers reflecting more conservative views), partisanship (measured on a 1–7 scale, with higher numbers for strong Democrats), and their expressed satisfaction with Congress and their own state legislature (each measured on a 1–7 scale ranging from very satisfied to very dissatisfied). All manipulations are included, as is the interaction between them in the full ordered probit model. The issue is coded 0 for participants who received the immigration scenario and 1 for those who received the gun control article. The consensus variable is operationalized from 1 to 3 (clear authority consensus = 1, divided opinion = 2, no authority consensus = 3) and majority opposition is dichotomous (1 = majority opposition, 0 = majority support). In the disaggregated analyses the authority variable and its interaction with majority support fall away as the models test for the influence of political factors in each consensus condition.

The results for the full model, given in table 3, demonstrate that authority consensus is statistically significant. As the level of consensus that Congress does not have the authority to act increases, participants' legitimacy ratings go down. Moreover, the marginal effects set forth in table 4 indicate that the variable is substantively important. As expert consensus moves from clear agreement among experts that Congress has authority to take such action to a mixed consensus, experimental participants were 8.1 percent less likely to say the action was "clearly legitimate." Consistent with results from the ANOVA analysis, we also see that majority opposition was not significant in the full model, although where participants are told that a majority of citizens oppose congressional action on gun control measures or tuition benefits, participants were less likely to see the proposed action as an appropriate exercise of national legislative authority.

The preference measures indicate that participants' feelings about the policy proposal clearly had an influence on their legitimacy ratings. Those who supported restrictions on guns and government benefits to citizens and those residing in the United States legally were more likely to rate congressional action pursuing those policies appropriate. Marginal effects for the main model in table 4 indicate that those who strongly agreed with the implications of proposed measures were 7.8 percent more likely to judge such actions as "clearly legitimate" than those who supported them to a lesser extent. Moreover, the variable is significant in the full model and for all three expert

TABLE 3. Ordered probit regression for legitimacy of congressional action

| | | Authority consensus conditions | | |
	Full model	Clear authority	Divided consensus	Clearly no authority
Manipulations				
Authority consensus	−.33*** (.09)	—	—	—
Majority opposition	−.42 (.28)	−.18 (.19)	−.28 (.18)	−.10 (.18)
Issue	−.11 (.29)	.06 (.20)	−.09 (.20)	.21 (.20)
Issue × Majority opposition	−.02 (.39)	.01 (.26)	.04 (.27)	.10 (.26)
Authority × Majority opposition	.15 (.13)	—	—	—
Issue × Authority	−.09 (.13)	—	—	—
Issue × Authority × Majority opposition	.04 (.18)	—	—	—
Preferences				
Policy agreement	.32*** (.02)	.31*** (.04)	.33*** (.04)	.34*** (.04)
Too much federal authority	−.15*** (.03)	−.12* (.06)	−.13** (.05)	−.19*** (.06)
Controls				
Female	−.03 (.08)	.06 (.13)	.10 (.14)	−.23+ (.13)
Conservative	.02 (.03)	−.05 (.06)	.00 (.05)	.07 (.05)
Democrat	.03 (.02)	.00 (.04)	−.01 (.04)	.06+ (.04)
Dissatisfied with Congress	.05+ (.03)	.19*** (.05)	.02 (.05)	−.07 (.05)
Dissatisfied with state institutions	.01 (.01)	.04+ (.02)	.00 (.03)	.02 (.03)
N	786	274	251	261
Likelihood ratio	262.99***	97.96***	77.16***	102.40**

+$p < .10$, *$p < .05$, **$p < .01$, ***$p < .001$ (two-tailed test). Standard errors in parentheses.

TABLE 4. Significant marginal effects (full model): Probability of "clearly legitimate" response on legislative authority

Variable	Variable change	Probability change	95% CI
Authority consensus	Clear authority to divided consensus	−.081	−.130 to −.040
Policy agreement	Somewhat to strongly support gun control measures or the restriction of tuition benefits	.078	.065 to .091
Federal authority	Agree to strongly agree federal government has too much authority	−.037	−.053 to −.021

Note: CI, confidence interval.

consensus conditions; thus, rules do not seem to moderate the role of preferences in judgments of appropriateness as the constraint hypothesis suggests. Those who strongly agreed that the federal government has taken too much authority from the states were 3.7 percent less likely to deem national authority clearly legitimate than those who somewhat agreed with that proposition; the variable is significant in the main analysis and across all consensus conditions. The effects of controls for ideology, partisanship, and satisfaction with legislative bodies are inconsistent across models. Thus participants' *feelings about the policy* at issue influence assessments of appropriateness more consistently than general political orientations do.

Discussion of Results of Assessments of Legislative Authority

Table 5 summarizes the results of the experimental hypotheses in the experiment regarding assessments of legislative authority. Rules regarding the appropriate exercise of government authority clearly matter in assessments of whether citizens think proposed congressional action is appropriate when it is pitted against state prerogatives in our federal system. Participants' feelings about policy and the distribution of federal authority are also significant. Although the level of public support for congressional action acted as anticipated, it was not significant in such assessments. Disaggregated analyses demonstrate that relevant political factors are important in legitimacy assessment regardless of what participants were told about experts' assessments

TABLE 5. Results of experimental hypotheses concerning assessments of legislative authority

Hypothesis	Results of experiment on legislative authority
Institutional rule hypothesis: Do rules matter in legitimacy assessments?	Expert consensus is significant; relative ratings of appropriateness are in the order predicted.
Policy preferences hypothesis: Are preferences significant in judgments?	Policy preferences are significant in the main analysis and in all three expert consensus conditions.
Public support hypothesis: Is public support significant?	Public support is not significant.*
Federal authority hypothesis: Are feelings about distribution of federal authority significant?	Feelings about federal authority are significant in the main analysis and in all three expert consensus conditions.
Constraint hypothesis: Do rules constrain role of political factors?	The constraint hypothesis does not receive support.

*The public support variable is marginally significant for the immigration scenario involving the restriction of tuition benefits (Braman 2021).

of congressional authority to act. This result is contrary to the constraint hypothesis.

Assessments of Unilateral Executive Authority

Chapter 1 discussed much of the research on the expansion of presidential authority in times of crisis. In addition to the research cited previously, it is important to note that chief executives are issuing more and more unilateral executive orders to respond to matters of public concern, even in the absence of any "emergency" situation. Indeed, Carmines and Fowler (2017) effectively demonstrate that the number of executive orders issued by presidents making significant policy changes has increased as Congress has become more polarized. They argue that chief executives are using unilateral action as a tool to achieve policy goals when they are worried about getting their agenda implemented through legislative action, and that this tendency has increased particularly since the Obama administration. This is noteworthy in light of evidence from Lowande and Rogowski (2021) that people do not necessarily prefer executive action to legislative measures in times of emergency. Carmines and Fowler suggest presidents no longer feel any compunction about taking matters into their own hands when there are not any exigencies other than a Congress that may flout or delay their policy goals.

When presidents do employ unilateral policy action, charges of chief executives improperly usurping legislative authority are becoming more and more prevalent. Consider litigation about whether President Obama overstepped the bounds of his executive authority into matters more properly addressed by Congress when he issued executive orders allowing undocumented individuals born in the United States (and later their parents) to remain in the country without fear of deportation. Notwithstanding the popularity of the DREAMers program, referenced in the previous chapter, many believed that those orders crossed the line from enforcing the law to pronouncing it, and that such action, if it was to be taken at all, should have been taken by representatives in Congress.

I use this sort of conflict about institutional authority between branches in the experiments on citizens' assessments of unilateral executive power. A previous study using undergraduate and MTurk participants that investigated assessments of executive actions during the Obama administration used scenarios involving raising the debt ceiling and committing troops to foreign states in times of humanitarian crisis. The results showed different factors were significant in judgments about the desirability and appropriateness of unilateral action. Participants' policy preferences were significant in assessments of the desirability of presidential action, but rules were not (Braman 2016). What experimental participants were told about constitutional rules, however, did matter in the *legitimacy* assessments of both undergraduate and MTurk participants. Evidence indicated that participants' policy views on these matters did not influence their judgments of the appropriateness of executive action.

Participants' level of satisfaction with President Obama also influenced assessments of the appropriateness of unilateral executive authority. Significantly, what participants were told about rules constrained the role of presidential satisfaction in different ways across the two samples. For undergraduate participants, consistent with the constraint hypothesis, satisfaction with Obama was significant only where expert opinion about authority was divided. This, however, was not the case in the MTurk sample. Among nonstudent participants the level of satisfaction with President Obama was at least marginally significant across all consensus categories but reached conventional levels of statistical significance only when participants were told that experts agreed Obama did not have authority to act. A likely explanation for the difference between samples was that undergraduates were more deferential to the opinion of experts. Rules did less to constrain the preferences of participants in the nonstudent sample, where participants were particularly sensitive to the idea that the president was violating rules. In line with the findings of Hibbing and Theiss-Morse (2002), it seems that for nonstudent participants, the potential violation signaled an impending constitutional crisis where it was important to choose sides, triggering participants' personal feelings about the president.

The change from the Obama administration to the Trump administration allows us to observe the influence of constitutional rules and political context not only across issues but also with a different president at the head of the executive branch. As with the inquiry into legislative authority, I conduct a fully specified ANOVA of the manipulated variables in the CCES administration and then ordered probit regressions for full and disaggregated models across consensus conditions to test the influence of measured variables. Consistent with prior findings, I expect that constitutional rules and presidential satisfaction will both be important in judgments of the appropriateness of executive action.

Experiment on Assessments of Unilateral Executive Authority

In the experiment on how individuals assess the appropriateness of unilateral executive authority, participants read an article stating that President Trump was considering issuing an executive order that would take away federal funding from sanctuary cities that declined to report undocumented individuals to federal authorities. Again, one-third of participants read an article stating that the consensus among experts was that the president had the authority to do so, one-third were told that experts agreed he did not have such authority, and one-third were told that expert opinion was divided on the question of authority. Half of the participants were told that 85 percent of the population supported the measure and the other half were told that only 15 percent of the population supported the action. Before participants read the article, they were asked about their support for sanctuary cities. The CCES also measured their satisfaction with the president's job performance, both houses of Congress, and state institutions. As in the study of legislative authority, participants were asked whether they thought constitutional experts of the sort cited in the article were "credible experts" on this matter of government authority.[11]

ANOVA Results for Assessments of Unilateral Executive Authority

Strikingly, in the ANOVA testing the effect of constitutional rules and public support in judgments of the appropriateness of unilateral action, what participants were told about the president's compliance with rules is not statistically significant. Although the relative order of marginal means is as predicted (participants judged the restriction of funds from sanctuary cities to be most appropriate where experts agreed Trump had the authority to take such action and least appropriate when they agreed he did not), the marginal means, illustrated in figure 3, are not statistically distinguishable (F (2, 488) = 1.98, p = .14). This it at odds with previous findings from when Obama was president. The ANOVA also reveals that the degree of public support for the action is not significant in assessments (marginal means are 3.92 versus 3.84 for majority support and opposition, respectively (F (1, 489) = .19, n.s.). Finally, the interaction between rules and support is not statistically significant (F (2, 488) = .06, n.s.).

Ordered Probit Analyses for Assessments of Unilateral Executive Authority

In the ordered probit models, I include measures of participants' preferences on the support for sanctuary cities (measured on a 1–7 scale, with higher numbers representing more opposition to cities that do not report undocumented individuals) and the level of satisfaction they express regarding President Trump's job performance (measured on a 1–5 scale, from very satisfied to very

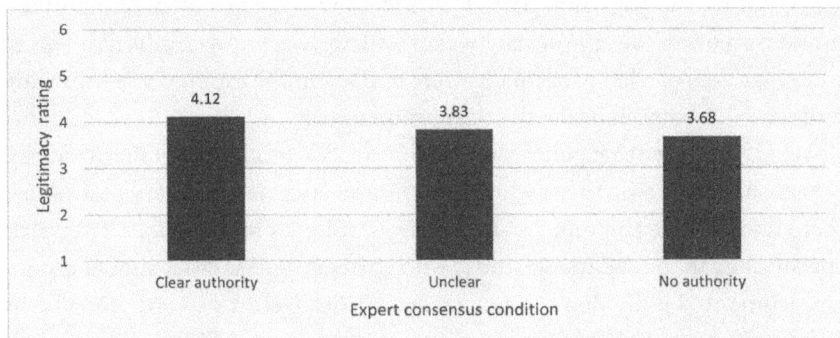

FIGURE 4. Marginal means for expert consensus conditions in executive authority experiment

dissatisfied). I also include controls for ideology (measured on a 1–5 scale, with higher numbers representing more conservative views), partisanship (on a 1–7 scale, with higher numbers for strong Republicans), satisfaction with Congress (on a 1–10 scale, with higher numbers representing greater dissatisfaction with the House and Senate), and satisfaction with participants' state governor (on a 1–5 scale, with higher number representing less satisfaction). I include the manipulations and the interaction between them as variables in the full model. Authority consensus is operationalized as an ordinal variable (1 = expert consensus of clear presidential authority to act, 2 = divided authority, 3 = no authority consensus) and level of support for the action is dichotomous (1 = majority opposition, 0 = support). The consensus variable and its interaction with support fall away in disaggregated models testing the role of political variables in each consensus condition.

In the full model set forth in table 6, we again observe that the authority consensus variable is not significant. Although the direction of the variable is negative, as expected, signifying ratings of appropriateness are lower where experts agree the president does not have authority to take the proposed action, the coefficient is not significant ($p = .14$). We also see across models that ratings of appropriateness are lower when a majority opposes the restriction of funding to sanctuary cities, but the influence of the variable is not significant.

Among the political measures of interest, participants' level of satisfaction with the current president is significant across all the probit models. The influence of the variable is also substantively important. Table 7 sets forth the marginal effects for selected variables in the full model. Those who strongly disapproved of Trump were 5 percent less likely to "strongly agree" that the action was appropriate compared to participants who somewhat disapproved of his job performance. Thus, how participants feel about the president is important in assessments of the appropriateness of unilateral executive authority. This is true regardless of what participants were told about the expert consensus with respect to his compliance with constitutional rules.

We also observe that policy support for sanctuary cities is significant across consensus categories: those who express opposition to sanctuary cities were more likely to see the unilateral restriction of funds by President Trump as appropriate. In the full model, those who strongly agreed cities should report undocumented individuals to federal authorities were 2 percent more likely to strongly agree that Trump's action was legitimate than those who agreed to a lesser extent. Again, this is at odds with prior studies, which found policy

TABLE 6. Ordered probit regressions for legitimacy of presidential action

	Full model	Authority consensus conditions		
		Clear authority	Divided consensus	Clearly no authority
Manipulations				
Authority consensus	−.13 (.08)	—	—	—
Majority opposition	.00 (.28)	−.05 (.18)	-.05 (.18)	−.02 (.18)
Authority × Majority opposition	.01 (.13)	—	—	—
Preferences				
Policy agreement	.18*** (.03)	.12** (.04)	.19*** (.05)	.29*** (.05)
Trump disapproval	−.45*** (.04)	−.36*** (.07)	−.49*** (.09)	−.57*** (.10)
Controls				
Ideology (conservative)	.16** (.06)	.15 (.10)	.18+ (.11)	.16 (.12)
Party ID (Republican)	−.04 (.04)	.04 (.06)	−.10 (.07)	−.11+ (.07)
Dissatisfied with Congress	.03 (.03)	.05 (.04)	.00 (.04)	.01 (.05)
Dissatisfied with state governor	.02 (.04)	.04 (.06)	.02 (.07)	.03 (.06)
N	443	152	146	145
Likelihood ratio	352.78***	92.55***	126.14***	148.75***

+p < .10, *p < .05, **p <.01, ***p < .001 (two-tailed test). Standard errors in parentheses.

views were not relevant in assessments of the appropriateness of executive action when Obama was president (Braman 2016). This could be because immigration was such a highly salient issue in the fall of 2017 when the CCES was administered.[12]

The only control variable that reaches statistical significance in the full model is ideology, indicating that participants who identify as conservative were more likely to support unilateral restrictions than those who are liberal. As we observed in the model for legislative action, it appears that participants' views about the desirability of the proposed action are more consistently

TABLE 7. Marginal effects (full model): Probability of "clearly legitimate" response on executive authority

Variable	Variable change	Probability change	95% CI
Policy agreement	Somewhat to strongly agree sanctuary cities should report to federal authorities	.02	.01 to .03
Presidential disapproval	Somewhat to strongly disapprove of Trump	−.05	−.07 to −.04
Ideology	Somewhat to strongly conservative	.02	.00 to .04

Note: CI, confidence interval.

important than general political orientations in judgments of appropriateness across models.

Discussion of Results of Assessments of Unilateral Executive Authority

Table 8 sets forth the results of the hypotheses tests in the experiment on the use of executive authority. The evidence confirms that how citizens feel about the president is important in judgments of the appropriateness of unilateral executive authority. Participants' feelings about the issue were also consistently significant across all expert consensus categories, contrary to the constraint hypotheses. Contrary to findings for judicial and legislative outputs, what participants were told about the president's compliance with constitutional rules did not significantly influence judgments of the appropriateness of his action.

Moreover, what participants were told about rules mattered less in assessments of executive authority than has been evident in previous research. This could be the case for three reasons. First, it could be that the general population is less attentive to constitutional rules as they are operationalized in this study than participants in previously studied convenience samples. Alternatively, it might be that in the context of immigration specifically, rules are less important in judgments of unilateral executive authority than in other issue contexts. Finally, there could have been an erosion in people's attentiveness to rules during the Trump administration. Indeed, participants did seem to

TABLE 8. Results for experimental hypotheses for assessments of executive authority

Hypothesis	Results of experiment on executive authority
Institutional rule hypothesis: Do rules matter in legitimacy assessments?	Rules are not significant, although relative ratings of appropriateness are in the order predicted.
Policy preferences hypothesis: Are preferences significant in judgments?	Policy preferences are significant in the main analysis and in all three expert consensus conditions.
Public support hypothesis: Is majority support significant?	Majority support is not significant in any of the analyses.
Presidential approval hypothesis: Are feelings about President Trump significant?	Feelings about the president are significant in the main analysis and in all three consensus conditions.
Constraint hypothesis: Do rules constrain the role of political factors?	The constraint hypothesis does not receive support.

attend to rules *on some level;* relative ratings were as predicted, although expert consensus manipulation was not significant.

No doubt, some readers may see this as a particularly attractive explanation, given the change in administrations and Trump's emphasis on "fake news" and the fallibility of experts who disagreed with his policy agenda. Still, we cannot be sure whether one of these explanations or a combination of two or three is driving this result. The assessments involve complex mental phenomena where political context, including *who* is taking *what* particular action, seems to matter a great deal. Clearly, more work needs to be done on such assessments, but each empirical "snapshot" adds to our knowledge and provides fodder for future research.

Conclusion

Table 9 summarizes the results of hypotheses tests across all three experiments. Several important findings emerge when we look across how citizens think about the authority of judicial, legislative, and executive actors. First, what participants are told about rules matters. There is a significant difference across motivation conditions in the experiment on judicial authority and across consensus conditions in the legislative authority experiment. Although

TABLE 9. Results of experimental hypotheses for assessments of official authority

Hypothesis	Judicial authority	Legislative authority	Unilateral executive authority
Institutional rule hypothesis			
Are rules significant?	Yes	Yes	No
Is relative ordering as predicted?	Yes	Yes	Yes
Policy preferences hypothesis			
Are preferences significant in judgments?	Yes	Yes	Yes
Public support hypothesis			
Is majority support significant?	No	No	No
Federal authority hypothesis			
Are feelings about the distribution of federal authority significant?	N/A	Yes	N/A
Presidential approval hypothesis			
Are feelings about President Trump significant?	N/A	N/A	Yes
Constraint hypothesis			
Do rules constrain the role of political factors?	Partial support	No	No

the difference between consensus conditions is not significant in the executive context, legitimacy ratings across conditions are in the order predicted.

Second, although majority support for action seems to matter in the direction predicted in all the experiments, it is not significant in any of the assessments of appropriateness. Third, citizens' policy support for the specific action at issue is consistently important in judgments of appropriateness across institutions, rather than general orientations involving partisanship and/or ideology. Moreover, the results indicate that participants' feelings about the distribution of federal authority influence their assessments of the legitimacy of congressional action when it is pitted against state prerogatives, and how people feel about the chief executive is clearly an important factor in assessing the appropriateness of unilateral executive authority. Finally, where political factors are significant, what citizens were told about compliance with decision-making or (constitutional) rules does very little to moderate the influence of such rules on assessments of the appropriateness of state action, contrary to the constraint hypotheses.

As with all experimental studies, it is appropriate to acknowledge that the findings are contextually dependent on the issues that are the subject of this inquiry. Assessments of government action related to other domestic and foreign policy matters are likely to differ depending on such factors as issue salience and the level of deference citizens may be willing to extend to office holders based on the officials' expertise. This study, however, does provide an accurate picture of how citizens think about government authority regarding the specific scenarios tested in the inquiry. This picture is valuable in and of itself and as a "first cut" in attempting to see how rules and political context matter in citizens' judgments about state authority.

It is also important to consider the extent to which the results here could reflect the timing of these studies. This seems particularly relevant when one considers (1) findings that although rules are significant in judging the appropriateness of judicial and legislative authority, they are not significant in citizens' evaluations of executive action, and (2) the suggestion (also raised by this finding) that there may be an erosion in the importance of constitutional considerations in citizens' judgments of the appropriateness of executive action. Indeed, there has been a good deal of rhetoric about how politics has come to dominate everything else in an increasingly partisan environment in the United States over the past several years. The findings reported here demonstrate that rules can (and do) matter in judging the appropriateness of judicial and legislative outputs. Unquestionably, preferences are also important, and indeed, more important than the constraint hypotheses suggest may be appropriate. Still, consistent with the logic in conducting the inquiry, the results illustrate that *each plays an important role* in citizens' assessments.

Findings concerning the evaluations of executive authority suggest that the new conventional wisdom regarding preferences predominating over institutional considerations may be correct, at least in part. Indeed, the erosion of the importance of constitutional rules is most evident exactly where some would expect it to be—in evaluating the appropriateness of the actions of a particularly polarizing president. Whether this is a blip or the start of a more widespread erosion of the importance of rules generally in thinking about official government action remains to be determined. Only more testing will shed light on the issue. Hopefully this study provides a worthwhile start for thinking about such issues.

What do these findings mean for the ability of government officials to expand their authority generally? The findings here clearly imply that popular officials who take action that is widely supported by the citizenry may have more success expanding their authority by citing public acquiescence to questionable assertions of power. On the bright side, they may also suggest that in our current divided political climate, concerns about unilateral executive action augmenting presidential authority might be overstated (Howell and Moe 2020). This is because *just as many citizens are likely to deem questionable government action inappropriate, as perceive it as legitimate.* Thus it may be harder for officials to use widespread public acquiescence to the action to expand the precedential legacy of institutional powers beyond specific measures enacted to deal with particularized problems.

3 | Assessing the Credibility of Constitutional Experts

ONE ISSUE THAT was not discussed in the last chapter is how participants in the legislative and executive authority experiments viewed the credibility of the constitutional experts commenting on government action in ways that were consistent (or inconsistent) with their own policy views. This is an interesting question and one that, as set forth below, the experimental scenarios provide significant leverage to explore. I turn to that question in this chapter because there is clearly something more that we can learn from these data about how citizens think about constitutional expertise in the context of contested policy action.

In chapter 4, I analyze how participants justify their assessments of government authority in light of the information provided in the experimental scenarios about legislative authority on gun control and immigration.[1] A brief look at some of the explanations that mention expertise reveals that responses fell into four broad categories:

1. Responses expressing *naivete* about constitutional matters:
   I'm unclear and do not understand the current and prospective laws surrounding this and I am not a constitutional scholar. (legitimacy/immigration)
   This question needs to be considered by those who really know the Constitution and its amendments. I am not that person. I simply have an opinion guided by a prejudiced media. (desirability/gun control)

2. Responses *deferring* to experts:
   According to the presumed experts this is a matter better left to the individual states to decide. (legitimacy/gun control)
   If constitutional law scholars and lawyers say it can be done, I accept their perspective because they ARE the scholars. Those saying it goes against the Second Amendment are typically mouthing what they hear on conservative TV and radio shows. Those people are NOT experts. (desirability/gun control)

3. Responses expressing *resistance* to expertise:

Disagree with constitutional law scholars on their interpretation. (desirability/immigration)

I don't need a law scholar to make a commonsense decision. Those who are not here legally should not receive ANY benefits paid for by the working tax dollars of citizens of the USA. Along with federal money is federal rules. States are to provide money for the people who paid for it. (legitimacy/immigration)

4. Responses that *question expert consensus* in some regard:

I think you can find constitutional law experts on both sides. In the end, the will of the people should prevail. I think we have seen the danger of lax gun control, and most people agree with gun control. (legitimacy/gun control)

The constitutional law scholars of today view the Constitution of the United States very differently than our forefathers intended. Most of them have been taught through a liberal filter and view the Constitution as such. To truly understand what was meant by our forefathers you must also read the Federalist Papers as it applies to the Constitution. That is why I believe the proposed legislation is wrong and should not be passed. (desirability/gun control)

The range of responses indicates it might be useful to see what is behind citizens' deference to, and skepticism about, constitutional expertise. Because all participants in the experiments on executive and legislative authority were randomly assigned to conditions in which they were exposed to consensus views that were either consistent, mixed, or inconsistent with their own and then asked whether they deemed the experts mentioned in the article "credible," we can explore demographic and attitudinal factors underlying responses to that question. Fortunately, as detailed further below, there is well-developed theory about the acceptance of expertise in other domains to guide the inquiry about how people think about constitutional authorities.

Experts and Credibility

In the highly specialized American society, citizens cannot be expected to have the knowledge or inclination to comprehend the implications of every socially relevant behavior. To deal with this, journalists have developed a norm in reporting on complex issues where they commonly seek the opinions of experts on matters of public concern (Merkley 2020a). Expert commentary is often used by news outlets to aid their consumers in understanding complicated causal relationships, historical events, and factors that can be relevant in the policy decisions of government officials. Where those who are knowledgeable in some recognized field tend to agree about the effects of some phenomenon of interest, journalists might even refer to "expert consensus" to alert readers to the weight of evidence regarding a particular claim (Johnston and Ballard 2016; Merkley 2020a, 2020b).

One domain where reporters commonly employ expert commentary is in matters related to the novel assertion of authority by government actors such as Congress and the president. As mentioned earlier, conceptions of procedural justice suggest citizens want to be confident that appropriate government actors are working to address matters of public concern and that they are doing so within the bounds of their rightful authority. Individuals, however, can find it difficult to directly monitor officeholders in this regard. Questions about which branch or level of government is empowered to act to address specific problems concerning issues like immigration, mask mandates, or the debt ceiling can be challenging because constitutional provisions regarding institutional powers are often unclear. Many of the rules constraining the behavior of government actors involve esoteric constitutional provisions and opaque bodies of doctrine from past historical eras. Thus journalists commonly cite academics, including law professors and political scientists, as "constitutional experts" to help citizens understand how legal and institutional constraints may relate to the actions of government officials. As such, these authorities can play an important role in our constitutional system; they are often the first to signal a problem if officeholders take actions that exceed the bounds of their legitimate authority.

According to long-standing research on persuasion, cited experts, as "high-credibility" sources, can yield substantial influence in moving people's opinions toward the evidence and the arguments they express (Petty and Cacioppo 1986). Hovland, Janis, and Kelley (1953) originally theorized that the power of persuasion for such authorities depends on the extent to which citizens believe those authorities are competent and trustworthy (see also Whitehead 1968; Pornpitakpan 2004). In our current polarized environment, constitutional experts may not be uniformly considered the high-credibility sources they once were. Research on the acceptance of scientific findings and expertise indicates growing trends in anti-intellectualism prompted by populism (Nichols 2017) and skepticism about the motives, methods, and findings of researchers who produce results contrary to one's own worldview (for a review, see Hornsey and Fielding 2017).

Recent studies reveal that journalists' allusions to "experts" or even "expert consensus" do not necessarily sway citizens' thinking in a direction that is consistent with the views of the authorities who are cited.[2] This is true with respect to social science authorities such as economists (Johnston and Ballard 2016) and "hard science" experts in regard to such issues as global warming (e.g., Kahan, Jenkins-Smith, and Braman 2011; Bolsen and Druckman 2018), vaccine effectiveness (Jolley and Douglas 2017), and the safety of nuclear power and genetically modified organisms (Merkley 2020b).

Academics, politicians, and pundits have all expressed a good deal of concern about citizens' resistance to scientifically recognized facts that pertain to public policy. One might expect such tendencies to be amplified in the realm of reporting involving the behavior of government officials asserting powers in our democratic system. In this age of academic skepticism, where political figures on both sides of the political aisle are constantly touting alternative versions of what the Constitution forbids and requires, it is not at all clear that citizens will see cited legal experts as "credible" on issues of national authority. Research on affective partisanship shows that citizens increasingly think of copartisans as "team members" and often demonstrate antipathy toward members of partisan outgroups (for a review, see Iyengar et al. 2019). Do we see experts on constitutional authority in a similar light, their credibility depending on whether they are expressing opinions that are compatible with our predispositions?

I begin to delve into these questions using evidence from the legislative and executive authority experiments described in the last chapter. I conduct the inquiry in a manner that should reveal factors that are important when people *credit* and *discredit* cited authorities. Moreover, I explore which citizens are likely to express *uncertainty* about constitutional experts. Investigating assessments in this way helps shed light on *different reasons why individuals might engage in motived reasoning* about constitutional expertise based on their agreement with the content of the views expressed, distinct from other factors that have been found to be important in assessments of experts such as partisanship.

Thinking about the Credibility of Constitutional Experts

Numerous studies published in the last decade have looked at individual cognition with respect to expertise in several disciplines, including psychology, political science, and sociology. Many of these studies are specifically interested in citizens' thinking with respect to climate change (for a review, see Hornsey et al. 2016). Others consider how individuals respond to social scientists' input about policy matters (Johnston and Ballard 2016) and scientific consensus with regard to other matters involving state regulations (e.g., Merkley 2020b; Milosh et al. 2021, investigating COVID-19 policy).

Druckman and McGrath (2019) offer a process-based argument as to why people may resist expert authority. Specifically, they argue that as people's ability to directly assess information decreases, the complexity of processing (and, thus, the points for sincere questioning) increases. As such, it is difficult to parse "directionally motivated" skepticism from the differing requirements of evidence that could be necessary to sway people's opinion. These scholars point out that when evidence is presented by an intermediary, people must first determine whether they find the expert credible before they assess the weight that the expert's argument and evidence should have in their judgments.

This point is well taken, but perhaps contemplates cognitive processes that are more independent in theory than in practice. There is experimental evidence, for instance, from one of the earliest studies on motivated reasoning that people given studies that produce evidence contrary to their opinions about the death penalty are less inclined to find them effectively conducted than are individuals given identical studies who are led to believe the results are consistent with their opinions (Lord, Ross, and Lepper 1979). This finding suggests that decisions about expert credibility and the soundness of scientific methods may be inexorably tied to whether the proffered evidence is compatible with one's prior beliefs.

While there is quite a bit of research in law and psychology exploring the persuasiveness and credibility of expert witnesses in the context of civil and criminal litigation, there are scant studies on the role of legal experts in shaping public opinion. One exception is a study by Simon and Scurich (2013) investigating the influence legal experts can have in shaping individual judgments about the factors that are relevant in judges' decisions in particular cases. These authors also explore what shapes people's confidence in legal experts. They find that legal commentators do not shape individuals' evaluations of jurists' decisional processes as much as people's agreement with the outcome of those decisions themselves. Moreover, people's views on the *competence and reliability* of legal commentators are determined by whether the expert is expressing a view consistent with their preferred outcome.[3] Simon and Scurich's findings suggest that compatibility with the views legal analysts express can have a substantial influence on citizens' assessments of expert credibility.

Another factor that is important in the evaluation of experts is political orientation. Studies demonstrate that Democrats and liberals tend to defer to expertise more than Republicans and conservatives (Gromet 2015; Suhay and Druckman 2015; Bolsen and Druckman 2018; see also Blank and Shaw 2015 on the role of conservatism in dampening the influence of expertise, and Johnston and Ballard 2016, which uses a combined measure of partisanship and ideology). One might suspect that the rhetoric of former president Trump plays an important role in this observed disparity. Though he may certainly exaggerate partisan differences in citizens' reliance on experts, evidence of partisan (and/or ideological) bias in the interpretation of expertise predates Trump's becoming a major focal point in American politics (Gauchet 2012; Suhay 2017).[4]

There are also studies demonstrating that where findings threaten the values of those who identify with the Democratic Party, Democrats seem to be the partisans who are less likely to defer to expertise (Kraft, Lodge, and Taber 2015; Nesbit, Cooper, and Garret 2015). These studies exploit a problem with some of the extant research on the acceptance of scientific evidence. Often the agreement with findings of a particular study (or scientific consensus on a policy matter) is conflated with partisanship. For instance, Republicans who have been found to be more resistant to scientific evidence also tend to be against the specific policy measures involved with reducing global warming or requiring citizens to wear masks.

Here, by randomly assigning participants to conditions where experts express views that are consistent (or inconsistent) with participants' own views, and controlling for partisan identity in my analyses of credibility assessments, I can distinguish the relative influence of each on evaluations of constitutional experts. This is important, to separate the causal influence of these distinct factors. Moreover, *different goals may be relevant* for individuals engaged in motivated reasoning based on their agreement with the views authorities express compared to motivated reasoning that is attributable to partisan identity. For instance, the studies by Lord, Ross, and Lepper (1979) and Simon and Scurich (2011, 2013) suggest people tend to find experts whose findings they agree with more credible than experts whose findings they disagree with. This sort of motivated reasoning serves self-esteem by helping individuals believe that their attitudes are correct or are based on sound reasoning (Kunda 1990). These cognitions can bolster self-perception by helping us feel more intelligent. Moreover, saying that scientists who conduct that research are competent, skilled, and effective also serves individuals' ego by attributing positive traits to others who have expressed similar viewpoints (Brewer 2007).

Other researchers (Kahan, Jenkins-Smith, and Braman 2011) have suggested that people engage in motivated reasoning about expertise for entirely different reasons, to feel close to relevant social groups in order to solidify valued social identities. Hornsey and Fielding (2017, 465) elaborate on this idea with respect to partisanship:

> To the extent that people identify with a certain group—and to the extent this group prescribes antiscientific beliefs—internalization of antiscientific views is likely. . . . In the last three decades . . . scientific debates have been caught up in political debates. . . . Republicans sought to discredit the moral integrity of the scientific community such as stem cell research and climate change. . . . For a self-identified Republican, the motivation would be to look favorably on their party's views and to dismiss or dispute contradictory evidence. Given this it is perhaps not surprising that trust in science has declined since the 1970s and that this decline is attributed exclusively to conservatives. (Citations omitted.)

Although bolstering social identity by attempting to forge close bonds with partisan allies can also enhance esteem, the mechanism for doing so is more indirect. Thus it is important to parse the influences that are a result of agreement with the views authorities express from those that are a consequence of partisanship.[5]

Another factor that could influence individuals' assessments of experts is their education, particularly where, as in this study, the constitutional experts cited are identified as academics. This might be so for two reasons. First, people who have attained high levels of education might recognize the value of knowledge gained through degree programs (or there may be an element of "sunk costs" such that they are more likely to value such knowledge because they have gone through the arduous task of attaining higher levels of education themselves). A second reason education may be important is that scholars have identified anti-intellectualism as a factor that is relevant in the evaluation of expertise (e.g., Merkley 2020b). These twin mechanisms suggest two distinct ways education might matter. If highly educated people value expert knowledge more, they should be more likely to say experts are "credible"; and if those with less education are acting against elitism, they should be more likely to dismiss experts as "not credible." To be sure, this is a fine distinction but one we can explore here by looking at factors that influence both of these distinct assessments.

There are several other demographic variables that could be relevant in the evaluation of expertise. People from traditionally privileged groups (i.e., Whites, males) could be more likely to recognize expert authority than those from nontraditional backgrounds (non-Whites, females); this could be particularly the case with constitutional authorities because certain demographics remain underrepresented in the higher echelons of the legal hierarchy where constitutional experts reside (Kay 1991; Hurwitz and Lanier 2008). Hornsey and Fielding (2007) suggest that this type of acceptance (or rejection) of expertise could be rooted in a kind of "system justification" motivation. Alternatively, some might expect women to be particularly deferential to expert authority based on traditional gender stereotypes (Anderson et al. 2012). A final characteristic that could be important in the assessment of expertise is age: younger individuals may be more likely to defer to experts than older individuals because of their relative lack of knowledge and experience.

Research Design

As set forth in chapter 2, scenarios in the legislative and executive authority experiments employed a consensus of experts on the exercise of national authority to address a matter of public concern. Just after participants were exposed to treatments in which experts expressed a view that was divided, consistent, or inconsistent with their expressed policy preferences, they were asked whether they thought such experts were "credible" regarding the question of government authority. As detailed below, there is some very interesting variance to explain in how study participants answered this question. Moreover, as participants were *randomly assigned* to conditions that can be slightly retooled to fit this inquiry, their answers are appropriate for exploration as a dependent variable to shed light on the question of how citizens think about constitutional expertise.

The experiment on assessments of legislative authority involved a design in which three variables were manipulated: (1) the issue that was the subject of congressional action, (2) expert consensus, and (3) the level of public support for proposed measures. Participants in the TESS administration read one of two articles that stated Congress was considering an action that would either (1) impose limits on the shipment of guns in interstate commerce or (2) cut off federal funds to states that allowed undocumented students to receive in-state tuition benefits. Prior to their reading the article about congressional authority, survey respondents were asked questions related to their support for (1) limiting gun access and (2) the restriction of benefits to US citizens and those residing in the country legally, as a way to gauge their policy views on the issues that were the subject of scenarios.

Each article stated that national legislative action could interfere with state prerogatives in the US federal system of government, specifically pitting congressional authority against states' rights. What participants were told about expert consensus concerning congressional authority to take each action was manipulated in the experiment. One-third of participants were told that the consensus among constitutional experts was that Congress was acting within its authority under Article I, one-third were told that expert opinion on the issue was divided, and one-third were told that legal experts agreed that the action would infringe on states' reserved powers in our federal system. This consensus was exemplified with a quotation from an authority identified as a constitutional law professor at George Washington University Law School.[6] The level of public support for such measures was also manipulated in the article. Half of participants read an article stating that 85 percent of the population supported such measures; the other half were told that only 15 percent of the population supported the proposed action.[7]

After reading the hypothetical article referencing expert consensus, participants were asked whether they thought constitutional law scholars were "credible" on the issue of government authority related the proposed measure and whether they thought the action was an appropriate exercise of legislative authority. The question about expert credibility is the dependent variable analyzed in this inquiry; respondents were given three options to indicate whether they thought experts were credible: yes, no, and don't know.

The design of an experiment on executive authority deployed in the CCES in the autumn of 2017 was purposefully quite similar. That administration involved a design in which participants read an article stating that President Trump was considering issuing an executive order that would take away federal funding from sanctuary cities that declined to report undocumented citizens to federal authorities. Before participants read the article, they were asked about their support for sanctuary cities. Again, one-third of participants read an article stating the consensus among experts was that the president had the authority to do so, one-third were told experts agreed he did not have such authority, and one-third were told expert opinion was divided on the question of authority. The quotation exemplifying consensus was attributed to a professor who was "a noted authority on government powers." Once more, half of participants were told that 85 percent of the population supported such measures and the other half were told that only 15 percent of the population supported the action. As in the study of legislative authority, after they read the article participants were asked whether they thought constitutional experts were credible on this matter of government authority, with the same three response options possible—yes, no, don't know.

For the purposes of the analysis in this chapter, I am interested in how individuals respond to experts who express views that are either consistent or inconsistent with their policy views on proposed government action controlling for other relevant variables. Participants in both surveys were randomly assigned to one of the three expert consensus conditions ("clear authority" consensus, divided consensus, and "clearly no authority" consensus). I combine these categories with the variable reflecting whether survey respondents agreed or disagreed with the policy implications of the proposed measures described in the articles on gun control, in-state tuition benefits, and sanctuary cities. This results in three new categories across administrations reflecting (1) participants who agreed with the consensus opinion cited in the article for the condition to which they were assigned ($n = 267$ TESS; $n = 156$ CCES), (2) participants whose responses left it unclear whether they agreed or disagreed because they were in the "divided consensus" treatment ($n = 254$ TESS; $n = 164$ CCES), and (3) participants who disagreed with the consensus opinion expressed in the article ($n = 273$ TESS; $n = 156$ CCES).

Results

Table 10 sets forth the distribution of responses to the credibility question across administrations. In each sample, responses were quite similar. A plurality of respondents indicated that they agreed the cited expert was credible. Approximately one-fifth of respondents said the expert was not credible, and

TABLE 10. Expert credibility ratings across experimental administrations (%)

	Experts are credible	Experts are not credible	Don't know
TESS 2016 ($n = 801$) (Legislative scenarios)	42.4	20.7	36.5
CCES 2017 ($n = 490$) (Executive scenario)	45.3	21.4	33.1

about a third of respondents said they were not sure. Thus here, as in previous studies (Blank and Shaw 2015), more people deemed experts cited in the article credible than not credible.[8]

A second observation worth noting is that the proportion of respondents who expressed uncertainty about the credibility of experts is not negligible. It is about a third of all participants in both samples. This suggests that individuals who find experts credible may not just be a mirror image of those who say legal experts are not credible. Different factors may be relevant in each assessment. Moreover, there might be systemic factors that explain who is more likely to express uncertainty about expertise. To explore this possibility, I run probit regressions on each of these distinct responses (credible, not credible, don't know) in addition to the ordered probit regression on the three-point response variable reflecting growing skepticism about expertise.

As I undertake multivariate analyses of judgments about expertise in several different ways, each model answers a different question about the cognitive processes involved in judgments of the credibility of constitutional authorities. I aim to answer three distinct questions in the analyses: (1) What variables explain skepticism about constitutional experts? (2) Are the same factors relevant in crediting experts' opinions and dismissing their views? (3) Who is most likely to express uncertainty about constitutional expertise?

Question 1: What variables explain skepticism about constitutional experts?
First, I employ an ordered probit model to see what leads to skepticism about expertise. The dependent variable in the analyses is the three-point response to whether the constitutional authorities are credible experts regarding the question of government authority described in the article. Responses are coded 1 for yes, 2 for don't know, and 3 for no, to reflect increasing skepticism. I employ each "agreement category" as a dichotomous variable to see how individuals in different categories respond to questions about expertise in

relation to one another. Participants who agree with the expert consensus in the condition to which they were assigned are the excluded category in these models.[9]

I also include measures of participant's partisanship (coded 1–7, with higher numbers representing strong Republican identity), race (1 White, 0 non-White), gender (1 female, 0 male), birth year (higher numbers reflect participants who are younger), and level of education (with higher numbers representing higher levels of education). The public support manipulation in each experiment is dichotomously coded (0 for 85 percent support, 1 for 15 percent). In the models for legislative authority, I control for whether the respondent was answering questions about gun control measures or limits on in-state tuition benefits for undocumented students (coded 0 and 1, respectively). Results for the ordered model regarding skepticism appear in table 11.

The results demonstrate that those who are in conditions where they disagree with the expert consensus are significantly more skeptical of experts than the excluded category of those who agree with the consensus across

TABLE 11. Ordered probit regressions for skepticism about expertise across administrations

Variable	TESS 2016	CCES 2017
Disagree with consensus	.25** (.10)	.33* (.14)
Unclear condition	.13 (.10)	.38** (.13)
Republican	.11*** (.02)	.09*** (.03)
White	−.35*** (.10)	−.27* (.12)
Female	.04 (.08)	.02 (.11)
Birth year (younger)	.00 (.002)	−.01[+] (.003)
Education	−.24*** (.04)	−.23*** (.04)
Majority opposition	.01 (.08)	.06 (.11)
Issue	−.13[+] (.08)	—
N	798	450
LR χ^2	77.40***	61.75***

[+]$p < .10$, *$p < .05$, **$p < .01$, ***$p < .001$ (two-tailed test). Standard errors in parentheses.

administrations. Marginal effects indicate that differences are substantively important. In the executive authority administration, for instance, participants in conditions where they disagree with expert opinion regarding sanctuary cities are 13 percent less likely to say experts are credible and 9 percent more likely to say they are not credible than are participants in conditions where they agree with experts. Those in the divided consensus category also tend to be more skeptical of experts than those who agree; this difference is significant in the administration regarding executive authority, but not in that legislative authority.

The models also reveal partisanship is significant in the assessment of experts, with Republicans more skeptical in judging experts than Democrats. In the executive authority scenario strong Republicans are 3 percent less likely to deem experts credible and 2 percent more likely to say they are not credible than Republicans who are not strong identifiers. Moreover, Whites are 11 percent more likely to say experts are credible and 7 percent less likely to say they are not credible than non-Whites. Education also plays a significant role in judgments, with those who are more educated expressing less skepticism about expertise. There is also evidence that younger individuals defer more to experts (in the CCES sample the birth year variable is marginally significant) and that participants who received the gun control treatment were more skeptical about experts than those who read about the restriction of in-state benefits in the study about legislative authority.

Question 2: Are the same factors relevant in crediting experts' opinions and dismissing their views?
A second question one may ask in the context of this inquiry is whether the same factors are relevant in deeming experts credible as in dismissing experts as not credible. To probe this question, I run identical probit models on each of those response categories, with the results reported in tables 12 and 13.[10] In table 12 the dependent variable is coded 1 if the respondent deemed the expert credible and 0 otherwise; in table 13 the dependent variable is 1 if the respondent said the expert was not credible and 0 otherwise.

Looking across results for the two responses, it appears that similar demographic factors come into play in both judgments. Republicans are significantly less likely than Democrats to say experts are credible and also significantly more likely to say they are not credible. Those who are educated are more likely to say experts are credible and less likely to dismiss them as not credible. Race also seems to be important; it is significant for both responses

TABLE 12. Probit regressions for "credible" responses across administrations

Variable	TESS 2016	CCES 2017
Disagree with consensus	−.25* (.11)	−.33* (.15)
Unclear condition	−.09 (.11)	−.29* (.15)
Republican	−.10*** (.02)	−.08** (.03)
White	.36*** (.11)	.25+ (.14)
Female	−.15+ (.09)	−.16 (.13)
Birth year (younger)	.00 (.002)	.00 (.004)
Education	.26*** (.05)	.24*** (.04)
Majority opposition	.01 (.09)	−.03 (.12)
Issue	−.13 (.09)	—
Constant	−1.21*** (.31)	−9.00 (7.00)
N	798	451
LR χ^2	64.43***	51.99***

+$p < .10$, *$p < .05$, **$p < .01$, ***$p < .001$ (two-tailed test). Standard errors in parentheses.

in the TESS administration and marginally significant in the CCES models. Whites tend to be more trusting of experts than non-Whites and less likely to dismiss their views.

One particularly interesting finding from looking across these models is that participants' agreement with expert consensus in the condition to which they are assigned appears to be more important in judging experts to be credible than in judging they are not credible.[11] This particular result is noteworthy because it is consistent with findings about self-esteem that suggest it is more satisfying to attribute positive attributes to people who are like you than it is to attribute negative attributes to those who are not like you (Brewer 2007). Viewed in this light, it seems attributing credibility to those who share our views makes us feel better about ourselves, while dismissing the opinions of those who disagree does not serve the same purpose as effectively. (See also Clark and Evans 2014 on the role of consistent high-credibility messages in self-validation).

To get a better idea of the substantive importance of variables in the

TABLE 13. Probit regressions for "not credible" responses across administrations

Variable	TESS 2016	CCES 2017
Disagree with consensus	.23[+] (.13)	.34[+] (.18)
Unclear condition	.17 (.13)	.50** (.17)
Republican	.12*** (.03)	.09** (.03)
White	−.30* (.12)	−.28[+] (.16)
Female	−.13 (.11)	−.20 (.14)
Birth year	.00 (.003)	−.01[+] (.004)
Education	−.22*** (.05)	−.19*** (.05)
Majority opposition	.00 (.10)	.10 (.14)
Issue	−.14 (.10)	—
Constant	.66[+] (.35)	14.74[+] (8.00)
N	798	451
LR χ^2	49.78***	43.94***

[+]$p < .10$, *$p < .05$, **$p < .01$, ***$p < .001$ (two-tailed test). Standard errors in parentheses.

analyses, table 14 sets forth predicted probabilities for credible and not credible responses in the executive authority scenario. First, it is clear that those who *agree with experts seem to be acting distinctly* from those who disagree with expert consensus and from participants in the divided consensus conditions; predicted probabilities for the latter two categories are quite similar.

The differences between those who agree with experts and those who disagree are quite pronounced. We observe that participants in conditions where they agree with experts have a .56 probability of saying the experts are credible and a .13 probability of saying they are not credible (with other variables held at their means), compared with .43 and .21, respectively, for participants in conditions where they disagree with the opinions expressed by constitutional authorities.

With respect to demographic factors, partisanship has a substantial effect on assessments of expertise; strong Democrats who agree with experts have a .64 probability of deeming them credible versus .45 for strong Republicans, with other variables held at their means. Thus, predictions indicate strong

TABLE 14. Predicted probabilities for expert assessments in executive authority scenario

	Prediction: Credible	Prediction: Not credible
Agreement condition		
Agree with consensus	.56	.13
Disagree with consensus	.43	.21
Unclear	.44	.26
Demographics under various relevant conditions		
Strong Democrat (agree)	.64	.08
Strong Republican (agree)	.45	.20
White (agree)	.59	.11
NonWhite (agree)	.49	.17
Highest education (agree)	.77	.05
Lowest education (agree)	.32	.26
Highest education (disagree)	.66	.10
Lowest education (disagree)	.21	.38

Note: Predicted probabilities are with demographic variables at their means and condition variables set to agree (disagree = 0, unclear = 0), disagree (disagree = 1, unclear = 0), or unclear (disagree = 0, unclear = 1), as indicated.

Republicans are about 20 percent less likely to say experts are credible and more than twice as likely to say they are not credible (.20 versus .08) than strong Democrats even when they agree with their views. Whites who agree with experts' views have a .60 probability of agreeing that experts are credible compared to .50 for non-Whites.

Education also has a powerful influence on assessments of constitutional expertise. Those with postgraduate education have the highest probability (.77) of finding experts credible when participants agree with the views that authorities are expressing. Moreover, even when experts express views that highly educated individuals do not agree with, they are still substantially more likely than not (.66) to deem them credible. Conversely, those without a high school diploma have the lowest likelihood of deciding experts are credible, particularly when they disagree with the views that experts express (.21); this group is also most likely to respond that experts are *not credible* when they disagree with the views authorities express (.38).

Question 3: Who is most likely to express uncertainty about expertise?
Table 15 displays probit models for "don't know" responses across administrations to explore whether there are systematic factors that explain the expression of uncertainty about expertise. Responses were coded 1 if respondents said they did not know whether experts were credible and 0 otherwise.

The results demonstrate that although those who disagree with experts are somewhat more likely to express uncertainty about expertise, there are no significant differences in terms of respondents' agreement with the consensus conditions they were in. Moreover, those who identify as Democrats and Republicans seem to respond with "don't know" similarly. We do, however, observe that a pair of demographic features are relevant. In both samples, female respondents are more likely than male respondents to respond with uncertainty about the credibility of experts; similarly, less-educated respondents

TABLE 15. Probit regressions for "don't know" responses across administrations

Variable	TESS 2016	CCES 2017
Disagree with consensus	.10 (.11)	.09 (.16)
Unclear condition	−.02 (.11)	−.08 (.15)
Republican	.01 (.02)	.03 (.03)
White	.17 (.11)	−.05 (.14)
Female	.24** (.09)	.35** (.13)
Birth year	.00 (.003)	−.00 (.004)
Education	−.10* (.05)	−.11** (.04)
Majority opposition	.00 (.09)	−.04 (.12)
Issue	−.02 (.09)	—
Constant	−.40 (.31)	−4.39 (7.19)
N	798	451
LR χ^2	17.09*	16.05*

$^+p < .10$, $^*p < .05$, $^{**}p < .01$, $^{***}p < .001$ (two-tailed test). Standard errors in parentheses.

are more likely than more-educated respondents to respond with uncertainty about the credibility of experts. Women who agree with experts have a .35 probability of responding that they do not know whether experts are credible in the executive authority scenario, compared to .23 for men. This is interesting, as female respondents were less likely than male respondents to give definitive answers—that experts were either credible or not credible—in each of the analyses above, although the differences were not significant. These findings, when taken together, perhaps demonstrate that men tend to be more decisive than women in their thinking about the credibility of experts.

Participants who don't have a high school diploma and who agree with the views experts express are about twice as likely to respond that they don't know whether experts are credible (.41) compared to participants who have graduate-level education (.21). Thus the analyses here demonstrate that those who are less educated are both more skeptical and more likely to express uncertainty about the expertise of constitutional authorities.

Conclusion

This chapter has examined how citizens assess the credibility of constitutional experts on matters of government authority. Findings were strikingly consistent across experiments conducted on 2016 TESS and 2017 CCES samples, using scenarios involving two government institutions and three different issues. This contributes to the overall confidence in findings about the factors and processes relevant in the evaluation of constitutional authorities from this inquiry.

Analyses showed that demographic factors, including partisanship, race, and level of education, were significant predictors of survey respondents' willingness to extend credibility to constitutional experts. Republicans, non-Whites, and those with less education all expressed more skepticism about expertise. The compatibility of the views expressed by experts with respondents' own policy views on the issues that were the subject of proposed government action was also important.

Looking at factors that were relevant in each response revealed that agreement with the views expressed by experts was more important in deciding that experts were credible than in deciding that they were not credible. This comports with research demonstrating it serves our self-esteem more effectively to attribute positive characteristics to those who are like us than to attribute negative attributes to those who are not. This may be especially true when evaluating experts. When we deem experts who share our views credible, those views themselves take on greater validity; deciding that experts who do not share our views are not credible does not have the same self-validating effect. This finding helps to distinguish the purpose of motivated reasoning that results from agreement with the views expressed by experts from the social identity benefits of motivated reasoning that have been theorized to be relevant in motivated judgments about experts driven by partisanship.

Although partisanship and agreement with the views expressed by experts both had considerable effects on assessments of expertise, differences between participants with the highest and lowest levels of education in our samples were most pronounced. It could be that the reason education has such a substantial influence on such judgments is that there is pressure from above and below, so to speak. Highly educated individuals are more likely to credit experts because of their own experience in academic environments, and those who are less educated are more likely to say experts are not credible because of a growing degree of anti-intellectualism, identified by such scholars as Merkley (2020b). The evidence provided here supports the notion that both mechanisms are at play. Moreover, the analysis of "don't know" responses suggests a third dynamic whereby those who are less educated are not only more skeptical, they are also more likely to express uncertainty about expertise than those who have achieved higher levels of education.

Expressing uncertainly about expertise did not seem to be tied to any passive-aggressive disagreement with the views authorities were expressing; there was no significant pattern between agreement conditions and the likelihood of giving a "don't know" response on questions addressing expert credibility. We observed that female respondents were significantly more likely to express uncertainty about the credibility of constitutional experts than male respondents. Moreover, uncertainty on the part of female respondents was more prevalent than deferring to experts, as gender stereotypes might suggest.

It is important to consider the implications of these findings for the constraining power of constitutional rules in our current political environment. One may question how findings about the credibility of constitutional experts influence the persuasive weight of arguments and the evidence they provide. The findings reported here suggest the relationship is somewhat complex. Although the distribution of responses regarding expert credibility across the TESS and CCES samples was quite similar, with over 50 percent of participants saying they did not think (or did not know whether) cited experts were credible, analyses of participants' ultimate judgments about the legitimacy of the government action in chapter 2 indicate that expert consensus significantly influenced participants' assessments in the legislative context. There was also evidence in the executive authority experiment that participants were heeding experts *in some respect,* as legitimacy ratings were highest when constitutional experts agreed the president had the authority to take the proposed action and lowest when experts agreed they did not.

This suggests a bit of a disconnect between participants' expressed assessments of expert credibility and the persuasive influence of the views those authorities profess. In their review of research on resistance to scientific authorities, Hornsey and Fielding (2017) suggest that such resistance may serve an independent *value expressive* function for individuals. It seems the various reasons we have to assess constitutional authorities in a biased manner may slant our assessments such that they do not accurately reflect the influence of expert information in our own judgments. The idea that this may cause some people to misjudge the influence of expert information in their own decision-making is an intriguing idea that seems worthy of further study.

Finally, it is appropriate to acknowledge the unique context in which the opinions of such authorities are relevant. Citizens are not judges, but widespread acquiescence to official assertions of authority that may be of questionable constitutional validity can certainly add to the appearance of appropriateness. Under such circumstances, public opinion can have real implications for government authority. We rely on the media to inform us about official acts we cannot observe directly. The media in turn rely on constitutional experts to alert citizens about dubious assertions of power on the part of government actors.

The findings presented in this chapter suggest that our willingness to credit experts, so that we may heed such warnings, depends in no small part on our opinions, our partisanship, and the extent to which we share the academic training of authorities that are cited. Ultimately, if we want constitutional rules to constrain government institutions in the manner they were designed to, there must be a way for individuals to recognize even socially constructed limits on state officials that is not so closely tied to our backgrounds and predispositions. In the absence of such limits, the only thing keeping officials in check in the current political environment may be the fact that we are so evenly divided. If Congress or the president takes some questionable action, similar numbers of people are likely to see it as appropriate and as inappropriate. Taken to its extreme, official authority that depends so substantially on political context may not have any real limits at all.

In the next chapter I delve more deeply into how people think about expertise by analyzing their open-ended justifications for assessments about the desirability and legitimacy of congressional action in experiments on legislative authority describing proposed congressional action on gun control and immigration. I look at how participants cite and refute the expert consensus mentioned in the conditions to which they were assigned. The analysis is quite interesting in several respects and provides additional evidence about some of the conclusions drawn here. I also explore the substance of those responses to gauge the extent to which participants mention constitutional and policy considerations in their justifications. The goal is to get a richer understanding of how people think about government powers in the context of important contemporary political debates.

4 | Examining Justifications for Citizens' Evaluations of Legislative Action on Gun Control and Immigration

I N THIS CHAPTER I analyze the open-ended responses of participants in the legislative authority experiment to questions asking them to explain their views on the desirability and appropriateness of proposed measures involving gun control and immigration. The focus is somewhat different from that in the preceding chapters, which tested hypotheses about how citizens think about government action and expertise. The analysis here is primarily descriptive. Gerring (2012) defines descriptive analysis as answering "what" questions about a class of phenomena. Here I explore what is in the minds of experimental participants as they think about government authority. The goal is to see how people employ different types of information to explain why they perceive the exercise of legislative authority as desirable and appropriate. In the relatively closed system provided by the experimental scenarios we can observe how distinct individuals respond to various kinds of information that can support or challenge their view of the role of government in particular policy areas.

The descriptive analyses in this chapter supplement findings from chapters 2 and 3. One reason to engage in this exercise it to acknowledge that the participants who take part in survey research are complex individuals who often vary in the extent to which they are interested in the political phenomena social scientists study and that they think about things in idiosyncratic ways that do not always fit neatly into the way we operationalize variables for statistical analysis. Of course, it is also true that people are not always aware of the influences on their decision-making. Analyzing open-ended responses to questions in the context of experimental research can help reveal whether there is a disconnect between what people say is behind their judgments and the observed influence of various considerations. For instance, investigating how legally trained individuals justified their decisions in an experimental study, Braman (2009) finds a discrepancy between the observed influence of attitudinal factors and participants' legalistic explanations of those judgments. Finally, looking at how individuals explain their own reasoning processes can lead to new insights into how people think about the exercise of government authority. In this regard, descriptive research may inductively lead to the advancement of knowledge of decision-making processes.

It can be difficult and expensive to obtain the kind of open-ended responses that I analyze here from national surveys.[1] As such, most experimental studies in the discipline do not collect or analyze this sort of data. Where open-ended responses have been employed by political psychologists to explore decision-making processes, however, they have resulted in interesting and important findings. Two prominent examples are particularly relevant to this inquiry. Work by Stanley Feldman and John Zaller looking at how people think about welfare policy, gleaned from open-ended survey questions, has led to important insights into the substantive content of conflicting considerations that come to mind in responding to survey questions about government aid and the cognitive processes involved in opinion formation itself (Feldman and Zaller 1992; Zaller and Feldman 1992). Like those researchers, I ask participants to explain their answers to questions about government authority to get an idea of the considerations in their minds as they respond to questions about the desirability and legitimacy of government action.

Work by Dennis Chong (1993) looks at the considerations in the minds of citizens in a different context. Chong explores how people think about constitutional frameworks involving civil liberties. He also finds a good deal of conflicting thoughts in the minds of citizens by analyzing how people talk about rights in interviews. He observes that people have a complex understanding of how civil liberties operate and that their responses are often powerfully influenced by the sort of questions they are asked because they have so many different considerations to draw on.

Similarly, citizens have a good number of concerns to weigh when thinking about the exercise of government powers. By drawing participants' attention to particular circumstances surrounding the exercise of that authority in experimental scenarios and then exploring how they justify their assessments, I hope to provide a realistic view of how citizens employ policy opinions, expertise, and their own understanding of constitutional frameworks in assessments of government action.

I start with a general overview of responses about each issue to get a sense of what participants' justifications look like. I discuss the coding scheme employed to see whether participants were more likely to mention certain considerations in answering questions about the legitimacy of official action compared to its desirability. I also explore whether some variables were mentioned more in discussing congressional action relating to gun control than in justifying participants' views of measures related to immigration. Finally, I consider whether different types of respondents were more likely to reference particular factors surrounding the exercise of authority in their justifications.

Justifying Assessments

Recall that in the experiment on legislative authority, respondents were given a hypothetical article describing a proposed national legislation that they were told might infringe on state prerogatives to regulate on particular matters. The measure involved either gun control (requiring background checks of private sellers and cutting down on ammunition sales) or immigration (preventing undocumented state residents attending public colleges from taking advantage of in-state tuition benefits). After they read the article and responded to questions about whether they thought the experts cited were credible, respondents were asked whether they agreed that "Congress *should take*" the proposed action (measure of perceived desirability) and whether they thought it was a "legitimate, or appropriate, exercise of legislative authority" (measure of perceived legitimacy).

Following both the desirability and legitimacy measures, respondents were asked, "Can you please explain your answer to the last question in a sentence or two?" (See the chapter 2 appendix for specific scenarios and wording.) The answers respondents gave were not intended to be exhaustive (although, as set forth below, some responses were rather long and complex). Rather, the prompt was designed to get an idea of the most pertinent thoughts in the minds of respondents as they answered questions relating to each type of assessment. The aim was to develop some additional understanding of how participants' own knowledge and preferences combined with information in the scenario to shape assessments of the proposed legislative action that was the subject of the article in each condition.

Of the 801 participants who took part in the legislative authority experiment, not everyone answered open-ended questions. Of the 396 participants assigned to the gun control condition, 65 did not respond to the open-ended question about why they thought Congress should or should not pass the proposed legislation; another 27 provided answers that were not responsive. This leaves 304 responses (or 77 percent) for analysis. The corresponding number for legitimacy justifications in the gun control condition is 265 (67 percent).[2]

In the immigration condition, 326 (80 percent) and 270 (67 percent) of the 405 participants provided substantive answers to the desirability and legitimacy justifications, respectively. The justifications people gave for their evaluations of official authority were sometimes simple and sometimes complex. In the spirit of the prompt, most respondents kept things relatively brief, averaging two or three sentences. In some cases, responses to the prompts were just a few words; other responses were quite a bit longer.

There was a good deal of variability in the sort of thing respondents discussed in response to open-ended prompts. Some respondents talked about the issues in explicitly constitutional terms:

> The Second Amendment was for when the country was just coming into being. It doesn't pertain to today. (desirability/gun control)

> No gun control shall be allowed by the Constitution! (desirability/gun control)

> Article I gives Congress the authority to [decide] how money is spent. Similar to how in the '70s and '80s the federal government wouldn't give highway funds unless the state had a 55 mph speed limit. (legitimacy/immigration)

> We need to have tighter restrictions on assault weapons and guns in general. The NRA and its members run the Second Amendment up and down the flagpole every chance they get. Have they read it? I don't think so because the first and most important [thing] it says [is] "A well regulated Militia, being necessary to the security of a free state, the right of the people to keep and bear arms, shall not be infringed." Are these people members of Militias, are they arming themselves to protect the Free State? NO. (desirability/gun control)

Others did not mention the Constitution at all but did seem to refer to their understanding of federalism, or how they thought our federalist system should operate:

> I believe in states' rights. The federal government is overstepping the right of the states to regulate. (desirability/gun control)

It should be up to each individual state to decide. (legitimacy/immigration)

States vary in the numbers of undocumented people living in the state. It is probably best that the state therefore be left to make this decision. While illegally entering the US is not to be encouraged, they are supporting the state they live in through sales, property, and (in some cases) income taxes. Thus they should be entitled to the state benefit of in-state tuition. Plus it seems best to help all people living in our country to attend college and get the education necessary to get a good job. (desirability/immigration)

Still other participants relied primarily on their views of whether this was sound policy to justify their assessments.

It would be the best place to start [with] better gun control. (legitimacy/gun control)

I believe that any law that protects the lives of children, as well as adults, should be passed! The language of the Constitution is far from being transparent and let us not forget it was created a long time ago when priorities were quite different than today. (legitimacy/gun control)

Illegals should not get the same privileges as legals. (desirability/immigration)

Don't restrict education. (desirability/immigration)

Funds for Americans only!! (desirability/immigration)

I just don't like it. (legitimacy/immigration)

Some participants discussed their own experiences in explaining their views:

I believe that illegal immigrants should not get all the benefits that legal citizens enjoy. I am an immigrant that came to America legally and did not get things for free. I worked hard and so did my siblings. We went to school, worked hard and are not rich but live according to our means and are getting Social Security. I am against deportation. The illegal immigrants that are here for many years and have children here and are law-abiding citizen should be awarded legal status, get jobs, learn the language, and pay the taxes. (desirability/immigration)

Others invoked constitutional history and their views of what the framers intended:

The federal government oversteps its constitutional bounds so often that the states' power has become compromised. Our original founders intended for states to have individual authority, but slowly the government strips that away, and it uses federal money to do it. (desirability/immigration)

This isn't just about "hunting." That is a canard. This is about the citizen's right to arm himself for his own security and to protect himself from others INCLUDING the government if they violate his rights. The founders understood this all too well. Would we have EVER gained our freedom from an oppressive government if we were all unarmed? The truth is that the government wants to do anything it can to determine where every gun is. For what purpose? So they can confiscate them or arrest the owners when it's deemed "appropriate." Which will be precisely the time the citizens will need their arms to protect themselves from said government. You can limit magazines to ten rounds if you want. I can buy a hundred magazines. That's fine. But because this would likely be only part of a larger bill taking away more rights, I could not support it in part. (desirability/gun control)

To impose some structure on the analysis of open-ended responses, a coding scheme was developed to keep track of different types of considerations respondents mentioned in their justifications. The scheme was not intended to be exhaustive but to keep track of factors particularly relevant to the inquiry about how citizens think about official action. Thus policy considerations, constitutional factors, and variables that were specifically manipulated in the experimental scenario, such as expert opinion and public opinion about the action, each figure prominently in the coding scheme.

The Coding Process

An undergraduate research assistant aided the classification of the opened-ended responses discussed in this chapter. The process started with each investigator coding the same subset of responses to calibrate the coding and refine the scheme for each scenario. Once we were satisfied with the scheme for both conditions and achieved a high level of intercoder reliability (.96 for all responses and .94 for substantive responses), the research assistant took over the lion's share of open-ended coding. Coders met periodically to discuss coding issues and categorize responses that were difficult to code over the course of the study.

Tables 16 and 17 set forth the coding scheme for each treatment condition. Responses to the desirability and legitimacy questions were coded separately, although, as discussed below, it does not seem as though most participants distinguished between the two prompts a great deal in justifying their assessments. Generally, answers were coded for responsiveness and whether the respondents mentioned specific factors in their justifications that were coded as dichotomous variables (1 mention, 0 no mention). The schemes for the gun control and immigration scenarios were somewhat different to reflect the distinct considerations raised by each issue. Each had codes for responsiveness and fifteen additional variables.

Both coding schemes noted whether respondents expressed uncertainty in their answers, whether they cited experts or expertise, and whether they explicitly said they were not an expert on the subject. Moreover, we noted when participants expressed policy opinions in justifying assessments for both questions. Responses in both conditions were also coded for references to the Constitution, federalism, Congress, the states, constitutional history, and public opinion about the issue. The gun control scheme included codes for references to the Second Amendment, gun rights, general safety, citizen safety, and the safety of gun owners. The immigration scenario included additional codes for references to education rights, the Supreme Court, citizenship, public funding, and the payment of taxes.

All variables were dichotomously coded for each response for every participant. Mentions could be coded for as many variables as was appropriate. The coding did not distinguish between positive and negative mentions of variables because such determinations are often difficult to make and can introduce a good deal of subjectivity into the coding process.

To illustrate, justifications stating "I support the Second Amendment and

TABLE 16. Open-ended coding scheme for gun control scenario

Variable name	Coding criteria
Blank	Response is blank.
Nonsense	Response has content but it is nonsense (e.g., "Kjshdf").
Not responsive	Content is not responsive to question (e.g., "yes," "no," N/A, "refer to previous").
Don't know	Respondent says don't know or not sure.
Expertise	Response mentions constitutional experts or expertise.
Not an expert	Respondent says they are not an expert in some regard.
Policy opinion	Response includes any sort of policy opinion.
Constitution	Response mentions the Constitution or any part of the Constitution.
Gun rights	Response refers to gun rights.
2nd Amendment	Response specifically mentions Second Amendment.
Federalism	Response references federalism.
Gun safety	Response reference safety of gun owners or citizens.
Citizen safety	Response mentions safety of citizens.
Owner safety	Response mentions safety of gun owners.
Congress	Response mentions Congress.
States	Response mentions states.
Constitutional history	Response mentions constitutional history or founding fathers.
Public opinion	Response mentions public opinion about the issue.

dislike the government having ANY say about guns" and "F*** the Second Amendment" were both coded similarly, even though one demonstrates negative feelings about the Second Amendment and the other expresses support. Each of the responses was coded 1 for referencing the Constitution and the Second Amendment. The first response also contains a policy opinion; the latter was not coded as containing policy content. Although there can be an argument that it does, we coded for clear indication of participants' views with respect to policy rather than broad references to legal frameworks.

Even with the conservative coding scheme, it is clear that a good number

TABLE 17. Open-ended coding scheme for immigration scenario

Variable name	Coding criteria
Blank	Response is blank.
Nonsense	Response has content but it is nonsense (e.g., "Kjshdf").
Not responsive	Content is not responsive to question (e.g., "yes," "no," N/A, "refer to previous").
Don't know	Respondent says don't know or not sure.
Expertise	Response mentions constitutional experts or expertise.
Not an expert	Respondent says they are not an expert in some regard.
Policy opinion	Response includes any sort of policy opinion.
Constitution	Response mentions Constitution or any part of the Constitution.
Education rights	Response refers to education rights.
Supreme Court	Response specifically mentions Supreme Court.
Federalism	Response references federalism.
Citizenship	Response references citizenship or prioritizing citizens.
Funding	Response mentions funding in any way or lack of resources for colleges.
Taxes	Response mentions citizens or immigrants paying or not paying taxes.
Congress	Response mentions Congress.
States	Response mentions states.
Constitutional history	Response mentions constitutional history or founding fathers.
Public opinion	Response mentions public opinion about the issue.

of justifications included some sort of policy content. This was true not only for prompts asking about the desirability of congressional action but also for responses to the legitimacy question as well. Moreover, many respondents talked about the Constitution when discussing the desirability of legislative measures, even though one might think such considerations would be more relevant in response to prompts about the legitimacy of congressional action. This was particularly true in the gun control scenario. As detailed below, some variables were discussed more commonly in response to one type of question than in response to the other.

As each of the desirability and legitimacy prompts probes the thinking of citizens with regard to these distinct assessments, I set forth the incidence of mentions for each type of response separately for both issues. I also present rankings of the five most discussed variables and the five least-mentioned considerations for each type of question across conditions. Finally, I compare the total number of mentions for commonly coded variables in the gun control and immigration scenarios to see if there were differences in how people thought about these different issues in the context of the government power dilemma raised in the articles.

Open-Ended Responses for the Gun Control Scenario

Table 18 reports the frequencies for each variable in responses to questions in the gun control scenario.[3] Several interesting findings emerge. First, people are more likely to express uncertainty when answering questions about the legitimacy of legislative action than when answering questions about its desirability. They are also somewhat more likely to say that they are not an expert on the matter in response to the legitimacy question. Finally, they are more likely to refer to expertise in this context. Taken together, these findings lend credence to the idea that people think differently about legitimacy than about desirability (see also Braman 2016). Respondents are more likely to reference outside guidance and acknowledge they are uncertain when answering questions about the legitimate exercise of legislative authority.

Moreover, respondents are more likely to mention policy opinions in responding to questions about the desirability of congressional action. This particular finding, however, should perhaps be treated with a grain of salt. As table 19 demonstrates, policy considerations were the most frequently mentioned of all the coded variables when participants answered questions about both desirability *and* legitimacy. Still, it does make sense that people are more likely to discuss policy when talking about the desirability of government action. The fact that over 70 percent of desirability responses contain policy content versus about 30 percent of responses to the legitimacy prompt suggests that the relative prominence of policy considerations in desirability justifications is substantively meaningful.

The frequencies reported in table 18 also reveal that people are significantly

TABLE 18. Open-ended coding for gun control responses, frequency of mentions

Gun control variable	Desirability mentions ($n = 304$)	Legitimacy mentions ($n = 265$)	Total mentions ($n = 569$)
Don't know	6	20	26
Expertise	11	17	28
Not an expert	2	7	9
Policy opinion	218	76	294
Constitution	55	60	115
Gun rights	48	23	71
2nd Amendment	40	21	61
Federalism	26	43	69
Gun safety	79	28	107
Citizen safety	57	18	75
Owner safety	19	2	21
Congress	24	71	95
States	18	40	58
Constitutional history	23	7	30
Public opinion	6	6	12

more likely to mention gun rights, the Second Amendment, safety in general, and the safety of both citizens and gun owners in discussing the desirability of policy than when they are justifying assessments of its appropriateness.

The fact that they are also more likely to discuss constitutional history when talking about desirability is a bit puzzling. It may reflect just how much views of what the framers intended have influenced perceptions of what *should happen* when it comes to congressional action matters related to the regulation of firearms. The frequencies reported in table 18 also indicate that respondents are more likely to talk about federalism and Congress and to mention states when discussing the appropriateness of legislative action than when justifying assessments of its desirability. Indeed, these three variables are among the most mentioned in justifications of the appropriateness of state action.

One noteworthy finding is there is little difference in references to the

Constitution in discussing the desirability or legitimacy of policy related to gun control. Indeed, as table 19 shows, references to the Constitution are among the top five variables mentioned in response to both types of questions. Again, this may reflect the fact that constitutional arguments, and specifically Second Amendment arguments, are commonplace these days in discussions of what the national government should do with respect to regulating firearms. The fact that the Second Amendment is more likely to be mentioned in statements concerning desirability than in statements about the appropriateness of government power may be additional evidence of this. It is also true, however, that the experimental scenario raises concerns about legislative authority in the context of the US federal structure, such that Second Amendment considerations might play less of a role in judgments about the appropriateness of congressional action under the specific circumstances raised in the hypothetical article.

One of the more interesting findings with regard to respondents' justifications concerns their awareness of the influence of various factors in their decision-making. For instance, expertise is among the least-mentioned

TABLE 19. Open-ended variable rankings for gun control condition

Desirability, open-ended rankings			Legitimacy, open-ended rankings		
Rank	Variable	Percentage of mentions	Rank	Variable	Percentage of mentions
1	Policy opinion	71.7	1	Policy opinion	28.7
2	Safety	26.0	2	Congress	26.8
3	Citizen safety	18.8	3	Constitution	22.6
4	Constitution	18.1	4	Federalism	16.3
5	Gun rights	15.8	5	States	15.1
—			—		
11	Owner safety	6.7	11	Expertise	6.4
12	Expertise	3.6	12	Constitutional history	2.6
13	Don't know	2.0	12	Not an expert	2.6
13	Public opinion	2.0	14	Public opinion	2.3
15	Not an expert	1.0	15	Owner safety	1.0

variables in justifying legitimacy assessments, even though the findings reported in chapter 2 clearly demonstrate that expert consensus has a significant effect on assessments of the appropriate exercise of congressional authority. Policy attitudes and respondents' feelings about federalism were also significant in the analysis of the legislative assessments in chapter 2; each figures prominently in rankings of the variables mentioned in participants' justifications for legitimacy assessments analyzed here. As we will see, this same pattern is evident in findings regarding justifications of responses in the immigration scenario. Thus it appears that people are either more aware of or more willing to acknowledge the influence of some factors than others in their decision-making about government authority.

Open-Ended Responses for the Immigration Scenario

A look at the justification for assessments of authority in the immigration scenario reveals both similarities and differences in how people talk about legislative action. Tables 20 and 21 report the frequencies and rankings for variables in response to each type of question. As in the gun control condition, respondents are more likely to express uncertainty and also more likely to say they are not experts with respect to the matter in response to the legitimacy prompt.

There seems to be a lot more policy content and quite a bit less constitutional content in discussions of the immigration issue than in justifications for assessments of the gun control measure. Again, respondents are more likely to mention policy views in talking about the desirability of government action, but that is also the most referenced variable in justifications of responses to the legitimacy question. The absolute number of policy references is higher in the immigration scenario and the absolute number of references to the Constitution is quite a bit lower. This finding likely occurs because specific concerns about violations of the Tenth Amendment are less commonly raised in public discourse than concerns about the Second Amendment. As such, citizens appear to be more comfortable talking in explicitly constitutional terms when it comes to legislative action concerning gun control than in discussing action on immigration, even where similar concerns about national authority are invoked. It could also be the reason more people are likely to express uncertainty regarding legislative action concerning immigration than about legislation concerning gun control (forty-two versus twenty-six total mentions). Citizens may feel more confident talking about government authority related to gun control because they hear about it on the news so often.

TABLE 20. Open-ended coding for immigration responses, frequency of mentions

Immigration variable	Desirability mentions ($n = 326$)	Legitimacy mentions ($n = 270$)	Total mentions ($n = 596$)
Don't know	9	33	42
Expertise	3	6	9
Not an expert	0	3	3
Policy opinion	233	109	342
Constitution	7	13	20
Education rights	14	2	16
Supreme Court	0	7	7
Federalism	42	51	93
Citizenship	141	28	169
Funding	30	23	53
Taxes	31	9	40
Congress	20	75	95
States	64	53	117
Constitutional history	1	2	3
Public opinion	0	0	0

Participants were especially likely to mention citizenship in justifying their opinions about the desirability of congressional action on immigration. Education rights and the payment of taxes were significantly more likely to be mentioned in justifications about the desirability of national legislation. As table 21 demonstrates, citizenship and taxes were among the most referenced variables in justifications of the desirability of congressional action.

In contrast to what we saw in the gun control scenario, respondents were also relatively more likely to mention federalism and the states than other variables in response the desirability question. They were equally likely to mention these variables in justifying the appropriateness of congressional authority. Both Congress and the Supreme Court were more likely to be referenced in response to the legitimacy prompt, with Congress being the second most referenced variable in that context.

TABLE 21. Open-ended variable rankings for immigration condition

Desirability, open-ended rankings			Legitimacy, open-ended rankings		
Rank	Variable	Percentage of mentions	Rank	Variable	Percentage of mentions
1	Policy opinion	71.4	1	Policy opinion	40.3
2	Citizenship	43.3	2	Congress	27.7
3	States	19.6	3	States	19.6
4	Federalism	12.9	4	Federalism	18.8
5	Taxes	9.5	5	Don't know	12.2
—			—		
11	Expertise	1.0	11	Expertise	2.2
12	Constitutional history	0.3	12	Not an expert	1.1
13	Supreme Court	0	13	Constitutional history	1.0
13	Public opinion	0	13	Education eights	1.0
13	Not an expert	0	15	Public opinion	0

Once more, we see participants were unlikely to reference expertise, notwithstanding the influence of expert consensus in their legitimacy assessments. Also, even though popular support for the policy was marginally significant in the assessment of the appropriateness of legislative action in the immigration scenario (Braman 2021), public opinion was not mentioned by respondents in their justifications. Again, this finding suggests a disconnect between the demonstrated effect of certain variables in respondents' legitimacy assessments and their explicit justifications for those judgments. Both federalism and policy views are referenced prominently in assessments about the legitimacy of congressional action on immigration.

Differences in Justifications across Issues

Table 22 sets forth the differences in total mentions for commonly coded variables across issues. Generally, the frequencies confirm that participants are more likely to speak in explicitly constitutional language and to reference

TABLE 22. Comparison of total mentions across issue scenarios

| Variable | Total mentions | | χ^2 result |
	Gun control ($N = 569$)	Immigration ($N = 596$)	
Don't know	26	42	3.25[+]
Expertise	28	9	11.01[***]
Not an expert	9	3	.06[+a]
Policy opinion	294	342	4.09[*]
Constitution	115	20	75.39[***]
Federalism	69	93	2.94[+]
Congress	95	95	0.12
States	58	117	20.31[***]
Constitutional history	30	3	24.20[***]
Public opinion	12	0	.002[a]

[+]$p < .10$, [*]$p < .05$, [**]$p < .01$, [***]$p < .001$ (two-tailed test).
[a] Fisher's exact test was used in place of the χ^2 test where cell counts are less than 5.

constitutional history when justifying assessments of gun control legislation. They are also more likely to mention public opinion and expertise, and to explicitly say they are not an expert in this context.

Individuals are more likely to say they are uncertain when justifying assessments of government action relating to immigration, and they are significantly more likely to mention policy opinions about the issue. Participants are also more likely to refer to federalism and the states in these justifications, perhaps because the immigration scenario involved federal action in the realm of education benefits, a matter many consider to be squarely within the prerogative of state legislatures.

Considerations across Different Types of Respondents

Besides looking at the differences in mentions for each type of question and across conditions, it is possible to see whether there were differences in the types of considerations raised by distinct types of respondents. Although many different types of comparisons can be drawn, here I focus on comparisons that seem particularly relevant to the inquiry. Specifically, I look at differences in factors mentioned by (1) Republicans versus Democrats, (2) participants who were randomly assigned to conditions where they *agreed with the expert consensus* versus those who were not randomly assigned to such conditions, and (3) participants who expressed the view that *experts were credible* versus those who did not express that opinion.

There were some differences between Republicans and Democrats in the types of considerations they mentioned in the gun control experiment in response to each question. For instance, 23 percent (33 of 143) Republicans mentioned the Constitution in their desirability responses versus 14 percent (22 of 154) Democrats (χ^2 (1, 297) = 3.80, $p < .05$). There was no difference in the extent to which they mentioned the Constitution in response to the legitimacy prompt. Republicans were also more likely to reference states in answers to questions about the legitimacy of the proposed measure on gun control (20 percent versus 11 percent, χ^2 (1, 254) = 4.31, $p < .05$). Democrats were significantly more likely to mention general safety (33 percent versus 16 percent, χ^2 (1, 297) = 11.43, $p < .001$) and citizen safety (25 percent versus 12 percent, χ^2 (1, 297) = 8.91, $p < .01$) in their responses to questions about the desirability of the proposed measure.

In the immigration condition, Republicans mentioned their political opinions more often than Democrats in response to prompts about the desirability *and* legitimacy of proposed congressional action (77 percent versus 66 percent for desirability, χ^2 (1, 319) = 4.85, $p < .05$, and 66 percent versus 58 percent for legitimacy, χ^2 (1, 264) = 3.84, $p < .05$). Republicans were also more likely to mention citizenship when explaining their view of the desirability of the proposed immigration measure (54 percent versus 34 percent, χ^2 (1, 319) = 12.60, $p < .001$) and more likely to mention Congress in explaining legitimacy assessments (35 percent versus 20 percent, χ^2 (1, 264) = 7.66, $p < .01$). Democrats were more likely than Republicans to express uncertainty in responding to the legitimacy prompt (19 percent versus 5 percent, χ^2 (1, 264) = 12.55, $p < .001$).

There were some interesting patterns concerning mentions of expertise, particularly in the gun control scenario.[4] Participants who agreed with policy supported by the expert consensus in the conditions to which they were assigned were more likely to mention experts or expertise than other participants in answering questions about legitimacy (12 percent [11 of 96] versus 3 percent [6 of 156], χ^2 (1, 252) = 5.89, $p < .01$). Moreover, those assigned to conditions where expert views were consistent with their views about federalism were also more likely to mention experts when responding to the legitimacy prompt (12 percent [11 of 91] versus 4 percent [6 of 161], χ^2 (1, 252) = 6.91, $p < .01$). People who were assigned to conditions where expert consensus supported their policy views about gun control were also marginally more likely to mention the Constitution in at least one of their responses than were participants who were assigned to other conditions (13 percent [14 of 108] versus 7 percent [14 of 203], χ^2 (1, 310) = 2.86, $p < .09$).

The fact that participants were more likely to mention experts and constitutional arguments when assigned to conditions suggesting that those factors supported their views lends credence to the notion that they were referencing those authorities and evidence to reinforce their opinions rather than to disparage the views of others. This supports the suggestion raised in chapter 3, that individuals employ the opinions of experts to bolster their own argument in service of self-esteem.

There is also evidence suggesting that those who agreed that experts were credible were more comfortable answering questions about the appropriate exercise of congressional authority. Specifically, they were less likely to express uncertainty when answering legitimacy questions in both scenarios than those who replied that they were unsure about the credibility of experts or responded that experts were not credible (5 percent [6 of 123] versus 10 percent [14 of 135], χ^2 (1, 258) = 2.72, $p < .09$ for gun control, and 6 percent [9 of 142] versus 17 percent [22 of 127], χ^2 (1, 269) = 7.93, $p < .01$ for immigration). Those who said experts were credible were also more likely to mention the Constitution in explaining their assessments of the legitimacy of proposed action across both the gun control and immigration scenarios (29 percent [36 of 123] versus 17 percent [24 of 135], χ^2 (1, 258) = 4.72, $p < .05$ for gun control, and 8 percent [11 of 142] versus 2 percent [2 of 127], χ^2 (1, 269) = 7.93, $p < .05$ for immigration).

Discussion

What does this analysis of open-ended responses tell us about how people think about government authority? Most people will not be surprised to learn that Democrats are more likely to mention safety when discussing the desirability of gun regulations and that Republicans tend to emphasize citizenship when explaining their views of immigration policy. Still, the effort has been worthwhile in several respects.

First, the open-ended responses people gave to explain their assessments reveal a good deal of variation in the specificity of individual answers and the considerations mentioned in response to each questions. Many of the open-ended answers convey strong attitudes about the desirability and legitimacy of government action on these issues, but there were also quite a few responses professing ignorance about how different levels of government should function these important policy questions.

Second, although there was a good deal of policy content in response to probes about both the desirability and legitimacy of official action, there were also indications that people thought about these questions somewhat differently. We observed that policy content was relatively more common in explanations about the desirability of proposed measures. Also, people were more likely to profess uncertainty and refer to outside sources of information when justifying their assessments about the appropriateness of legislative action. Finally, the rankings of relevant considerations reveal a good deal of variation in the most frequently mentioned factors across the two types of questions for both issues. Perhaps more telling are the *similarities* in how people thought about the legitimacy of legislative authority surrounding gun control and immigration. Besides policy preferences, considerations involving Congress, federalism, and the states all figured prominently in how people justified their views about the legitimacy of proposed measures. Given the sort of contested authority described in each scenario, this is evidence that a good number of participants were thinking about the appropriateness of legislative authority in terms of relevant institutional frameworks.

There were also clear differences in how respondents justified their views of government action that seem to reflect public discourse on matters related to gun control and immigration. The analysis of open-ended questions revealed people were much more likely to discuss the regulation of firearms in constitutional terms and more likely to raise policy concerns about citizenship and the fair distribution of tax burdens and benefits in explaining their views about policy pertaining to undocumented individuals. The fact that policy opinions were so commonly mentioned in participants' explanations of why they thought legislative action was *appropriate* may also reflect current debates about public policy referenced in the introduction to this book, in that citizens may be mimicking the behavior of elites they commonly observe contesting the legitimacy of policies with which they disagree.

We also observed that some of the factors that influenced participants' assessments of the appropriateness of legislative action were not frequently mentioned in their justifications of those evaluations. As referenced in the last chapter, although some participants did specifically mention experts or expertise, it was not commonly invoked in justifications, even though the consensus of cited experts played a significant role in judgments about the appropriate exercise of authority. The same thing was observed with respect to the marginally significant role of public opinion in the immigration scenario. It could be that people were not necessarily aware of the role these factors play in their assessments about government action. It seems quite likely, for instance, that widespread support for or opposition to government action may influence judgments about the appropriate exercise of authority in unconscious ways.

The analyses of participants' views about experts in chapter 3 suggests the influence of expertise on legitimacy judgments may be more complex. Some people clearly acknowledged the need to rely on expertise, while others disavowed its role in their judgments, specifically questioning the wisdom and motives of constitutional authorities. In this chapter we observed that people who were in conditions in which experts supported their views were more likely to mention those experts in explaining their assessments of government action related to gun control. Those who said experts were credible across issues were less likely to express uncertainty about the exercise of legislative authority where expert views on the matter were referenced and more likely to justify their assessments in explicitly constitutional terms. This finding suggests that for people who credit constitutional authorities, experts can serve a useful informational function that makes such individuals more comfortable commenting on the appropriateness of government action using constitutional evidence. As mentioned earlier, the fact that participants were more likely to reference experts when the views those experts expressed were consistent with the participant's predisposition also suggests that citing experts plays a role in reinforcing our confidence in our own views in service of self-esteem.

Creative research minds can certainly think of ways to test the implications of how people think about and cite expertise more directly. As such, the analyses in this chapter not only give us a richer understanding of the various considerations citizens use to talk about the exercise of government authority, they also provide fodder for future research. I hope that in utilizing the experimental data collected on these questions, I have made the case that this is an important and worthwhile endeavor.

III

Thinking about Institutions and Fundamental Change

Laws and institutions must go hand in hand with the progress of the human mind. As that becomes more developed, more enlightened, as new discoveries are made, new truths discovered, and manners and opinions change, with that change of circumstances, institutions must advance also to keep pace with the times.

—Thomas Jefferson, excerpt from letter to Samuel Kercheval, July 12, 1816, memorialized on Southeast Portico of the Jefferson Memorial

5 | Valuing Institutions
The United States Supreme Court

THIS CHAPTER MOVES up a level of complexity from looking at how people assess the legitimacy of government action to investigating how they think about democratic institutions, specifically the US Supreme Court. My approach to thinking about institutions contemplates that citizens come to value institutions as they perceive (or expect) personal and societal benefits from the institutions' outputs. I propose that by shifting our focus slightly from "support for" to "perceived benefits from" institutions, researchers can take advantage of theoretical frameworks that link people's thinking about outputs to their willingness to protect democratic institutions in a way that realistically reflects how people think about fundamental government change.

Although this logic about valuing institutions in terms of the perceived benefits and risks they provide can certainly be extended to other governing bodies, I choose to focus on the Supreme Court in this chapter for several reasons. First, it is an incredibly important institution that sits at the pinnacle of the US legal hierarchy. Though the court's pronouncements are not self-enforcing, they have the power to influence policy across state and national levels of government. Second, the vulnerable nature of the institution in American democracy has prompted a good deal of scholarly interest in how people think about the court. As such, theory and findings about how people think about the court qua institution, distinct from its individual outputs and particular judicial officials, are better developed than for the other branches.

Finally, despite all the scholarly attention given to how people think about the court, to my knowledge, no one has taken the sort of subjective interest-based approach that I propose here. Perhaps this is a result of the court's fabled reputation of being above politics, famously characterized by Harold Lasswell as "who gets what, when, and how" (1936). Whatever the reason, this is not only surprising, it also represents a missed opportunity to look at some fundamentally interesting questions. Do some segments of society see themselves as beneficiaries of the court's previous outputs more than others? Who feels threatened by decisions that could emanate from the institution in the near and more distant future? How are these perceptions influenced by societal understandings of previous decision-making legacies and our current political environment?

Experimental methods provide a powerful tool to explore these important questions. I describe factors that may influence citizens' subjective perceptions of personal and societal benefits from the Supreme Court, focusing on several features, including (1) the court's reputation for preserving democratic and minority rights, (2) the decision-making legacies of particular court eras, (3) the current political environment, and (4) differing levels of uncertainty about the court's outputs and composition in the near and more distant future. I then discuss the design and results of twin experiments included in the 2019 CCES to probe influences on the assessment of "retrospective benefits" and "prospective risks" emanating from the court's judgments. I undertake these analyses to answer some of the questions set forth above, but also to explain the alternative conceptualizations of "risk domain" used in chapter 7 to see whether insights from prospect theory can help us understand support for changes to the court.

Valuations: Thinking about the Court in Terms of Perceived Benefits

Law and courts scholars are interested in how citizens think about the Supreme Court as an institution for two important reasons that are both aptly captured in Hamilton's famous observation about the third branch in the *Federalist,* no. 78: "The judiciary . . . may truly be said to have neither FORCE nor WILL, but merely judgment." The decisions of the Supreme Court are not self-enforcing. Often the justices make pronouncements that are not popular, and so the court must rely, at least to some extent, on respect for the institution from members of the other branches, and from citizens themselves, for compliance. Moreover, the court inhabits a somewhat precarious position in our constitutional structure. The justices rely on Congress for their jurisdiction and budget; Congress also determines how many justices serve on the court, a decision that can fundamentally change how the court functions.

As referenced in chapter 1, in a series of publications starting in 1992, Greg Caldeira and James Gibson apply legitimacy theory to the Supreme Court to explain how the court exercises influence and survives in our democratic system. Borrowing from David Easton (1965), they argue legitimacy is fundamentally comprised of two types of support for the court as an institution:

specific and diffuse support. Specific support involves "a set of attitudes toward an institution based on fulfillment of demands for particular policies or action" (Caldeira and Gibson 1992, 637). Diffuse support can be thought of as a "reservoir of good will" for the institution that encourages individuals to comply with decisions of the court even if they do not agree with them, and litigants to respect court judgments even when they do not prevail. This aspect of the theory is captured in the frequently cited phrase "legitimacy is for losers" (Gibson 2015). A second characteristic of this reservoir of good will is that it protects the court from threats to its institutional integrity that may be posed by other branches of government or political actors.

I propose that rather than looking at different aspects of support for the institution, we can understand citizens' willingness to support change by considering how individuals value the institution. To do so I employ two theoretical traditions that have been used in social science investigations: rational choice and prospect theory. In this chapter I focus on how citizens think about institutional benefits from the Supreme Court, using intuitions political scientists have borrowed from economics. The next two chapters rely more explicitly on insights from prospect theory to explore how citizens think about institutional change.

Political scientists have long been fascinated with how the pursuit of benefits shapes politics. This is perhaps best embodied by "rational choice" approaches in which individuals are presumed to act in a manner that serves their own self-interest. Researchers have developed rational choice models to explain the behavior of governing elites, including members of Congress (Shepsle 2006) and Supreme Court justices (Epstein and Knight 1998). Studies also show that interests can play a role in the decisions of ordinary citizens with respect to voting behavior, public opinion, and support for regulatory policy (Green and Gerken 1989; Dixon et al. 1991; Funk 2000). There is evidence that broader concerns about others can influence political behavior and policy opinions. Kinder and Kiewiet's (1979, 1981) work on sociotropic voting is a classic illustration of this phenomena. Shapiro and Gilroy (1984) have suggested that collective interests may be more important than individual self-interest in thinking about government intervention. This could be especially important for thinking about governmental institutions like the Supreme Court because it is commonly portrayed as providing benefits to society at large.

Significantly, how citizens value the court is likely to be influenced both by socialization processes and by ideological considerations that have been theorized to have an impact on diffuse support. Individuals' valuations should reflect the fact that there is a *range of sometimes conflicting attitudes* that people can experience in response to the court's decisions, beyond ideological agreement or performance satisfaction, that have been the focus of research looking at support for outputs.

As Gibson and Caldeira (2009) effectively argue, from our earliest days, citizens are taught the importance of the court in protecting democratic freedoms and minority rights. Although the idea that appointed judges could invalidate the actions of democratically elected representatives may have been controversial when the Constitution was written, today citizens generally see judicial review provided by the Supreme Court as a "democratic good" that protects important rights and keeps government actors within the bounds of their constitutional authority.

It is precisely *because* most individuals hold the court in such high regard that citizens may experience disappointment when Supreme Court justices make decisions they do not agree with because they believe those pronouncements go against their own personal or broader societal interests. In small doses, this sort of disappointment may not influence support for the court as an institution, but the steady accumulation of such decisions may cause individuals to question the wisdom of keeping the institution as it is currently structured. A mixture of considerations involving (1) the role the court plays in our democracy, (2) citizens' feelings about particular outputs, and (3) any potential enthusiasm or disappointment individuals feel about how the justices are exercising their substantial influence in our society should be reflected in how citizens value the court in terms of the benefits and losses they perceive devolve from its outputs.[1]

As such, the valuations that I measure here are related the assessment of judicial outputs analyzed in chapter 2. People are likely to say the court is providing benefits when they perceive its decisions as predominantly legitimate. Alternatively, if they see the court as making illegitimate pronouncements or if they do not feel those judgments are serving important interests, they are more likely to say the court's decision-making is resulting in personal or societal harms. Of course, this may not be a strictly additive process; some pronouncements may weigh more heavily in assessments than others.

Assessing Benefits and Risks from Supreme Court Decision-Making

To explore how citizens think about gains and losses emanating from Supreme Court decisions, I employ a distinction that has been used by political scientists in other contexts. Researchers commonly differentiate between personal and societal benefits in studies of the influence of interests on voting (Kinder and Kiewiet 1981) and support for policies (for a review, see Funk 2000). This distinction seems particularly important for outputs of the Supreme Court. Sharp operationalizations of "societal interest," however, can be hard to come by. Researchers commonly assume survey respondents are socially oriented when they endorse broad values such as egalitarianism and humanitarianism (Feldman and Steenbergen 2001) in the absence of specific questions about how society benefits from outcomes.

Here I employ relatively direct measures of societal and self-interest by simply asking participants how "society" and "people like you" have been influenced (or may yet be influenced) by Supreme Court pronouncements over relevant court eras. Two additional benefits of the approach are that it allows me to determine whether there are meaningful differences in how people think about personal versus societal benefits and whether particular groups (i.e., non-Whites, females) see themselves as distinct personal beneficiaries of the court's outputs.

I investigate valuations of the court via experimental methods by using questions that purposely call participants' attention to different past (and future) decision-making eras. I do so for several reasons. Although people may be thinking of different aspects of the court's decision-making over the different periods I employ, asking survey respondents to think about particular eras should bring some standardization to the measure so that that we know what set of past outputs and what set of future expectations are relevant to judgments. Asking respondents about assessments of court outputs over multiple years also increases the likelihood they will consider various decisions and trends in decision-making that have occurred (or that they expect may yet occur) over relevant periods. This comes closer to approximating their feelings about the court as an institution, separate from how they feel about particular outcomes or justices. Finally, by focusing participants' attention on perceived gains and losses over different eras, I can test the influence of several factors that should, in theory, have an impact on their assessments of "retrospective benefits" and "future risks" emanating from the court's pronouncements.

Specifically, I test whether citizens have different feelings about benefits and losses over past decision-making eras based their partisanship and the distinct decision-making legacies of each era. Considering the court's current composition, I also investigate whether Democrats and Republicans perceive different levels of threat over the near and more distant future because of increasing levels of uncertainty moving forward in time. In investigating perceptions of future expectations of the court, I specifically explore the influence of question wording to see whether citizens are more likely to expect gains or losses from future pronouncements of the court depending on how future outputs are framed.

In both experiments I manipulate the *relevant time span* individuals are asked to consider when making judgments to see how citizens with distinct partisan identities think about gains and losses. I do so for different reasons in the experiments looking backward and forward in time. For the experiment on retrospective benefits, half of respondents are asked to assess gains and losses over the last seventy-five years, the other half are asked to assess them over the last fifteen years. I do this to manipulate the legacy of Supreme Court decision-making that is brought to mind. The two reference points were chosen because they roughly approximate what most people think of as the "modern" Supreme Court era, which includes the Warren court through the Roberts court (seventy-five years) and the start of the Roberts court (fifteen years).

THE MODERN SUPREME COURT ERA

The impression of the court as a protector of minority rights has been solidified by decisions of the court that have occurred in the last seventy-five years, including *Brown v. Board of Education* (1954), *Heart of Atlanta Motel v. United States* (1964) (ending racial segregation in public schools and places of public accommodation), and *Reynolds v. Simms* (1964) (announcing the one person, one vote doctrine). Many of these storied landmark decisions were made during the Warren court era (1954–69), named for former governor of California Earl Warren's tenure as chief justice.

In addition to protecting minority rights and voting rights, the Warren court has a reputation for expanding civil liberties in such decisions as *Griswold v. Connecticut* (1965) (declaring citizens' constitutional right to privacy) and the rights of criminal defendants through such decisions as *Mapp v. Ohio* (1961) (announcing the exclusionary rule, which provides that evidence obtained through an illegal search cannot be used at trial) and *Miranda v. Arizona* (1966) (requiring that citizens be apprised of their Fifth Amendment right against self-incrimination before they can make a knowing and voluntary waiver of that right). These decisions are somewhat more controversial, contributing to the Warren court's reputation as a substantially "liberal leaning" body. Indeed, in the late 1960s Richard Nixon was able to capitalize on the court's reputation for liberal decision-making, particularly in the realm of criminal justice, to argue that the "activist" justices on the court needed to be "reined in." This political stance is thought to have substantially contributed to his presidential victory in 1970 (McMahon 2011).

Thus the Warren court has a somewhat complex decision-making legacy. It is commonly thought of as initiating the modern Supreme Court era, with its increased attention to civil rights and liberties relative to previous courts, which focused on cases involving economic or federalism issues (Baum 2021). Many of its decisions are generally perceived by citizens as advancing equality and the American representative system of government, but others are judged through a more critical partisan lens. Many Republicans, for instance, see *Griswold v. Connecticut* as particularly problematic because it has provided the constitutional foundation for controversial rights including abortion and gay marriage.

THE ROBERTS COURT AND BEYOND

Since the Warren court era, the court's membership and its decision-making have grown increasingly conservative. This is because the vast majority of openings on the Supreme Court since 1970 have been filled by Republican presidents. Thus the Burger (1969–85) and Rehnquist (1986–2005) courts are known for being significantly less liberal than the Warren court. This trend toward conservatism has continued during the Roberts court era (2005–present), particularly as some of the more moderate Republican appointees, including Justices Sandra Day O'Connor and Anthony Kennedy, retired and were replaced by more conservative judges. With the appointment of Brett Kavanaugh in 2018, conservatives gained a clear majority of seats on the court. Moreover, with Amy Coney Barrett's replacement of Justice Ruth Bader Ginsburg in 2020, conservatives now have a 6–3 advantage on the bench.

All this bodes quite well for Republican policy interests that may come before the justices in the foreseeable future, particularly as many of the justices appointed to the court since 2000 have been relatively young (at or around age fifty at the time of appointment). And insofar as Supreme Court justices enjoy life tenure, the impact of those appointments will be felt for quite a while. Partisan fortunes become more uncertain, however, as we move further into the future: it is impossible to tell who may be in power in thirty or forty years as these conservative justices leave the court. Thus it seems important to consider both past decision-making legacies and uncertainty about the future in exploring how people think about risks and benefits from the institution.

EXPERIMENTAL HYPOTHESES

My hypotheses with respect to the retrospective time span are as follows:

> H1. All respondents will recognize more benefits over the seventy-five-year period than over the fifteen-year period because it is associated with widely valued advancements in equal treatment and voting rights via important landmark decisions, including *Brown v. Board of Education.*

> H2. There will be an interaction between the time span manipulation and respondents' political identification such that Democrats and Republicans will perceive retrospective benefits in different ways over decision-making eras.

Republicans, for instance should be more likely to perceive benefits emanating from the court during the last fifteen years because the era is associated with growing conservatism on the court; similarly, Republicans should be less likely to acknowledge benefits in the longer term because of the historical association of the Warren court with liberalism. Including partisanship in the analysis of retrospective benefits also allows me to test for the possibility that individuals who identify as Republican might also be less likely to acknowledge benefits emanating from court outputs in general, owing to years of negative partisan rhetoric about "judicial activism," largely coming from Republican politicians.

In the experiment looking at prospective risks, the time span manipulation (fifteen versus seventy-five years) is used to alter respondents' *degree of uncertainty* about what the court will look like in the future. Uncertainty should act differently for Democrats and Republicans in light of the current composition of the court.

> H3. There will be an interaction between time span and partisanship such that Republicans should perceive less threat to their interests in the short term than over the long term.

This is because the court currently has a majority of conservative justices, and their influence will likely be felt for the foreseeable future. Conversely, Democrats will likely respond that they feel more threatened by the court's outputs over the next fifteen years than over the longer seventy-five-year period.

In the experiment looking forward, I also manipulate *question phrasing* to see how framing may influence the perception of future benefits and risks (Tversky and Kahneman 1981). One-third of respondents are asked how they think society and people like themselves will "be influenced" by Supreme Court decisions. One-third are asked how much they think they "will benefit," and one-third are asked how much they think society and people like them "will be hurt" by decisions of the court in the relevant time frame.

> H4. I expect the question phrasing to influence assessments such that those who are asked how much society "will benefit from" decisions should rate future prospects higher than those who are asked how much society will be influenced, and how much society will be hurt, because the question itself focuses on gains. Similarly, I expect those in the "hurt by" phrasing conditions will predict fewer benefits than [those in] the other phrasing conditions as the question focuses on losses.

Experiment 1: Exploring Perceptions of Retrospective Benefits

One thousand respondents to the 2019 CCES were asked relevant questions about the Supreme Court as part of a university team module. Participants in the team module were asked how much they thought (1) society and (2) "people like you" have been influenced by decisions of the Supreme Court. These questions were prefaced with the following manipulation so that half of the respondents were prompted to think about retrospective influence over the last seventy-five years and the other half were prompted to think about the last fifteen years.

> People often talk about the Supreme Court in terms of specific decision-making eras. Since (1945/2005) the Supreme Court has made many decisions about individual rights and liberties, economic issues, and politics.

TABLE 23. Response percentages for retrospective benefits

	Last 75 years			Last 15 years		
	Benefited	Not Influenced	Hurt	Benefited	Not Influenced	Hurt
Society	61	15	24	36	24	39
People like you	50	29	21	24	42	33

Responses were measured using a seven-point Likert scale ranging from 1 (benefited a great deal) to 7 (been hurt a great deal). I also created an additive scale of the two questions (ranging from 2 to 14) to summarize assessments.

Analyses for Experiment 1

Table 23 displays the percentages of responses in each condition. It is clear that respondents recognize more benefits over the past seventy-five years than over the past fifteen years and are less likely to say society or people like them have been hurt by decisions by the court.

It is also worth noting that there is a very modest correlation ($r = .16$) between those who identify as Democrats and the scaled recognition of benefits emanating from the court's past decisions; the same is true for those who identify as liberals ($r = .19$). This suggests the perception of retrospective benefits is *distinct from both partisanship and ideology*.

This observation, however, does not really tell us much about who sees themselves and society as beneficiaries of the court's judgments over the respective eras. To delve into this question and directly test my hypotheses, I present an analysis of results on influences in judgments of retrospective benefits two ways: first, via ANOVAs on both questions and an additive scale of the two measures, and second, with confirmatory regression analyses.

EXPERIMENT 1: ANOVA ANALYSES

In the 2 × 2 ANOVAs I use the retrospective time span condition to which respondents are assigned and whether they identify as Democrat or Republican as factors.[2] The model also includes the interaction between these two factors to test my hypotheses about differential effects by partisanship across the time spans.

The results indicate that both variables and the interaction between them are significant at at least at the .01 level in the analyses of both questions and the additive scale. Marginal means indicate that respondents in the seventy-five-year span condition recognized more benefits to society than those in the fifteen-year span condition. Scores on the seven-point scale (reverse coded so that larger numbers represent more benefit) averaged 4.71 for the past seventy-five years versus 3.90 for the past fifteen years in answers to the question regarding benefits to society $(F (1, 816) = 46.91, p < .001)$.

Moreover, ratings were 4.58 for those who identified as Democrats and 4.04 for those who identified as Republicans $(F (1, 816) = 20.45, p < .001)$. This confirms the suspicion that Republicans might be less likely to see past decisions of the court as beneficial, in general. Finally, the interaction of the two factors was significant such that the difference between ratings of benefits across decision-making eras was more pronounced for Democrat than for Republican respondents $(F (2, 815) = 8.34, p < .004)$.

It is important to note that results for the "people like you" question and the additive scale were substantively identical. For the "people like you" question, the significance tests were $F (1, 817) = 50.80, p < .001$, for time span; $F (1, 817)$ 11.54, $p < .001$, for partisanship; and $F (2, 815) = 6.90, p < .01$, for the interaction; for the additive scale they were $F (1, 814) = 55.89, p < .001$, for time span, $F (1, 814)$ 18.37, $p < .001$, for partisanship, and $F (2, 813) = 8.30, p < .01$, for the interaction.

Figure 5 sets forth marginal means for the interaction from the ANOVA on the additive benefits scale for illustrative purposes. Like Democrats, Republicans rated benefits higher over the past seventy-five years, but on average, the Republican ratings are lower than Democrats' ratings. Moreover, the difference

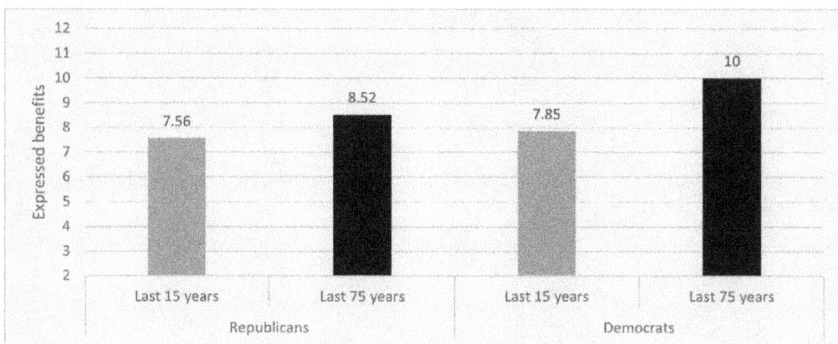

FIGURE 5. Marginal means for retrospective benefits from Supreme Court decisions

in ratings between the time spans was more pronounced for respondents who identified as Democrat than for those who identified as Republican. Democrats acknowledged more benefits over the long term than did Republican respondents, although both groups tended to assess the short term similarly.

RETROSPECTIVE BENEFITS REGRESSION ANALYSES

The results of regression analyses on both questions and the additive scale are set forth in table 24. Coefficients and standard errors for the two questions are from ordered probit analyses and the scale coefficients are from an ordinary least squares (OLS) regression. The models include the time span manipulation (with respondents in the seventy-five-year condition coded as 0 and those in the last-fifteen-year condition coded as 1). Partisanship is included as a seven-point measure (with higher numbers indicating stronger Republican identification). As in the ANOVAs, an interaction between those variables is included.

TABLE 24. Regression results for assessments of retrospective benefits

Variable	Societal benefits (ordered probit)	Personal benefits (ordered probit)	Additive benefit scale (OLS regression)
Constant	—	—	−11.16 (11.58)
RETRO 15 treatment	−1.01*** (.14)	−.96*** (.14)	−2.80*** (.37)
Republican	−.13*** (.02)	−.10*** (.02)	−.32*** (.06)
RETRO 15 × Republican	.12*** (.03)	.11*** (.03)	.31*** (.08)
Younger	.003+ (.002)	.003 (.002)	.01+ (.006)
Female	.08 (.07)	.12+ (.07)	.29 (.19)
Education	.04+ (.02)	.05* (.02)	.12+ (.07)
White	−.13+ (.08)	−.12 (.08)	−.37+ (.21)
Subjective ideological agreement with court	−.001 (.03)	.04 (.03)	.05 (.09)
N	906	908	904
Pseudo-R^2 // R^2	.035***	.032***	.13***

$^+p < .10$, $^*p < .05$, $^{**}p < .01$, $^{***}p < .001$ (two-tailed test). Standard errors in parentheses.

Although this is an experiment with random assignment to conditions (and so controlling for other variables is not strictly necessary), doing the regressions allows me to test for the influence of partisanship along its entire seven-point range (whereas it is operationalized as a dichotomous factor in the ANOVAs). I employ several demographic variables on CCES in the regressions, including age (operationalized by birth year), education (measured on a six-point scale, with higher numbers representing more education), gender (1 male, 2 female), and race (1 White, 0 other), to observe their influence on perceptions of retrospective benefits. I also control for subjective ideological agreement with the current court in the regressions via the four-point measure used by Bartels and Johnston (2013), with higher numbers indicating more agreement with the court.[3] The chapter 5 appendix includes specific question wording.

As we observe in the ANOVAs, the time span manipulation, partisanship, and the interaction between them are significant in all three models. With respect to the interaction, the negative Republican coefficient signifies that in the seventy-five-year condition (where RETRO 15 = 0), strong Republicans were less likely to see benefits than others. Similarly, the negative coefficients for RETRO 15 indicates that in the fifteen-year condition, respondents who were lower on the partisanship scale (i.e., strong Democrats) tended to rate benefits lower than they did for the retrospective seventy-five-year condition. The interaction indicates that when both variables are high (strong Republicans in the RETRO 15 treatment), benefit assessments get a significant boost over baseline.

The significance levels of the control variables are different across analyses but the direction of the coefficients across models is the same for four of the five controls. Generally speaking, younger individuals, female respondents, non-Whites, and those who have achieved greater levels of education are more likely to perceive societal and personal benefits from the court's past decisions. Subjective ideological agreement with the current court does not consistently influence retrospective assessments of benefits for the eras investigated.

Experiment 2: Exploring Perceptions of Prospective Risk

After the questions about their retrospective assessments, respondents were asked questions about the benefits and losses they expected from Supreme Court decisions in the future. As with the questions about retrospective benefits, half of the respondents received a question asking about their expectations concerning the next seventy-five years and half of the respondents received questions about the next fifteen years. In addition to the prospective time frame manipulation, I also included a manipulation of question phrasing. Thus experiment 2 involves a 2 × 3 design where the time span that respondents are asked to consider prospectively is manipulated, as well as the way the question frames outcomes from court decisions. All answers were measured on a six-point scale ranging from 1 (indicating society or people like them would be "substantially better off") to 6 ("substantially worse off"). (Note that the order of responses reversed for the "hurt by" conditions to further emphasize losses in the question phrasing.)

Similar to the retrospective benefits measured in experiment 1, the prospective benefit scale is quite modestly correlated with both partisanship ($r = -.22$ with Democratic identification) and ideology ($r = -.26$ with liberalism). Moreover, the scales measuring the perceptions of retrospective and prospective benefits are each *positively correlated with the other* ($r = .30$), though one is positively related to these general political orientations and the other is negatively correlated with them. This finding further supports the notion that perceptions of benefits and risk are each conceptually distinct from partisanship and ideology.

As with results about retrospective benefits, I present significant results from fully saturated ANOVA models (so that all three factors and all the interactions between them are included in the model). Then I discuss results from confirmatory regression analyses for each question and an additive twelve-point scale. Controls in the regression models are identical to those set forth previously.

EXPERIMENT 2: ANOVA ANALYSES

Once again, the pattern of significant results was identical across both questions and the prospective benefits scale. The results showed that both the phrasing condition and partisanship had significant main effects on prospective evaluations at least at the $p < .01$ level; the time frame manipulation did not have a significant main effect on prospective evaluations. However, as predicted, the *interaction* between time frame and partisanship is consistently significant across models at the .01 level.

While the phrasing manipulation was significant in the ANOVAs, it did not work entirely as predicted. Analyses for all three questions indicate that respondents in the "hurt by" condition predicted significantly fewer benefits than those in the other phrasing conditions but that there was no significant difference in the "influenced by" and "benefit from" conditions. Indeed, for all prospective measures, those in the "influenced by" phrasing conditions predicted higher benefits than those in the "benefit from" conditions, though differences were not significant. For example, when rating prospective benefits for society $(F (2, 803) = 9.55, p < .001)$, those in the "hurt by" condition manifested a marginal mean of 3.12 on the six-point scale compared to 3.60 in the "influenced by" condition $(p < .001)$ and 3.48 in the "benefit from" condition $(p < .01)$. The difference between the latter two groups was not significant. Significance tests for this main effect were $F (2, 807) = 5.51$ $(p < .01)$ for the "people like you" assessment and $F (2, 796) = 8.67$ $(p < .001)$ for the scale.

Partisanship also had a significant main effect across measures. Interestingly, and in contrast to what happened with the retrospective assessments, Republicans are more likely to be optimistic about what they have to gain from future court pronouncements than Democrats. In rating prospective benefits to society, Republicans averaged 3.82 versus 2.97 for Democrats $(F (1, 804) = 84.90, p < .001)$. Significance tests for this main effect were $F (1, 808)$ $= 47.85$ $(p < .001)$ for the "people like you" assessment and $F (1, 798) = 75.79$ $(p < .001)$ for the scale.

Finally, as predicted, the interaction between the prospective time frame and partisanship is significant across all models such that Republicans expected more benefits in the next fifteen years than in the next seventy-five years. Conversely, Democrats expected more benefits over the longer period and expected more risk over the short term. Significance tests for the interaction were $F (2, 804) = 10.68$ $(p < .001)$ for the society assessment, $F (2, 807)$ $= 8.71$ $(p <. 01)$ for the "people like you" assessment, and $F (2, 797) = 9.77$ $(p < .01)$ for the scale.

Once more, figure 6 sets forth marginal means for the interaction in the ANOVA on the additive scale for illustrative purposes. One can see that Republican respondents have higher prospective ratings on average and that Republicans rate benefits higher in the short term than in the long term, but those relative assessments reverse for Democrats: they perceive more threat from losses in the short term and more prospective benefits over the longer, seventy-five-year period.

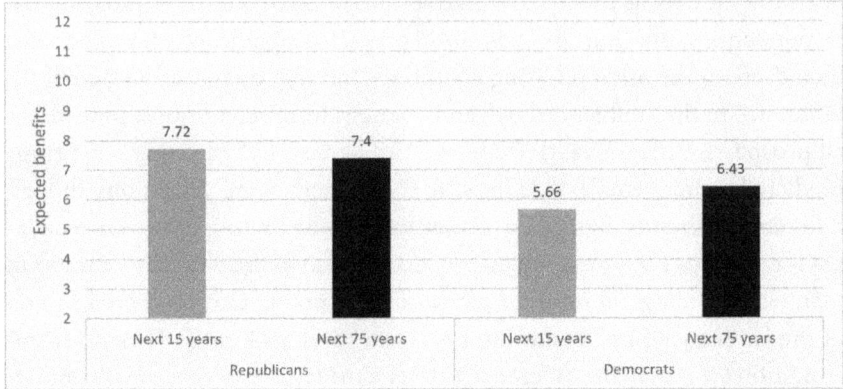

FIGURE 6. Marginal means for expected benefits from Supreme Court decisions

REGRESSION ANALYSES ON PROSPECTIVE ASSESSMENTS

As in the regressions of the retrospective benefit measures, the time span manipulation is included in the regressions of prospective measures with a dichotomous variable (coded 0 for those in the prospective seventy-five-year conditions and 1 for those in the fifteen-year condition), and partisanship is measured on a seven-point scale ranging from strong Democrat to strong Republican. The question wording manipulation is coded ordinally such that the variable is 1 for those in the "hurt by" conditions, 2 for those in the "influenced by" conditions, and 3 for respondents in the "benefit from" condition. An interaction term for time span and partisanship is included, as well as one with the manipulated variables (time span and question phrasing). All controls that were included in the previous analyses are included here with the same coding.

The regression analyses in table 25, with partisanship operationalized along its entire seven-point range, generally confirm what we observed in the ANOVAs. Although the substantive interpretation of coefficients is a bit more complex owing to the multiple interactions in the model, we see that the time span coefficient does not achieve traditional levels of significance across analyses (although it is marginally significant in the regression of respondents' assessment of personal benefits). The question phrasing and partisanship variables are significant across models (except for phrasing in the personal benefit model). Finally, the interaction between the time span manipulation and partisanship is consistently significant in all three models. The direction

TABLE 25. Regression results for assessments of prospective benefits

Variable	Societal benefits (ordered probit)	Personal benefits (ordered probit)	Additive benefit scale (OLS regression)
Constant	—	—	2.53 (9.98)
PRO 15 treatment	−.28 (.22)	−.39$^+$ (.22)	−.78 (.52)
Question phrasing	.14** (.06)	.08 (.06)	.31* (.14)
Republican	.06** (.02)	.04* (.02)	.15** (.05)
PRO15 × Republican	.11*** (.03)	.10*** (.03)	.26*** (.07)
PRO15 × Question phrasing	−.12 (.09)	−.05 (.09)	-.23 (.20)
Younger	.000 (.002)	.001 (.002)	.001 (.005)
Female	.11 (.07)	.11 (.07)	.27$^+$ (.16)
Education	−.01 (.02)	−.02 (.02)	−.06 (.06)
White	−.09 (.08)	−.05 (.07)	−.20 (.18)
Subjective ideological agreement with court	.06$^+$ (.03)	.05 (.03)	.11 (.08)
N	895	897	887
Pseudo-R^2 // R^2	.03***	.02***	.09***

$^+p < .10$, $^*p < .05$, $^{**}p < .01$, $^{***}p < .001$ (two-tailed test). Standard errors in parentheses.

of the control variables is consistent across models, although none of them achieve traditional levels of significance. Generally, female respondents[4] and respondents who agree with the ideological decisions of the current court tend to be more optimistic in assessing their future prospects, while Whites and those who are more educated tend to be more pessimistic.

Discussion

In this chapter I used questions on the 2019 CCES to explore respondents' retrospective and prospective evaluation of benefits from court outputs. Consistent with experimental expectations about retrospective assessments, the results of experiment 1 demonstrate a main effect for the time span manipulation, with all respondents, regardless of partisanship, more likely to acknowledge benefits over the longer, seventy-five-year period than over the shorter, fifteen-year term. As suspected, we also observe a main effect for partisanship, with Republican respondents generally rating benefits from past outcomes of the court lower than Democrats. The anticipated interaction between time frame and partisanship is also significant; Republican respondents are less likely than Democrats to acknowledge benefits over the longer era, which included the famously liberal Warren court. Evidence from the regression analyses for experiment 1 also indicate that women and more educated individuals are more likely to perceive personal benefits from the court and that non-Whites, younger respondents, and those with more education perceived greater societal benefits from the court's previous decisions.

In terms of prospective assessments, Republican respondents are clearly more optimistic about the benefits they expect to receive in the future than are Democrats. This is likely due to the majority conservative composition of the court in 2019. It seems that this optimism outweighs any concerns about "judicial activism" theorized to contribute to the main effect for partisanship in the opposite direction observed in experiment 1. We also observe that although time span in and of itself does not influence prospective evaluations, it interacts with partisanship, so that Republicans are more likely to predict more benefits in the short term and more losses in the longer term; this relative ordering shifts for Democrats, who perceive more risk in the short term and greater benefits in the long term.

The question phrasing manipulation is also significant, but results indicate it was primarily the "hurt by" frame that depressed benefit responses. This is probably because when individuals think about prospective influences from the court, they are generally thinking in terms of gains rather than losses. This could be the result of the court's storied history of protecting individual and political rights, but it is probably a version of self-positivity bias, whereby we are more likely to expect good outcomes than bad outcomes for ourselves in the future (Salgado and Berntsen 2019). As such, respondents in the "influenced by" frame were perhaps closer to those in the "benefit from" frame in terms of mind-set when answering the questions about future benefits. Viewed in this light, the reason the "hurt by" wording results in significantly lower assessments is because calling respondents' attention to potential losses shifts their relative thinking about court outputs more than it does the thinking of individuals in the benefits framing condition.

Conclusion

In this chapter I theorized that citizens come to value institutions such as the Supreme Court as they perceive (or come to expect) benefits from their outputs. My experimental findings tend to confirm intuitions that individual assessments of retrospective benefits are powerfully influenced by conceptions of relative partisan gains over particular decision-making eras. Democrats see more benefits over the modern Supreme Court era than Republicans do. Moreover, future expectations of benefits seem to be influenced by partisan anticipation, given the court's current composition, and uncertainty about the future. This explains why Republicans expect more benefits in the short term and Democrats anticipate more risk.

What remains to be seen is whether these assessments of retrospective benefits and prospective risks influence people's willingness to change the way the court functions as an institution. I turn to important questions about how people think about fundamental changes to democratic institutions in the following chapters. Contrary to portrayals of citizens as resistant to such measures, the findings indicate that people may be more open to the idea of altering governing bodies than conventional wisdom suggests. The valuations I measure here figure prominently in the analysis of support for changes to the Supreme Court in chapter 7.

In the next chapter I explain why individual perceptions of gains and losses are very likely to shape individual thinking about institutional change and also test that intuition across all three branches using people's expectations about their party's likelihood of winning national contests in the 2020 election.

6 | Electoral Expectations and Support for Constitutional Change

RECENT SUGGESTIONS TO alter the Supreme Court appear to be part of a larger movement that exposes citizens to arguments that we should change the way democratic institutions function to make our system work better and to address governmental inefficiencies. Similar arguments have been raised concerning changes to the Electoral College and rules such as the filibuster in the Senate to help prevent legislative gridlock. Conventional wisdom suggests that people are reluctant to entertain suggestions about fundamental government change because it is too difficult or too risky.

Levinson and Blake (2016) cite some rather dated survey evidence, collected around the constitutional bicentennial in 1987, demonstrating that Americans are largely reluctant to alter our founding document. More recent studies by law professors Stephanopoulos and Versteeg (2016) and Blake and Levinson (2016) indicate more of a mixed picture. Stephanopoulos and Versteeg report that in 2015, citizens on average gave the Constitution a nine out of ten rating on their approval scale. Blake and Levinson reference a 2011 *Time* magazine survey showing that 33 percent of the population agreed that we should hold a constitutional convention. That question, however, had only two response options, and two-thirds of citizens indicated that the Constitution had "held up well" (67 percent). One might wonder how giving respondents more choices, including a neutral response option, might influence evidence of support for change.

A handful of studies in political science generally support the idea that citizens who hold state or federal constitutions in high esteem are more reluctant to support changes to those documents (Zink and Dawes 2016; Brown and Pope 2019; Dawes and Zink 2022). As these studies are more interested in the effects of constitutional faith than its prevalence, however, they do not report the proportion of individuals in their samples that exhibited strong constitutional "reverence" or "veneration" in the various ways it is defined.[1] Moreover, by conceptualizing veneration as "a diffuse, implicit attitude, or feeling toward the Constitution" that, in theory, relates to support for broad constitutional frameworks (Dawes and Zink 2022, 402), these studies do not ask about specific suggestions to alter the way institutions operate, and so likely underestimate the extent to which people may be willing to support such measures.[2]

Contrary to portrayals of US citizens as unable or unwilling to entertain proposals to revise the American democratic system, the evidence in this chapter and the next indicates a good deal of support for fundamental government change. The findings show, for instance, that survey respondents are quite willing to agree that the United States is in a "constitutional crisis" and are not at all hesitant to "blame the system" for problems of governance. Thirty-eight percent of survey participants in the 2020 CCES responded that it would be a good (or excellent) idea to amend the Constitution to address specific problems of governance, and a striking 44 percent endorsed the idea of calling for "a constitutional convention to rethink how our system works." Thus, although it may be challenging to get people to agree on what changes should look like, it appears that there is not as much citizen resistance to changing the way our institutions operate as is often assumed.

Fundamental institutional change also requires political entrepreneurs who know how to navigate the system to put change in motion. Sometimes, however, it is not in the interest of elites holding power to champion such causes. Consider the popularity of congressional term limits in the 1990s. After the Supreme Court declared them unconstitutional in *U.S. Term Limits, Inc. v. Thornton* (1995), a term-limit amendment was highly unlikely. Passing a constitutional amendment requires that two-thirds of both houses of Congress vote to propose that amendment and then that three quarters of the states vote to ratify it. Following the decision in *Thornton,* two-thirds of members of Congress were not about to propose a measure that would work against their own electoral interests. Of course, one could argue that members could have approved a term-limits amendment that would not apply to incumbents, only to future members of the institution. Supporting such a measure, however, would likely involve a complex calculus by individual members involving not only whether they agreed such limits were good for democracy but also how they had fared in the absence of term limits, and how politicians with similar policy views might be affected if limits were imposed in future electoral environments.

Here I suggest that the decision processes of citizens may not be very different from that used by government officials. Fundamentally, decisions about institutional change involve whether we should risk making some alteration to how government operates or maintain the status quo, considering uncertainty about what conditions will be in the future. In the language of behavioral economics, this involves a "decision under risk," where insights from prospect theory should be particularly useful (Tversky and Kahneman 1981, 1987).

In this chapter, I investigate how citizens' assessments of their own party's prospects for political gains or losses can influence their support for strategies and solutions involving constitutional change. My main hypotheses, derived from prospect theory, is that individuals who are in the "domain of gains" should be less likely to support risky strategies and proposed institutional changes than individuals who are in the "domain of losses." This is a direct application of the primary insight of prospect theory's logic of decision-making under risk: people tend to be "risk averse" when they stand to gain something and "risk seeking" when facing the prospect of loss. If we consider institutional change as a potential risk (compared to maintaining the status quo of how government operates), then those who think they are likely to win control of democratic institutions should be more likely to resist change; conversely, those who feel they will lose elections should be more amenable to taking the gamble of changing how the system works.

Next, I discuss the intuition behind using prospect theory to explore support for constitutional change in more detail. I also describe an empirical test of the idea involving survey questions from the 2020 CCES. Specifically, the questions asked participants whether they agreed with claims that the United States was in a "constitutional crisis." Questions also asked how likely they thought it was that their party would win control of national institutions in the 2020 election, along with questions about their support for (1) different strategies and (2) different solutions for fixing government inefficiencies. In the following section I detail the logic of using prospect theory to explore support for constitutional change before describing my empirical inquiry and findings.

Prospect Theory and Support for Constitutional Change

Prospect theory (Tversky and Kahneman 1981, 1987) is a model of decision-making under risk that comes from behavioral economics and is often cited for its inherent critique of purely rational notions of decision-making. The main insight of the theory is that decision-makers do not necessarily weigh the utility of objects (or targets) in decision-making objectively. Whether they conceive of themselves as having something to gain or lose is critically important to most individuals' valuations when making judgments.

This is because "losses loom larger than gains": put simply, it hurts more to lose something than it feels good to receive that same object. In a classic demonstration of this phenomenon, Kahneman, Knetsch, and Thaler (1990) did an experiment with undergraduates that involved simple transactions. They asked one group of students what they would be willing to pay to acquire university mugs and pens, while another group was given the very same items at the start of the study and then asked how much they would require to sell them. The price students in the first group were willing to pay to acquire the objects was consistently lower than what students in the second were asking to part with those identical items. This is referred to as the "endowment effect." It demonstrates that there is value in the very concept of possessing something over and above the value of the thing itself.

Critically for my purposes, another important implication of the theory involves the nature of risk orientation when dealing with gains versus losses. Most individuals tend to be *risk averse* when they are thinking in the domain of gains and *risk seeking* when thinking in the domain of losses. Research demonstrates that, when facing statistically equivalent outcomes, if those outcomes are presented as losses, individuals will generally take a chance on losing nothing, even if it means they could stand to lose twice as much by taking that risk, because losing hurts so much. Conversely, if outcomes are presented as gains, individuals generally prefer a sure thing, rather than taking a chance and facing the prospect of getting nothing, even if taking that chance meant they could earn substantially more than promised. These tendencies are not universal. Some people have a greater tolerance for risk than others, but according to studies, between 70 and 80 percent of the population fall victim to this type of bias. (See, e.g., Tversky and Kahneman's [1981, 1987] famous "Asian disease" scenario).[3]

Intuitions from prospect theory have been applied to interesting questions in creative ways in political science. Rose McDermott (2001) uses prospect theory to explain how prominent leaders make important decisions. She argues, for instance, that part of the reason President Carter decided to attempt the perilous rescue of hostages from Iran in 1980 was because he was thinking in terms of losses; he was behind in the polls and the United States was embroiled in the energy crisis. The decision, of course, turned out to be unsuccessful, costing many American lives. Carter in effect ended up worse than where he started, but when he took the risk, according to McDermott, he was hoping to regain some of his dwindling popularity.

Other scholars who study international relations have used the theory to explain decisions during the Cuban missile crisis (Haas 2001), decisions to go to war (e.g., Niv-Solomon 2016), and the success and failure of deterrence policy during the Cold War (Berejikian 2002). In the field of comparative politics, prospect theory has been employed to explain such phenomena as European governments' level of support for welfare reform policies, in light of electoral risks (Vis 2010), and cross-national differences in political party platforms, considering leaders' aspirations for political office (Schumacher et al. 2015).

In the context of American politics, Kam (2012) has used the concept of risk orientation to explain why some individuals are more likely to participate in political activities and support candidates with particular characteristics (Kam and Simas 2012). Eckles and co-authors (2014) provide evidence that those who are risk averse are more likely to support incumbents in elections, and Arceneaux (2012) effectively demonstrates that political arguments that emphasize losses are more effective in the minds of citizens because of this basic cognitive bias.

Mercer (2005, 4) notes one common problem that researchers have encountered when employing prospect theory in the discipline: "Political scientists using prospect theory all wrestle with the problem of determining an actor's or group's frame." He notes that several different strategies to assess decision-making domains have been utilized over the years. This is especially problematic when researchers write about prominent decision-makers or groups of individuals "from a distance," without direct access to their subjective frame of mind. In her 2011 review of the literature, Vis echoes this observation: "It is unclear how to determine when political actors consider themselves to be in a gains or losses domain" (338).

Insights from prospect theory apply intuitively to thinking about institutional change. In an early study demonstrating the usefulness of the framework, Quattrone and Tversky (1988) demonstrate individuals are more likely to support the Equal Rights Amendment when they are primed to consider setbacks women faced from discrimination. More recently, Blake and Anson (2020) use individuals' perceptions of their states' government and economic performance to demonstrate that those who have a positive view of these factors are more likely to resist calls for a state constitutional convention. They also show that framing could "deflect perceptions in a more positive direction" (2020, 339). In the same study, using survey data from Rhode Island and New York, Blake and Anson demonstrate that negative perceptions of state government (and economic conditions in Rhode Island) increase support for constitutional conventions in those states, consistent with predictions from prospect theory. As set forth below, I employ a similar strategy here, by using respondents' *expressed evaluations* to determine their risk domain. I explicitly ask respondents how they feel about particular government institutions and whether they expect to win or lose electoral control of those bodies in 2020.

To my knowledge, this is the first study that uses electoral prospects to explain public support for strategies and measures involving fundamental government change. As such, it should be useful for both students of American politics and scholars who study comparative institutions. The findings should also be of interest to those who study international relations, where insights from prospect theory commonly inform research; this particular inquiry lends itself to a relatively clean test of prospect theory itself. Unlike other political phenomena that the framework has been employed to explain "from a distance," we can determine whether individuals are in the domain of gains or losses with respect to their thinking about governmental institutions and electoral prospects by asking survey respondents directly about how they feel about government and the likelihood of their side winning elections.

Why Should Electoral Expectations Matter?

Citizens' expectations about national elections should influence their thinking about strategies and institutions in a manner consistent with prospect theory for several reasons. There is a long-standing tradition of the media framing elections as "horse races," with candidates jockeying for position to win elections and parties strategizing about how to win control of national institutions. Psychological evidence indicates that people tend to see their partisan identities as an extension of themselves, in line with social identity theory (West and Iyengar 2020). Moreover, research on affective partisanship (Huddy et al. 2015; Abramowitz and Webster 2016) demonstrates that there is an emotional component to this thinking, giving rise to in-group favoritism and outgroup antipathy. We see copartisans as similar to ourselves and members of the other party as quite different. As such, citizens take some personal satisfaction in seeing candidates from their party succeed in elections. Viewed in in this light, there is good reason to think our favored party's electoral prospects are felt directly, such that a win for the party is perceived as a win for ourselves.

Another reason electoral expectations should matter is instrumental. Our personal and political interests are better served when our preferred party is in power; those same interests can suffer when it is not. Republicans who want tax cuts are more likely to get them if Republicans are in control of national institutions. Democrats seeking tuition relief are in in a better position to achieve that goal when copartisans win elections. Citizens understand that their personal interests may be substantially influenced by the outcome of political contests. As a result of constant campaign coverage, they often have a sense of "cautious optimism" or "impending doom" as elections approach.[4] These feelings should influence citizens' risk orientations toward maintaining the status quo, so that they can realize anticipated gains from elections, or, alternatively, changing "the rules of the game" to prevent imminent loss, in line with intuitions from prospect theory. In the next sections I describe an experiment looking at how people respond to charges of constitutional crisis in the 2020 CCES. I also discuss my survey measures and specific findings about the influence of electoral expectation on support for constitutional change in more detail.

The Survey

Empirical evidence for this inquiry comes from a pre-election module of the CCES. The survey was out in the field in fall of 2020, just prior to the November elections. One thousand participants took part in the module. Significantly for my purposes, 2020 was a presidential election year during which control of the executive branch and both houses of Congress would be determined by the outcome of the pending races. Several items in the module were designed to explore citizens' thinking about constitutional crisis and change.

RESPONSES TO CLAIMS OF CONSTITUTIONAL CRISIS: EVIDENCE FROM AN EXPERIMENT

Before being asked questions relevant to the prospect theory analyses in this chapter, participants were exposed to an experimental treatment in which either legal experts, Democratic officials, or Republican officials were asserting that the United States was facing a "constitutional crisis." Specifically, the experimental prompt read:

> Some see the current situation in Washington, D.C., including congressional gridlock and events surrounding investigations into the President's conduct, as "politics as usual," but an increasing number of [legal experts / Democratic officials / Republican officials] are arguing that

we are in the middle of a constitutional crisis that needs to be addressed as soon as possible.

To what extent do you agree there is a constitutional crisis?

In light of the prevalence of such arguments in recent political discourse, the experiment was intended to see how likely individuals were to accept such claims from copartisans compared to legal experts and members of the opposite party. In mentioning the investigations into former president Trump's conduct there was no intention to stack the deck in any partisan direction. Democrats might perceive a crisis prompted by Trump's alleged behavior, while Republicans reading the same prompt could attribute a crisis to officials engaging in what they perceived as "relentless" efforts to hold the former president accountable. The prompt was purposely counterbalanced with the notion that some citizens believed this was all just "politics as usual."

The results demonstrate that survey respondents were surprisingly amenable to such claims regardless of their source. Overall, only 17 percent of respondents disagreed with the proposition that there was a constitutional crisis, 67 percent agreed, and 16 percent said they were neutral or unsure. An ANOVA of responses demonstrates partisan differences in the strength with which participants expressed this view. As illustrated in figure 7, participants who identified as Democrats were more likely to strongly agree there was a constitutional crisis than Republicans (F $(1, 797)$ = 163.58, $p < .01$). The interaction between the experimental treatment conditions and partisanship (F $(2, 795)$ = 23.12, $p < .001$) reveals that participants were significantly more likely to agree that there was a crisis when claims were being made by a copartisan than by officials from the opposing party ($p < .01$ for Democrats and $p < .001$ for Republicans).

There was no significant difference between the propensity of Democrats to agree with experts versus copartisans. Republicans were marginally more likely to agree with claims of constitutional crisis coming from copartisans than from experts making similar claims ($p = .056$); they were also significantly more likely to agree with such claims coming from experts than from officials from the opposing party ($p < .001$).

Because a score of five on the scale signifies participants agreed there was a crisis, the results reported here demonstrate that both Democrats and Republicans were generally more likely to agree with claims about constitutional

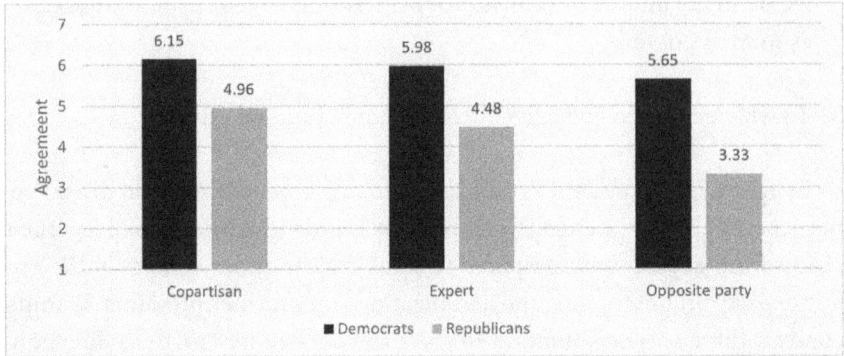

FIGURE 7. Marginal means for agreement with claims of constitutional crisis by party identification

crisis than disagree. Indeed, the only condition in which answers of Republican respondents revealed that, on average, they "slightly" disagreed with the
proposition was when such claims were made by officials from the opposing
party. Thus it appears citizens in general are quite likely to endorse the view
that our democracy is not functioning as it should. The questions I turn to next
involve the attributions people make for such difficulties and their support for
different kinds of strategies and solutions to fix problems of governance.

QUESTIONS ABOUT ATTRIBUTIONS, SUPPORT FOR
STRATEGIES AND SOLUTIONS, AND ELECTORAL PROSPECTS

Besides probing how people responded to claims of constitutional crisis,
questions on the survey asked about attribution of blame for problems of governance, as well as participants' level of support for strategies and solutions
to address such issues. As detailed below, some of those tactics and proposed
measures involved fundamental constitutional change. Examining the influence of people's electoral expectations on their support for various strategies
and solutions is the main object of inquiry in this chapter.

Following the experiment, questions asked how citizens assessed responsibility for problems of governance in Washington, D.C., what strategies they
supported to address governmental inefficiencies, and about their support
for specific solutions involving government powers and decision rules. The
survey also asked respondents to indicate how likely they believed it was that
the Democratic Party would win the presidency and a majority in the two

chambers of Congress. The text of all relevant questions is given in the appendix to chapter 6.

Before turning to the multivariate analysis, I start with some descriptive data that are relevant to the inquiry. According to arguments put forth by Levinson (1988) and Lazare (1996), citizens are much less likely to blame problems of governance on "the system" than on individual officeholders and institutions; this is an empirical question inviting exploration. I explicitly ask people about how they attribute responsibility for problems of governance to explore this question.

In terms of attributing blame, figure 8 indicates that contrary to this thesis, 64.2 percent of respondents in the 2020 CCES said "a flawed government system" was at least somewhat responsible for problems in Washington, D.C. As one might expect, there are significant partisan differences in attributions of responsibility. Republicans (including leaners) are significantly more likely to blame Democratic officials and Congress, and Democrats are more likely to blame President Trump, Republicans, and "the system" (all these differences are significant at $p < .001$). Still, there does not appear to be a great deal of reluctance to attribute problems to fundamental problems with the government structure compared to other factors.

We also observe some important differences in the strategies respondents are willing to endorse to address governmental inefficiencies. Figure 9 demonstrates that 57.9 percent of respondents support engaging in conventional electoral politics. Higher percentages of respondents support mobilizing voters than support either "amending the constitution to address specific problems" or "convening a constitutional convention to rethink the system." This is not surprising and, indeed, may be taken as evidence that citizens perceive

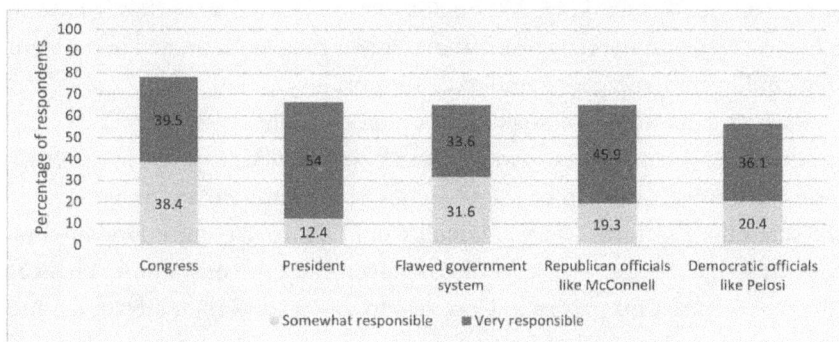

FIGURE 8. Attribution of responsibility for difficulties in Washington, D.C.

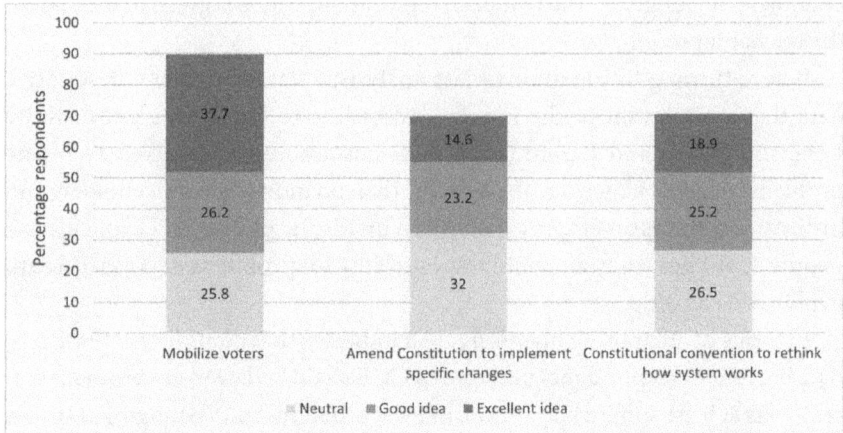

FIGURE 9. Support for alternative strategies to address problems with government

amending the constitution and holding a convention as more difficult and riskier strategies because they contemplate changes to our fundamental system of governance.

What is surprising is that 37.8 percent of respondents indicated it would be a good (or excellent) idea to amend the Constitution to implement specific changes and 44 percent endorsed holding a constitutional convention to rethink the system. As such, support for strategies involving fundamental constitutional change is likely higher than many people expect. Moreover, a substantial percentage of respondents said they were neutral with respect to strategies involving constitutional change (32 percent for amendments and 26.5 percent for calling for a convention). This suggests there are citizens who can be convinced to engage in such tactics to address problems with the way our government is working. Although super-majorities are certainly hard to achieve, these numbers suggest that intelligent proposals, framed in the right way, could gain significant democratic support.[5]

Respondents were also asked their opinions about seven specific changes to address problems with the way government is working. Three involved altering the powers of each of the branches of government and one involved changing the Electoral College, which would likewise require fundamental constitutional change. Two solutions involved rule and/or statutory changes (making it harder for parties in Congress to use rules to their advantage and changing the salaries and benefits of officeholders). The last is hard to categorize as a constitutional or rule change as it would involve changing the authority of officeholders with regard to foreign affairs.

Support for each solution appears in figure 10. Although it is unclear whether respondents were aware of which solutions represented changes that would require constitutional alteration and which would not, it is interesting that the two solutions that would not necessarily require constitutional alteration were the solutions that received the most support; 68.3 percent of respondents said they were likely or very likely to support measures making it harder for parties in Congress to change the rules to their advantage and 56.6 percent expressed support for changing the salaries and/or benefits of officials. These were the only two changes to governing institutions exhibiting no partisan differences in support.[6]

In terms of changes that would require constitutional action, survey respondents expressed the most support for changing the Electoral College; 49.3 percent of respondents said they were likely or very likely to support such changes. Support for altering the powers of government institutions ranged from 43 percent for the presidency to 30.3 percent for the Supreme Court; 34.1 percent of respondents said they would support changing the powers of Congress.

From looking at the data, it seems clear that that, in general, Democrats are more likely to support strategies for change and solutions to government inefficiencies involving institutional change. The question is whether adding the electoral risk domain and controlling for other relevant factors can tell us

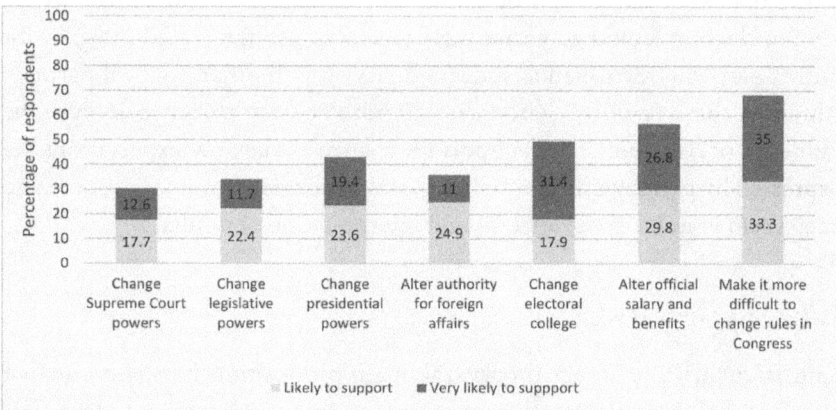

FIGURE 10. Support for specific changes to government institutions

TABLE 26. Electoral expectations 2020 for president, House of Representatives, and Senate

	Party will win	Could go either way or other	Party will lose
Presidential race	500	425	75
House majority	457	455	98
Senate majority	396	528	76

more about such preferences. Considering that aim, it seems relevant to mention that Democrats were more optimistic about winning the 2020 elections. Sixty-three percent of individuals who identified as Democrats said they expected to win the presidency versus 53 percent of Republicans;[7] 68 percent of Democrats expressed the view that Democrats would win the House, while 34 percent of Republicans indicated their side would win a majority of that chamber. Predictions for the Senate were not significantly different: 48 percent of Democrats predicted a win for their party and 47 percent of Republicans thought the Republican Party would prevail.

Besides these partisan differences, another thing that is evident about respondents' electoral predictions is that they were much more likely to indicate they thought their side would win than that it would lose. Table 26, setting forth the number of respondents in each category, demonstrates this tendency. As we can see, respondents were much more likely to say that they felt their party would win than lose in all three electoral contests. It seems that rather than say their party would lose the election, most individuals would say the election "could go either way" (this was also the coded category for individuals who identified as independents or with other political parties). Although these response tendencies do not deter my ability to analyze the influence of risk domain on support for change as electoral expectations are expressed by participants in the survey, it is important to note them here and keep them in mind in the analysis and interpretation of results.

Who Supports Risky Strategies?

Consistent with prospect theory, the main proposition I test here is that citizens who are in the domain of gains (i.e., those who expect to win elections and/or control of democratic institutions) should be resistant to risky strategies and fundamental institutional change, and citizens who are in the domain of losses (i.e., those who expect to lose elections and/or control of institutions) should be more risk acceptant and in favor of institutional change. Also, the more elections individuals expect to win, the more comfortable they should be with conventional political tactics (e.g., mobilizing voters in elections) and the more risk averse they should be with respect to tactics that involve changing the system.

This electoral operationalization of citizens' risk domain explicitly contemplates that whether individuals expect their party to be in control of a governing body reflects whether they see themselves as benefiting (or not benefiting) from that institution. Admittedly, this is not the only way to operationalize risk domain, and as we will see, in the analyses it seems to work better in some institutional contexts (i.e., for the presidency) than others (Congress and the Supreme Court). I discuss this more later in the chapter.

I am also able to control for several relevant attitudinal and demographic factors in the inquiry. Specifically, people who blame difficulties of governance on a "flawed government system" should be more likely to support change. Moreover, as the very understanding of the word conservative involves resistance to change, one might expect conservatives and Republicans to be more resistant to change than liberals and Democrats. I control for these political orientations in my models.

Another attitudinal factor that could influence support for change is how satisfied citizens are with current officeholders and institutions. This represents a somewhat sticky issue because how satisfied respondents are with the state of national institutions at the time the survey was fielded may indeed be an *alternative way to operationalize* whether individuals are in the domain of gains or losses that is distinct from electoral expectations. This is in line with what Mercer (2005, 4–5) refers to as the determination of risk domain based on one's "satisfaction with the status quo." In contrast, electoral expectations involve respondents' beliefs about what they have to gain (or to lose) from institutions *going forward*. This is closer to what Mercer refers to as the classification of risk domains in terms of "aspirational states" (2005, 5–6). In this light, respondents who expect to win pending elections may be characterized as being in the domain of gains and thus more averse to proposals to change the institution than those who expect losses.

As both status quo (satisfaction with current institutions) and prospective (electoral expectations) operationalizations of risk domains are entirely plausible, I explore their effect on support for the strategies and solutions that are the subject of this inquiry in separate regression analyses while controlling for other relevant factors. I also include a third model with both current satisfaction and electoral expectations in one analysis. The third model can be viewed as including both current and future conceptualizations of risk domain, or as a more complete test of electoral expectations, controlling for respondents' satisfaction with current institutions. As set forth below, findings do not differ very much across any of the three models.

As for demographic factors, I include controls for age, gender, race, and education. Younger individuals and those who are relatively disadvantaged in the current US system (women, non-Whites) could be more willing to take risks and support solutions that involve fundamental changes. Those who are more educated may be resistant to change because they understand how government currently works, and so may derive some advantage from retention of the status quo. Alternatively, those who are more educated may be more likely to embrace risk and institutional change because they perceive that fundamental changes can address problems, in a way those with less education do not; either way, it seems important to control for the influence of education.

The first set of analyses probes whether respondents' risk domain influences their support for conventional politics (mobilizing voters) versus strategies that entail constitutional change (amending the Constitution and calling for a convention). As responses to each question are measured on a 1–5 scale, I conduct ordered probit regressions examining the influence of several relevant factors. Here prospective risk domain is operationalized from negative 3 to 3, the number of net wins expected in all three races. The intuition is that those who expect to win elections to institutions are more likely to be in the domain of gains because those victories should result in benefits; conversely, those who expect their party will lose elections should be in the domain of losses. Moreover, on average, individuals who expect to win more elections should feel more optimistic about their prospects.[8]

Net institutional approval is coded from negative 3 to 3 as well. It is the additive sum of whether respondents express approval (1) or disapproval (−1) for President Trump, Congress, and the Supreme Court. This variable represents the current risk domain in the second set of analyses for all three strategies. A third model for each strategy includes both electoral expectations and net institutional approval.

I also control for respondents who are more likely to blame a flawed system of government for difficulties of governance (coded 1–4, "not at all responsible" to "very responsible") and for respondents' ideology (1–5, with higher numbers representing more conservatism) and partisanship (1–7, with higher numbers for strong Republican respondents). Age is coded by birth year; gender is coded 1 for male and 2 for female. Education is an ordinal variable coded 1–5, with higher numbers representing more education. Race is dichotomous (1 White, 0 other). The results of analyses for all three strategies appear in table 27.

As we can see, people who expect to win 2020 elections are more likely to want to engage in conventional electoral politics to deal with potential inefficiencies. Predicted probabilities indicate that those who expect their preferred party to win all three elections are 23.7 percent more likely to say it is an "excellent idea" to mobilize voters than those who expect to lose all three 2020 contests.[9] Unsurprisingly, those who expect their preferred candidates to win elections endorse the strategy when they anticipate substantial success.

These preferences, however, reverse for riskier strategies involving constitutional change. Predicted probabilities indicate that those who expect their preferred candidates to lose all three elections have a 15.5 percent likelihood of responding that it is an "excellent idea" to amend the Constitution to address government inefficiencies, compared with 9.3 percent for individuals who expect their preferred candidates to win all three elections. The corresponding figures are 19.2 percent and 12.8 percent for the question involving holding a constitutional convention. This is what prospect theory predicts. Those who expect to win are less likely to want to take chances with changing how our government operates and those who expect to lose are more amenable to risky systematic change, controlling for relevant attitudes and demographic factors. Some may argue this is also consistent with rational choice explanations. I cannot entirely refute this. Still, prospect theory seems the more appropriable framework; remember, the 2020 election had not yet occurred. Moreover, consistent with prospect theory, figure 9 suggests respondents perceive strategies involving fundamental change as inherently risky compared to conventional politics.

People who are unhappy with the status quo are more willing to use all three strategies to try to change things than those who are satisfied with the way the government is operating. Those who disapprove of the president, Congress, and the court are 21.2 percent more likely to say mobilizing voters is an excellent idea than those who are satisfied with all three institutions. Those who disapprove of current institutions are respectively 6.3 percent and 7.3 percent more likely to say it is an "excellent idea" to amend the Constitution and hold a constitutional convention than those who approve of all three branches of government.

TABLE 27. Ordered probit regressions for strategies for change

	Mobilize voters			Amend Constitution			Constitutional convention		
	Prospective gain or loss	Current gain or loss	Both perspectives	Prospective gain or loss	Current gain or loss	Both perspectives	Prospective gain or loss	Current gain or loss	Both perspectives
Net wins expected	$.10^{***}$ (.02)	—	$.10^{***}$ (.02)	$-.06^{*}$ (.02)	—	$-.05^{*}$ (.02)	$-.05^{*}$ (.02)	—	$-.04^{+}$ (.02)
Institutional approval	—	$-.08^{***}$ (.02)	$-.09^{***}$ (.02)	—	$-.06^{**}$ (.02)	$-.06^{**}$ (.02)	—	$-.06^{**}$ (.02)	$-.05^{**}$ (.02)
Flawed system	.04 (.04)	.04 (.04)	.03 (.04)	$.27^{***}$ (.04)	$.27^{***}$ (.04)	$.27^{***}$ (.03)	$.43^{***}$ (.03)	$.43^{***}$ (.04)	$.43^{***}$ (.04)
Conservative	$-.28^{***}$ (.05)	$-.25^{***}$ (.05)	$-.24^{***}$ (.05)	$-.31^{***}$ (.04)	$-.28^{***}$ (.05)	$-.29^{***}$ (.05)	$-.23^{***}$ (.04)	$-.20^{***}$ (.05)	$-.20^{***}$ (.05)
Republican	$-.04^{+}$ (.02)	-.03 (.02)	-.01 (.03)	$-.08^{***}$ (.02)	$-.05^{*}$ (.02)	$-.06^{**}$ (.02)	$-.04^{+}$ (.02)	-.02 (.02)	-.03 (.02)

	(1)	(2)	(3)	(4)	(5)	(6)	(7)	(8)	(9)
Younger	−.01**	−.01***	−.01**	.004⁺	.005*	.004*	.006**	.007**	.007**
	(.002)	(.002)	(.002)	(.002)	(.002)	(.002)	(.002)	(.002)	(.002)
Female	−.08	−.07	−.06	−.22**	−.20**	−.21**	.15*	.17*	.17*
	(.08)	(.08)	(.07)	(.07)	(.07)	(.07)	(.07)	(.07)	(.07)
Education	.14***	.13***	.13***	.04⁺	.04	.04	−.07**	−.07**	−.07**
	(.03)	(.03)	(.03)	(.02)	(.02)	(.02)	(.02)	(.02)	(.02)
White	.21*	.24**	.23**	−.06	−.06	−.06	−.29***	−.29***	−.28***
	(.09)	(.09)	(.09)	(.08)	(.08)	(.08)	(.08)	(.08)	(.08)
N	891	891	891	898	898	898	895	895	895
Pseudo-R^2	.08***	.08***	.09***	.10***	.10***	.10***	.11***	.11***	.11***

$^+p < .10$, $^*p < .05$, $^{**}p < .01$, $^{***}p < .001$ (two-tailed test). Standard errors in parentheses.

People who blame the system for problems with governance are not significantly more or less likely to want to mobilize voters than those who do not, but, as one might expect, they are significantly more willing to embrace strategies involving constitutional change. Not surprisingly, conservatives across the board are more likely to resist strategies for change. Republicans are similarly less likely to want to amend the Constitution, but they show preferences similar to those of Democrats in terms of the other strategies analyzed, while controlling for other variables in the model.

Younger individuals are significantly less likely to want to engage in electoral politics but significantly more likely to want to change the system. Both more educated and White individuals seem to show a preference for things as they are. They are more likely to want to engage in conventional politics and less likely to want to rethink the system, though there is no evidence of differences with less educated and non-White respondents in terms of amending the Constitution. The effects of gender are complex. Men and women are equally likely to endorse conventional political strategies. Women are significantly more likely to embrace having a convention to think about broad changes to the system, while men are more significantly more likely to endorse incremental constitutional change through the amendment process.

Support for Institutional Change

To explore whether electoral fortunes influence support for changing specific aspects of government, I conduct similar ordered probit regressions on participants' responses to questions concerning support for changing powers across the branches and the Electoral College. One difference in these regressions is that they are institution specific. Rather than operationalizing electoral prospects as a single ordinal variable, I create three dichotomous variables representing whether respondents said they expected their party to win the relevant election(s) for each institution, whether they expected to lose, or whether they said it was too close to call. For the Electoral College regression, I use the presidency as the relevant election. For Congress, winners are those who expressed the view their party would win *both houses* and losers are those who expressed the view their party would lose both houses. For the Supreme Court regression, respondents are coded as expectant winners (losers) if they expressed the view that their party would win (lose) the presidential race *and* a majority of the Senate as these are the officials responsible for appointments to the court.

By excluding those who expect to win in the regressions, we can observe how the groups move in relation to one another in terms of support for each proffered change. Institutional approval is similarly tailored to range from 1 to negative 1, depending on whether the respondent said they approved or did not approve of President Trump, Congress, or the Supreme Court, respectively. I use approval for the president in the regression regarding support for change to the Electoral College. All other variables are identical to those described in the previous section. Here I include models with both expected wins (prospective gains/losses) and institutional approval (status quo gains/losses) across all the analyses, noting that results across the two alternative models (including one of these measures and excluding the other) yield identical statistical results.

In table 28 we observe that electoral prospects influence support for changing institutions related to the presidency (i.e., altering executive powers and the Electoral College) but do not influence support to change congressional powers or altering the powers of the Supreme Court. Where the variable does influence support, it acts as prospect theory predicts. Those who expect to lose the 2020 presidential election are significantly more supportive of taking the risk of changing executive powers and marginally more supportive of changing the Electoral College than whose who expect to win. Predicted probabilities indicate that, holding other variables at their means, respondents who expect their party will lose the presidential election have a 25.8 percent likelihood of strongly supporting changes to executive powers versus 13.9 percent for respondents who expect to win that election. Corresponding percentages for changing the Electoral College are 32.8 percent for respondents who expect their party to lose the presidency versus 23.8 percent for those who expect their party to win the election.

There is no significant difference between those did not make any prediction and the excluded category of those who said they expected their side to win the presidential election in terms of altering presidential powers or the Electoral College; though the coefficients are small, they indicate winners are more supportive of change than those who express no opinion. This should not cause too much concern. Fundamentally, prospect theory predicts differences between those who are in the domain of gains verses individuals in the domain of losses without some undifferentiated median category. Moreover, prospect theory predicts asymmetric effects, such that losses loom larger than gains. Though there is not a significant difference between those who expect to win and respondents who express no opinion, identical regressions with

TABLE 28. Ordered probit regressions for support for constitutional changes (expected winners excluded category)

	Alter presidential powers	Alter legislative powers	Alter powers of the Supreme Court	Changes to Electoral College
Expect to lose election(s)	.44*** (.14)	−.12 (.18)	−.12 (.19)	.27+ (.14)
No prediction or other	−.01 (.08)	−.01 (.08)	−.09 (.08)	−.07 (.08)
Institutional approval	−.41*** (.06)	−.15*** (.04)	−.24*** (.04)	−.49*** (.05)
Flawed system	.22*** (.04)	.22*** (.04)	.19*** (.04)	.19*** (.04)
Conservative	−.15*** (.05)	−.09* (.04)	−.16*** (.04)	−.31*** (.05)
Republican	−.09*** (.03)	−.01 (.02)	−.12*** (.02)	−.10*** (.03)
Younger	.00 (.002)	.00 (.002)	.00 (.002)	.00 (.004)
Female	.03 (.07)	.17* (.07)	.24*** (.07)	.34*** (.08)
Education	.01 (.02)	−.01 (.02)	−.01 (.02)	.01 (.03)
White	.18* (.08)	.01 (.08)	−.05 (.08)	.12 (.08)
N	899	880	881	900
Pseudo-R^2	.13***	.03***	.10***	.21***

+p < .10, *p < .05, **p < .01, ***p < .001 (two-tailed test). Standard errors in parentheses.

the no-prediction category excluded (included in the appendix) indicate that those who expect to lose the election are significantly more likely to support both these changes than those who do not offer a prediction about the election. Taken together, these findings tend to support the theory's intuition that losses are felt more strongly than gains. This asymmetry might be taken as further evidence that prospect theory rather than rational choice is at play in decisions to support fundamental change.

The institutional approval variable indicates that those who disapprove of either President Trump, or Congress, or the Supreme Court are significantly more likely to support changing the powers of the respective branch of government. For instance, those who disapprove of Trump have a predicted probability of strongly endorsing changes to executive authority, at 22.7 percent, versus 5.7 percent for those who approve of him; a difference of seventeen percentage points. Those who disapprove of the current Congress and the court are 5.6 percent and 8.3 percent more likely to strongly support changing the powers of those institutions than those who approve of these institutions, respectively. This echoes Blake and Anson's (2020) findings with regard to support for calls for changes to state constitutions. Although this particular finding may not seem Earth-shattering, these results may be more important than they appear. It is not entirely obvious that disapproval of current government officials should *necessarily* lead to greater support for fundamental change to the institutions they inhabit. Evidence here suggests current dissatisfaction with institutions influences support for fundamental change across all three branches of government.

Those who blame the system for inefficiencies in governance are more likely to support changes to powers across the board. Conservatives are consistently more likely to resist change. Republicans are significantly more resistant to changing executive powers, the Electoral College, and the authority of the court, but express similar views about changing congressional authority controlling for other factors in the model. Female respondents are significantly more likely to favor changing the powers of Congress, the court, and the Electoral College than male respondents but express similar views with respect to executive authority.

One obvious difference between the presidency (where electoral prospects are significant) and Congress and the Supreme Court (where they are not) is that the variable involves a single election rather than some combination of elections and so it represents a cleaner operationalization of the concept. Still, given the rather conservative compound operationalization, such that those who expect to gain (lose) both chambers of Congress are coded only as winners (losers), it seems the variable reflects electoral prospects in *some* respect. Another possibility (which I consider further in the conclusion) is that electoral prospects are a better approximation of whether one is in the domain of gains or the domain of losses with respect to the unitary presidency than with respect to more complex institutions such as Congress. The same argument could also be made for the court, in perhaps stronger terms. For whatever reason, it seems that electoral prospects work as expected in the executive context but not in the others.

Conclusion

The evidence presented in this chapter demonstrates that people are more open to solutions involving fundamental constitutional change than the extant literature portrays. Moreover, citizens tend to agree that our government is not working as it should. Over two-thirds of experimental participants agreed that we are facing a constitutional crisis. Moreover, they showed no hesitancy in blaming problems of governance on a flawed system. Finally, 38 percent of participants expressed support for addressing problems by amending the Constitution and a striking 44 percent indicated it would be a good or excellent idea to have a constitutional convention to "rethink the system."

Some readers may argue that merely raising the idea of a constitutional crisis could have made respondents more amenable to supporting solutions involving fundamental changes to government. I cannot refute this. But it is also true that arguments of this sort appear quite commonly in our daily discourse (and in much stronger terms than the counterbalanced experimental prompt utilized in this investigation). Indeed, this was the impetus for investigating how people respond to claims of a constitutional crisis. Moreover, even if the arguments about crisis elevated the level of support for such strategies over what it might have been absent such claims, the sheer level of support for such measures stands in stark contrast to arguments suggesting people are completely unwilling to consider fundamental government change. Clearly, additional testing should be done to understand citizens' willingness to embrace strategies and measures involving such action. At the very least, the findings reported here suggest there is more openness to fundamental institutional change than most suppose.

Overall, insights from prospect theory have served quite well for exploring how electoral expectations can influence support for strategies and measures involving constitutional change. Satisfaction with current institutions influenced support for strategies and solutions involving change across all three branches of government. Also, as the theory predicts, those who expect their party to lose elections are more willing to support "risky" strategies involving both incremental changes (passing amendments) and broader approaches (convening a constitutional convention) to retooling our government system, while those who expect their party to win are more likely to want to engage in conventional political tactics. Moreover, we observed that expectations also influence specific measures involving the presidency, where the party candidate who wins the election is perhaps the best predictor of whether citizens have something to gain or lose from that institution in the next four years. Those who expected to win the 2020 presidential election were risk averse with respect to changing executive powers compared to those who expected their party to lose the election. This was also the case for supporting changes to the Electoral College, where differences were marginally significant.

One question that remains is, why do electoral expectations predict support for changes to the presidency but not for changes to Congress or the Supreme Court? As I hinted earlier, I think this is because electoral prospects capture the risk domain for thinking about institutional gains and losses somewhat unevenly. First, the president is a unitary actor, so future outputs of the institution are very closely tied to the political views of the person who wins the election. Both chambers of Congress and the Supreme Court are comprised of multiple actors. Outputs depend more on consensus and hashing out views with those on the other side. As such, the preferences of actors in legislative majorities may be diluted; the opinions of justices appointed by parties with which we are aligned are subject to influences other than pure ideology and partisanship. This is all to say that your side winning a particular chamber (or achieving a position of power to appoint justices) is not as clear a predictor of the future benefits or losses citizens may incur from legislative or judicial bodies.

Additionally, Congress is increasingly known more for stagnation arising from partisan differences than for policymaking; this is true no matter which party is in charge. Thus even citizens who believe their party will win elections in both houses might not feel they have much to gain from this particular institution. This is another factor that suggests electoral prospects may not translate directly to institutional prospects with respect to Congress.

As for the Supreme Court, using electoral prospects as a proxy for institutional prospects is also imperfect. One problem is that the operationalization here assumes that citizens understand which democratic officials play a role in appointments; this assumption may not be warranted. Moreover, there is a substantial disconnect between future court outputs and current party politics. First, it is hard to say for sure that current appointees will hold the party line with respect to all cases and issues. We know justices can undergo substantial ideological drift during their tenure on the court (Epstein et al. 2007). Also, there are other factors relevant in Supreme Court decision-making, including the views of other justices, precedent, and case facts, that influence decisions besides the justices' preferences. Thus electoral prospects may not be the best indicator of the future gains and losses that citizens can expect from the Supreme Court.

Where does that leave us? As I mentioned at the start of this chapter, electoral expectations, while certainly plausible and intuitively appealing, are not the only way to gauge how citizens feel about institutions and their future outputs. For instance, a better indicator of citizens' institutional prospects with respect to the court may be the sort of the assessments we explored in chapter 5, asking citizens how much they feel that have benefited from past decisions of the Supreme Court and how much they expect to gain from decisions going forward. I specifically test this proposition, using those assessments to approximate individuals' risk domain with respect to the court, in the next chapter. Gauging institutional prospects for Congress may be a harder nut to crack, but I am confident that creative researchers will come up with a way to do so. The findings reported here suggest it could very well be worth the effort. Insights from prospect theory seem to have a good deal to tell us about how people think about strategies and measures involving fundamental institutional change.

7 | Institutional Prospects

*Exploring Support for Changes to
the United States Supreme Court*

PROPOSALS TO CHANGE the Supreme Court are on the nation's agenda in a manner we have not seen since the Roosevelt era (Phillips 2020).[1] During the 2020 presidential primary season major Democratic candidates floated ideas that had been previously suggested by legal scholars (Cramton 2007; Carrington and Cramton 2008; Epps and Sitaraman 2019) and prominent public figures about how to change the institution. Former attorney general Eric Holder, for example, suggested adding justices to the Supreme Court's nine-person membership during an appearance at Yale Law School in 2019, after the Senate's failure to consider the nomination of Merrick Garland.[2] Other proposals included imposing term limits on Supreme Court justices.

As referenced in chapter 1, plans to change how the justices are selected and how the court operates are not new or limited to Democratic candidates (Badas 2019a). During the 2016 primary season Republican senator Ted Cruz suggested having Supreme Court judges sit for retention elections.[3] Still, the failed nomination of Garland, the controversial hearings surrounding the nomination of Justice Kavanaugh to the nation's highest bench, and the success former president Trump had appointing conservative justices to the federal bench seem to have created an environment in which Democratic officials were expressing an unprecedented degree of support for institutional change to the court. Indeed, to help voters during the 2020 primary season, the *Washington Post* displayed several graphics on its website indicating the candidates' stances on "court packing" and "term limits for Supreme Court justices," along with their positions on matters relating to such issues as health care and the environment.

After the Democratic primaries, it looked for some time as though the issue could go away because Joe Biden was not among those proposing alterations to the institution, but Donald Trump's eleventh-hour replacement of Justice Ruth Bader Ginsburg with conservative judge Amy Coney Barrett renewed calls to change the Supreme Court.[4] As part of his policy agenda during his first hundred days, President Biden called for a commission to investigate changes to the institution.

The fact that prominent scholars and politicians have so recently endorsed concrete plans to alter the Supreme Court provides a unique opportunity to look at how citizens think about institutional change as something other than a purely hypothetical exercise. In this chapter I explore an influence on public opinion about institutional change to the Supreme Court that goes beyond the well-worn suspects of partisanship (Badas 2019b), legitimacy theory (Gibson and Caldeira 2009), and subjective ideological agreement with the court (Bartels and Johnston 2013, 2020). My main hypotheses, derived from prospect theory, is that individuals who are in the domain of gains should be less likely to support proposed changes to the court than individuals who are in the domain of losses.

This is a direct application of the primary insight of prospect theory's logic of decision-making under risk: people tend to be risk averse when they stand to gain something and risk seeking when facing the prospect of loss. If we consider institutional changes to the court as a potential risk (vis-à-vis retaining the status quo of how the court currently operates), then those who see themselves as beneficiaries or who expect to benefit in the future from the court's judgments should be more likely to resist change. Those who feel they have not benefited from the court's judgments or who expect to be on the losing end of decisions in the future should be more amenable to taking the gamble of changing how the court functions.

In the following sections I discuss the intuition behind using prospect theory to explore support for institutional change in more detail. I also describe an empirical test of the idea involving public support for changes to the US Supreme Court using survey questions from the 2019 Cooperative Congressional Election Study (CCES). Specifically, questions asked participants about their support for generic "change" on the court and support for three specific measures: (1) adding justices to the court, (2) instituting an eighteen-year term limit for justices, and (3) the election (rather than appointment) of Supreme Court justices.

In assessing whether citizens think about the court in terms of gains or losses, I use measures from chapter 5 exploring (1) how people value the court as an institution in terms of societal and personal benefits derived from its outputs, and (2) how they think about prospective risk in terms of gains and losses they expect from the court going forward. Specifically, I assess the role that perceptions of retrospective benefits and prospective risks play in respondents' expressed level of support for institutional change to the court while controlling for other relevant factors, including partisanship and subjective ideological agreement with the current court.

Thinking about Institutional Change on the Supreme Court

Recently there has been a good deal of debate about the relationship between support for policy decisions of the court and support for the court as an institution. Diffuse support can be thought of as a "reservoir of good will" that protects the court from threats to its institutional integrity that may be posed by other branches of government or political actors. In their 2009 book and in articles with co-authors, Gibson and Caldeira (e.g., Gibson and Caldeira 2009; Gibson, Lodge, and Woodson 2014; Gibson and Nelson 2016) propose a strong socialization process where legal symbols and early education create a psychological attachment to the institution that is relatively resistant to change. Alternatively, Bartels and Johnston (2013, 2020) and Christenson and Glick (2015) provide compelling evidence that support for the court in fact depends on citizens' subjective ideological agreement with the court's decisions.

Commenting on the relationship between specific support and diffuse support, Gibson and Caldeira (2009, 39) write, "Diffuse support is institutional *loyalty*. It is support that is *not* contingent upon satisfaction with immediate outputs of the institution" (emphasis in original). Still, it makes a good deal of sense that citizens' feelings about the court's policy determinations would influence their willingness to protect the institution. Although Bartels and Johnston (2013) and Christenson and Glick (2015) do not include explicit measures of specific support in their research, each study suggests that specific feelings about the decisional outputs underlie feelings about diffuse support in research that explores individuals' subjective ideological agreement with the justices and the court's decisions as factors that influence diffuse support.

Gibson and Nelson (2015) have challenged studies tending to show citizens' feelings about particular outputs can diminish diffuse support by pointing out that calling individuals' attention to one decision that they do not like should not necessarily influence how they feel about the court as an institution. Moreover, specifically addressing research by Bartels and Johnston (2013), they argue that where such effects have been identified, they are likely to be short-lived, owing to a sort of psychological "rebound effect" in confidence for the court rooted in citizens' adherence to democratic values

(Mondak and Smithey 1997). They also posit that such effects will be limited by periodic exposure to symbols tending to reinforce the court's legitimacy (see Gibson, Lodge. and Woodson 2014) and that any reduction in support for the court as an institution that may be caused by displeasing outcomes will simply be counterbalanced by more attitudinally compatible judgments in the not too distant future.

Gibson and Nelson acknowledge, however, that there is some subset of individuals to which agreement with institutional outputs matters a great deal. They write, "There are undoubtably some individuals whose support for the Court is entirely contingent upon satisfaction with its decisions. For most, however, performance satisfaction and . . . [diffuse support] are only loosely related" (2015, 170–71). These authors go on to suggest a "'new math' of institutional legitimacy" to take account of this subset of citizens (2015, 173).

Rather than engaging in somewhat arbitrary guesses about what proportion of citizens disagree with any particular judgement (or the somewhat vague aggregation of judgments that contribute to specific support) *and also* do not extend legitimacy to the court—as Gibson and Nelson's new math contemplates (Gibson and Nelson, 2015, 173)—the approach I suggest here offers a more intuitive way of thinking about why individuals are likely to support changes to the institution and who is likely to do so.

By asking people about their perception of benefits and losses from the court, we do not have to make implicit assumptions as to what people value most about the institution or how many people hold that view. Prospect theory involves subjective perceptions. As I mentioned in chapter 5, citizens' valuations are likely to be influenced by a mix of considerations, including (1) their views of the role the court plays as the protector of rights in our democracy, (2) their level of agreement with its pronouncements (or anticipated outputs), and (3) their evaluations of how the justices are using (or will use) their substantial power in our democratic system. People may assign different importance to each of these considerations in assessing benefits from the institution. Part of the logic of using prospect theory in this context is that measuring individuals' subjective valuations of the court allows for this sort of individual variation.

This is especially important now. Scholars including Krewson and Schroedel (2020) and Zilis (2021) suggest we may be in a transitional period where the partisan views that are so rampant in politics generally are becoming more influential in how people think about the court as an institution. Some point to the decline in public approval for the court, and particularly the decline among Democrats following the Trump appointments, as evidence of this change (Bartels and Kramon 2021; Zilis and Blandeau 2021).

Positivity theory may very well apply to a large swath of the population. But even Gibson and Nelson (2015) admit it does not apply to everyone. Moreover, the swath of people who are open to support for institutional change may be growing. At least one of the trio of counterbalances to dissatisfaction with outputs of the institution proposed by Gibson and Nelson (2015) has been substantially eroded by the success of former president Trump in shaping the ideological balance of the court. A heavily balanced conservative court is less likely to make salient judgments that counterbalance the dissatisfaction and disappointment with the court and its justices many people feel after decisions like *Dobbs*. Based on research showing a decline in adherence to democratic values, discussed in the introduction to this book, it is also possible that the rebound effect for confidence in the court identified by Mondak and Smithey (1997) is not as strong as it has been previously.[5]

In making their arguments about what influences support for the court as an institution, researchers often talk about the effect of agreement with the court's pronouncements as an all-or-nothing proposition. According to the alternative characterization proposed by Gibson and his co-authors, diffuse support is either loyalty for the court that is "*not* contingent" (Gibson and Caldeira 2009, emphasis in original) or (for some individuals) "*entirely* contingent" (Gibson and Nelson 2015, emphasis added) on satisfaction with decisions. Bartels and Johnston similarly talk about the influence of subjective agreement with the court's pronouncements in rather absolute terms: "We are confident in our primary substantive take away that policy disagreement is a primary basis for Court curbing. Simply put, when citizens disagree with the Court's policy making, they are quite likely to attack the Court's independence and power" (Bartels and Johnston 2020, 249).

At this stage in our democratic life cycle, it is possible that both accounts of why people are loyal to (or choose to attack) the court are correct for different segments of the population. This may be why trying to establish a theoretical and empirical connection between support for outputs and support for the court as an institution that applies to our current situation as well it has in past eras has proven so elusive. It is also why it might be worthwhile to change our focus a bit, away from disagreements about how different types of support are or should be related and toward exploring what prospect theory's conception of decision-making under risk can tell us about support for fundamental change.

Testing Prospect Theory and Support for Change to the Court

My goal is to present a new way of thinking about support for institutional change that law and courts scholars have not previously considered. Using prospect theory as a lens to examine support for changing the court allows us to explore the role of interests in citizens' thinking about institutional change while simultaneously recognizing that individuals are not wholly rational.

As this discussion indicates, there are numerous explanations for why individuals might support or resist change to the Supreme Court as an institution. One possible explanation is partisanship. As mentioned earlier, in the current political environment it is clearly Democratic political figures who are proposing institutional change to the court. All else equal, Democrats should be more likely to support proposals for change than Republicans. Another factor that might influence support for fundamental changes to the court as an institution is diffuse support. Put simply, those with high levels of diffuse support should oppose change and those with lower levels should be more open to change. This presents a bit of a quandary because it would be problematic to have the often used measure of diffuse support predict support for the specific proposals I investigate here—the two concepts are highly endogenous. An admittedly imperfect solution that I use here involves controlling for education in analyzing support for changes to the institution.[6] Finally, borrowing an intuition from Bartels and Johnston (2013, 2020), a third factor that could drive support for change is subjective ideological agreement with the current court. Those who disagree with the court may be more likely to want fundamental changes in how it operates.

The fact that there are other potential influences on predispositions about changes to the Supreme Court is part of what makes this an interesting, and perhaps powerful, demonstration of the operation of prospect theory in a politically relevant context. The study of "retrospective benefits" and "prospective risk" assessments made by survey respondents with respect to the court provides a useful opportunity to do so. Those who feel they have gained from the court's past decisions are likely to value the institution more than those who do not. In this sense, one might think of retrospective benefits as a valuation of the court and also as a proxy for respondents' risk domain; those who feel they have benefited from the court could be thought of as being in the domain of gains, and so risk averse going forward. This is conceptually similar to a kind of "endowment effect" and in line with what Mercer (2005, 4–5) refers to as the determination of risk domain based on one's "satisfaction with the status quo."

An alternative operationalization of risk domain involves respondents' expectations about what they have to gain (lose) from the court's pronouncements going forward. This is closer to what Mercer refers to as the classification of risk domains in terms of "aspirational states" (2005, 5–6). In this light, respondents who expect to benefit from *future decisions* of the court may be characterized as being in the domain of gains and thus more averse to proposals to change the institution than those who expect losses.

As both retrospective and prospective operationalizations of risk domains are at least plausible, I explore their effect on support for changes to the court in separate regression analyses while controlling for other relevant influences. This should allow us to determine whether prospect theory is better conceived of as a status quo or a forward-looking framework with respect to support for change to the Supreme Court.

Analyzing Support for Institutional Change

Some readers may be concerned that the experiments embedded in the 2019 CCES about perceived benefits and losses could influence my ultimate findings about support for institutional change. Here I acknowledge that the percentages of support for different proposals should perhaps be interpreted with a grain of salt as they might differ from what respondents would express without having been previously exposed to questions about outputs and the manipulations of the embedded experiments. Clearly, manipulations *influence* assessments of retrospective benefits and prospective risk. My main purpose, however, is to investigate whether and how those expressed assessments *influence respondents' judgments* about support for change. In this light, calling respondents' attention to benefits and risks (and the factors that might influence their expression) arguably increases the internal validity of the inquiry with respect to the influence of those factors on decision processes.

Following questions on the 2019 CCES about retrospective and prospective benefits (analyzed in chapter 5), all respondents were asked questions about their support for changes to the court. The first of these questions asked respondents the extent to which they supported generic "changes" to the court. The next three asked about three specific proposals: (1) adding justices to the court above its current nine, (2) imposing eighteen-year term limits on the justices rather than granting life tenure, and (3) electing rather than appointing justices to the court. Each question was answered on a six-item scale from "strongly support" to "strongly oppose." There was no neutral option. The percentages

TABLE 29. Support for generic change and specific proposals to alter the Supreme Court (%)

Proposal	Support	Oppose	Missing/skipped
Generic "change"	62.4	37.6	1.0
Add justices	50.6	49.4	1.4
Eighteen-year term limit	72.8	27.2	.6
Elect justices	59.5	40.5	.8

of those demonstrating support and opposition for each question are set forth in table 29. The low rates of nonresponse indicate most people were willing to proclaim their support or opposition to changes to the court.

Similar to what we observed in the last chapter, responses to these questions demonstrate a surprising degree of support for fundamental change to the Supreme Court, one of our most valued democratic institutions. Sixty-two percent of respondents said they supported generic "changes." The degree of support for electing justices was quite similar, at 60 percent. Quite a few more respondents expressed support for term limits (73 percent). The proposal with the least support among respondents involved adding justices to the court (51 percent).

It is worth noting that experimental manipulations notwithstanding, the findings here on support for term limits and adding justices are quite similar to the results of a Marquette Law School national survey conducted about a year later, in September 2020, that asked voters analogous questions. Specifically, that survey indicated that 75 percent of citizens supported term limits and 46 percent supported adding justices to the Supreme Court; it did not include questions about generic change or electing justices.[7]

In addition to these measures of support for change I use an additive measure of support ranging from three to eighteen (summarizing support for adding justices to the court, term limits, and electing justices) as a dependent variable in the regression analyses that follow. My goal is to test how intuitions from prospect theory influence participants' levels of support for changes to the court. As both retrospective and prospective perceptions of benefits represent two plausible ways of determining whether respondents are in the domain of gains or losses with respect to the court, I use retrospective assessments and prospective assessments as *alternative operationalizations* for respondents' risk domain in the regression analyses set forth in table 30. The first five columns use the fourteen-point scale of retrospective benefits (societal and personal benefits) as the operationalization of risk domain for each measure, and the second five columns use the similar twelve-point additive scale of prospective benefits. Results for individual questions are from ordered probit regression models; results for the specific change scale measure are from ordinary least squares regressions. To be clear, those who believe they have benefited from the court's decisions (or believe they will benefit from decisions in the future) should be in the domain of gains, and therefore risk averse and *less likely to support changes*. Those who express more losses (or feel they will be worse off in the future because of decisions of the court) should be in the domain of losses and so *more likely to support changes*.

As Druckman (2004) cautions, perfect equivalencies rarely exist in real-word choice domains; there are usually contextual factors that influence individuals' preferences about decisions under risk concerning politically relevant phenomena. Therefore I control for other politically relevant factors in my analyses. I control for subjective ideological agreement with the current court in the regressions via the four-point measure used by Bartels and Johnson (2013), with higher numbers indicating more agreement with the court.[8] Subjective ideological agreement with the court should be negatively related to support for changes; those who agree with the current court should be less likely to want to change its institutional structure. The partisanship variable is the seven-point party identification scale, with higher numbers indicating respondents are strong Republicans. I expect this variable will be negative and significant as Democrats are more likely to support change in the current political climate. The appendix to chapter 7 includes specific question wording. I also employ several demographic variables on CCES in the regressions, including age (operationalized by birth year), education (measured on a six-point scale, with higher numbers representing more education), gender (1 male, 2 female) and race (1 White, 0 other) to observe their influence on perceptions of retrospective benefits.

Looking at the first five columns in the table 30, we see that the coefficients for the retrospective benefits operationalization of risk domain are generally in the direction predicted by prospect theory. The variable reaches conventional levels of significance for the generic "change" measure and for the question about support for term limits, but not the other measures. Coefficients for the prospective benefit operationalization in the latter five columns consistently indicate that those who expect more benefit from future decisions of the court are more resistant to changing the institution. The

TABLE 30. Support for change using retrospective versus prospective benefits as risk domain

	Risk domain: Retrospective benefits					Risk domain: Prospective benefits				
	Generic change	Add judges	Term limits	Elect judges	Specific change scale (OLS)	Generic change	Add judges	Term limits	Elect judges	Specific change scale (OLS)
Constant	—	—	—	—	-31.14[+] (16.39)	—	—	—	—	-27.34[+] (16.13)
Retrospective benefits	-.03*** (.01)	.02 (.01)	-.02* (.01)	-.001 (.01)	-.01 (.05)	—	—	—	—	—
Prospective benefits	—	—	—	—	—	-.15*** (.02)	-.08*** (.02)	-.10*** (.2)	-.06*** (.02)	-.34*** (.05)
Republican	-.16*** (.02)	-.15*** (.02)	-.13*** (.02)	-.17*** (.02)	-.71*** (.06)	-.14*** (.02)	-.14*** (.02)	-.10*** (.02)	-.15*** (.02)	-.62*** (.06)
Subjective ideological agreement	-.03 (.03)	-.01 (.03)	-.02 (.03)	-.05 (.04)	-.15 (.13)	-.01 (.03)	.00 (.03)	-.01 (.04)	-.05 (.04)	-.11 (.12)

Younger	.01***	.01***	.001	.006***	.02**	.01***	.01***	.001	.01**	.02**
	(.002)	(.002)	(.002)	(.002)	(.008)	(.002)	(.002)	(.002)	(.002)	(.008)
Female	.27***	.25***	.20**	.46***	1.43***	.32***	.27***	.22**	.47***	1.49***
	(.07)	(.07)	(.07)	(.07)	(.27)	(.07)	(.07)	(.07)	(.07)	(.27)
Education	-.03	-.04	-.05+	-.13***	-.36***	-.05*	-.04	-.06*	-.12***	-.36***
	(.02)	(.02)	(.02)	(.03)	(.09)	(.02)	(.03)	(.02)	(.03)	(.09)
White	-.21**	-.13+	.02	-.15+	-.45	-.19**	-.14+	.01	-.14+	-.44
	(.07)	(.08)	(.08)	(.08)	(.14)	(.08)	(.08)	(.08)	(.08)	(.30)
N	896	893	901	900	885	881	878	887	885	875
Pseudo-R^2/R^2	.06***	.05***	.03***	.06***	.20***	.08***	.05***	.04***	.07***	.23***

+p < .10, *p < .05, **p < .01, ***p < .001 (two-tailed test). Standard errors in parentheses.

variable is statistically significant at the .001 level across measures, with other relevant factors controlled for, including partisanship and subjective ideological agreement with the court. Respondents' partisanship is also significant across models, demonstrating that Republicans are more likely to oppose proposals for change, as predicted.

The substantive interpretation of the OLS coefficient for the scaled change measure indicates that respondents who respond that they have the most to gain from future decisions of the court are 3.4 points less likely to support change on the eighteen-point measure than those who feel they have the most to lose. This represents a 19 percent change in support for institutional change, consistent with what prospect theory predicts. Moreover, the magnitude of the effect is similar to the 3.7 point (or 20 percent) decrease in support for change as one moves from strong Democrat to strong Republican on the partisanship measure. This is strong evidence that intuitions from prospect theory can help us better understand support for institutional change in substantively meaningful ways.

Subjective ideological agreement is negatively associated with support for change, though it is not significant. Control variables indicate that women and younger individuals tend to be significantly in favor of proposals to change the court. Those who are more educated tend to be against such proposals. There is some facial validity to this finding in light of Caldeira and Gibson's (2009) evidence that those who know more about the court score higher on measures of diffuse support. As they put it, "to know the Court is to love it" (and to seek to protect it from proposals to change its institutional structure). On average, Whites seem more opposed to changing the institution than non-Whites, but the direction and level of significance of the coefficient are not consistent across models.

Do Valuations Predict Support for Change across Parties and Ideologies?

One last question to address is whether valuations predict support for change equally well across individuals with different partisan and ideological views.[9] There have been findings suggesting Republicans and Democrats may think differently about the court. For instance, Bartels and Kramon (2021) find Republicans shift their thinking about the court in an anticipatory manner and boost their evaluations of the institution when a copartisan is elected president, while Democrats are more likely to respond retrospectively, adjusting their evaluations in a negative direction only after a president from the opposing party makes an appointment that actually shifts the ideological makeup of the court.

To address how valuations work across different political groups, I conduct regressions analyzing the effect of valuations on support for the cumulative change scale for both Democrats and Republicans separately, controlling for ideology (measured on a five-point scale, with higher scores reflecting more conservative ideology). I then repeat the task for liberals, moderates, and conservatives, controlling for party identification (measured on the same seven-point scale used previously, where higher scores reflect stronger Republican Party identification). I also control for all the variables I have used in earlier analyses. All regressions are OLS regressions.

Results for these individual models appear in table 31. The analyses clearly indicate that, consistent with what we observed previously, prospective evaluations of benefits from the court are significant in predicting support for change across Democrats and Republicans and across all ideological groups (liberals, moderates, and conservatives).

Perhaps more interesting is that the evaluations of retrospective benefits, which were *not* significant in predicting support for the scaled change measure in table 30, appear to work differently across partisan and ideological groups. They are significant in predicting support for change for Democrats and liberals in the direction predicted by prospect theory: those who perceive fewer benefits are more supportive of measures involving change to the court. Assessments of retrospective benefits from the court do not significantly predict support for change among Republicans or moderates; they are marginally significant in predicting support for change among conservatives, but in the wrong direction.

Although this pattern of results seems to echo Bartels and Kramon's (2021) finding that Republicans (conservatives) tend to think about the court prospectively, expectations of future benefits are also relevant in predicting Democrats' (liberals') level of support for change. Moreover, it is not entirely clear why retrospective benefits should operate differently across party (or ideological) lines. These findings also suggest that retrospective benefits may work better than was previously evident in predicting support for change among Democrats and liberals than among others. The influence of some of the control variables also changes across models, reflecting how well they distinguish among those who support change within each partisan and ideological group. Overall, these disaggregated analyses demonstrate quite clearly that the expectation of future benefits is a consistent predictor of support for change to

TABLE 31. Support for specific change scale regressions by party identification and ideology

| | Retrospective benefits | | | | | Prospective benefits | | | | |
| | By party | | By ideology | | | By party | | By ideology | | |
	Democrat	Republican	Liberal	Moderate	Conservative	Democrat	Republican	Liberal	Moderate	Conservative
Constant	8.20 (19.77)	75.31** (26.39)	26.33 (23.60)	24.81 (30.0)	22.23 (30.20)	2.37 (20.19)	59.61* (28.22)	25.96 (23.89)	27.76 (28.90)	14.87 (30.57)
Retrospective Benefits	-.11* (.05)	.10 (.08)	-.13* (.06)	-.03 (.08)	.13+ (.08)	—	—	—	—	—
Prospective Benefits	—	—	—	—	—	-.20** (.07)	-.22* (.09)	-.22** (.07)	-.28** (.10)	-.21* (.10)
Ideology (conservative)	-.50** (.17)	-.78** (.17)	—	—	—	-.41* (.18)	.89*** (.24)	—	—	—
Party (Republican)	—	—	.02 (.13)	-.62*** (.14)	-.26+ (.14)	—	—	.06 (.13)	-.57** (.14)	-.27+ (.15)
Subjective ideological agreement	-.09 (.16)	-.52* (.22)	.24 (.19)	.57* (.25)	-.99*** (.23)	.07 (.02)	-.89*** (.24)	-.22 (.19)	.40+ (.25)	-.73** (.12)

Younger	.00	.05**	.02+	.007	.02	.01	.04**	.02+	.01	.01
	(.01)	(.01)	(.01)	(.02)	(.02)	(.01)	(.01)	(.01)	(.02)	(.02)
Female	.60+	2.00***	.37	1.17***	2.40***	.73*	1.89***	.50	1.70***	2.35***
	(.34)	(.45)	(.41)	(.47)	(.48)	(.35)	(.44)	(.41)	(.47)	(.48)
Education	-.29**	-.55***	-.31*	-.36*	-.40**	-.32**	-.49**	-.31*	-.40*	-.38*
	(.11)	(.16)	(.02)	(.16)	(.18)	(.11)	(.16)	(.13)	(.17)	(.18)
White	-.55	-.18	-.14	-1.11*	.07	-.48	-.13	-.01	-1.14*	-.02
	(.35)	(.17)	(.43)	(.50)	(.60)	(.36)	(.57)	(.43)	(.51)	(.61)
N	421	350	312	270	301	413	348	308	260	299
R^2	.05**	.18***	.05*	.20***	.20***	.06***	.19***	.05*	.21***	.20***

+$p < .10$, *$p < .05$, **$p < .01$, ***$p < .001$ (two-tailed test). Standard errors in parentheses.

the Supreme Court among different kinds of partisan and ideologues in the manner predicted by prospect theory.

Conclusion

In chapter 6 we observed that electoral prospects did a better job of predicting support for changes involving the presidency than for changes involving Congress or the court. I suggested that a sharper conception of whether individuals perceive themselves as being in the domain of gains or in the domain of losses with respect to those institutions may be necessary to get an idea of whether prospect theory can add to our understanding of support for changes to those particular governing bodies.

Here, using measures of citizens' perceptions of retrospective benefits and expectations of future risk from Supreme Court outputs analyzed in chapter 5, we observed that assessments of future risks significantly influenced respondents' level of support for changes to the court in the manner predicted by the theory. Although retrospective assessments generally influenced support in the expected direction in the analyses of all respondents, they were not consistently significant across proposed measures. In disaggregated analyses we observed that retrospective benefits worked better to predict support for the additive measure of support for change for certain types of respondents, specifically Democrats and liberals, than for others. This is an intriguing finding worthy of future investigation.

Using the expectation of future benefits as a proxy for risk domain revealed predictions across different groups of partisans and ideologues in a manner wholly consistent with predictions from prospect theory. It makes some theoretical sense that future expectations matter when thinking about potentially "sticky" changes to our democratic system. Demonstrating the effect of such perceptions while controlling for other influences on respondents' opinions about change, including partisanship and subjective agreement with the court, is a useful start in thinking about how the assessment of benefits may influence thinking about institutional change more generally. Prospect theory can add significantly to our theorizing about support for institutional change in the United States, and perhaps elsewhere. As I argue more explicitly in the conclusion, researchers will need to be creative about applying the theory to such questions, but it seems there is much to be gained from the endeavor.

Conclusion

To what purpose are powers limited, and to what purpose is that limitation committed to writing, if these limits, may at any time be passed by those intended to be restrained? The distinction between a government with limited and unlimited powers is abolished if those limits do not confine the persons on whom they are imposed.

—Chief Justice John Marshall, *Marbury v. Madison* (1803)

TODAY, MANY AMERICANS see our Constitution as something apart from themselves and perhaps even from the daily operation of the government it established. It is not. As I have argued in this book, the regime that our founding document created does not simply exist in the abstract. Our Constitution and the authority it envisions operate in a political context. It is particular governing officials, acting on issues of the day, that give the document's institutional powers, and the limits on those powers, concrete definition. That is why federal judges require that disputes be crystallized under the "cases and controversies" language of Article III. It is also why it is so important to understand how rules and the political environment shape people's views of government action.

The chapters in this book take advantage of insights across the social sciences to investigate how people think about government authority and fundamental change in our democratic system. The findings should be beneficial to those interested in constitutional law, political science, and psychology. There are also important practical lessons pertaining to how to get citizens to embrace changes inherent in the evolution of our democratic system. Making changes to our most valued government institutions certainly involves risk, but, as Thomas Jefferson reminds us, it is important for ensuring that those institutions continue to serve citizens' personal and societal interests as times change.

In this conclusion I discuss some of the specific findings and implications of this research for how people think about government authority and change, how findings in this book can help contribute to a continuing interdisciplinary discourse, and how the rather high level of latent support for fundamental governmental reforms uncovered here may be harnessed by those seeking to promote change using some of the lessons we have learned about why people support and resist potentially risky alterations in the way government operates.

Summary of Findings Regarding How Citizens Think about Government Action

In exploring how people think about official action, I purposely tried to get all the leverage I could from experiments that were conducted with national samples of citizens. The analyses of closed- and open-ended responses to questions in which survey respondents were exposed to counterfactual scenarios involving the use of judicial, legislative, and unilateral executive authority revealed a great deal about how citizens utilize various types of information in their assessments of official action and how they use that information to justify their views.

The findings demonstrate that both rules and the political environment matter in citizens' assessments of the appropriateness of government action. Consistent with findings on institutions from research on procedural justice, we observed that individuals clearly attend to compliance with institutional rules when assessing the legitimacy of official action. In all the experiments involving appropriateness of state action across the three branches, people rated action as most appropriate when they had reason to believe that officials were following procedural rules and least appropriate when they were under the impression that officials were not following required procedures. This particular result obtained not only in the experiments involving immigration and gun control that are reported in chapter 2 but also in studies with convenience samples exploring the assessment of unilateral executive action on issues involving the debt ceiling and the commitment of troops in times of humanitarian crisis (Braman 2016) and state court decisions on gay marriage and tort reform (Braman and Easter 2014). The replication of findings across experiments involving distinct issues and different kinds of democratic institutions is strong evidence that compliance with institutional rules matters in citizens' understandings of appropriate authority.

There is also evidence, however, that institutional rules are less important than perhaps they should be for government officials to be meaningfully constrained by constitutional dictates in the minds of citizens. Although rules influenced such assessments, they did very little to constrain the role of political factors across all three branches of government. Rather than observing an interaction between rules and context where institutional rules constrained the role of political factors in judgments, we saw that each had an independent influence on participants' assessments.

It is telling, however, that in previous experiments on executive authority, rules acted to constrain the role of political factors most powerfully for undergraduate participants (Braman 2016). As I mentioned in chapter 2, the reason the constraint hypothesis seems to work for undergraduates but not for participants in other samples utilizing similar experimental designs may be because student participants are particularly susceptible to the operationalization of rule compliance that was used in these studies because they tend to be more deferential to the views of constitutional experts. This particular characteristic actually increases the internal validity of the study with student participants for testing the *potential* for rules to constrain the influence of political factors in assessments of authority. If the intuition is correct, it suggests that when individuals *believe* what they are told about compliance with rules, those rules *can restrict* the operation of political factors in their assessments.[1]

Moreover, because similar experiments were subsequently conducted with MTurk workers and national samples, we were able to directly observe how rules and political factors acted to influence the assessments of individuals in those experimental populations. This speaks to the usefulness of experimental replication in general. Comparing results across experimental administrations helps us to have confidence in results where findings are similar and to identify theoretically relevant differences that could lead to discrepancies in results across experimental administrations.

Taken together, the experimental findings reported here bring us closer to understanding how people think about institutional powers across the branches. Notwithstanding evidence suggesting rules may be less important than they were previously in assessments of unilateral presidential authority, it seems clear that *rules matter* across institutions.[2] We also observed that, among the political factors examined, individuals' *policy preferences* mattered a great deal in assessments of the appropriateness of government action across all three branches; somewhat surprisingly, *widespread democratic support* for contested political action did not.

In light of the strong influence of political factors in assessments of state action, the findings reported here suggest that citizens are not particularly well equipped to enforce constitutional dictates. Perhaps it is too much to expect that they would be, or that constitutional limits should be enforced by political means. Citizens, after all, do not have the time or the inclination to pay attention to everything government officials do that may exceed the bounds of the officials' authority. Moreover, citizens have policy preferences that, at times, can be better served by politicians who flout formal rules. Finally, citizens may have trouble keeping track of how the individual encroachments that James Madison was so worried about can accumulate to erode limits on state authority.

Thus our specialized society utilizes judges, attorneys, and constitutional experts who are trained in the tools of legal analysis to enforce constitutional provisions and alert citizens to concerns about official overreach. The findings in chapter 3 reveal, however, that citizens' willingness to credit expert assessments of the appropriateness of state action can be powerfully influenced by their own policy preferences and by demographic factors such as partisanship and the extent to which they share the educational background of cited authorities. Although this is wholly consistent with findings about the assessments of expertise in other scientific and policy domains, it raises unique difficulties for the prospect of having a government that is meaningfully constrained by principled limits on its authority.

The analyses of justifications in chapter 4 give us a richer understanding of how people think about the desirability and legitimacy of proposed congressional measures involving gun control and immigration in the context of current policy debates. Some respondents professed ignorance of constitutional rules about how the different level of governments should function to address matters of public concern, while others gave very detailed explanations of why the Constitution forbids (or demands) congressional action with respect to both issues. Perhaps more than anything, the influence of popular discourse was evident in respondents' explanations. They were more comfortable talking about gun control in explicitly constitutional terms. Moreover, there was a good deal of policy content in the way respondents justified their assessments of the appropriateness of congressional authority, hinting they might be mimicking elites who invoke conceptions of the proper exercise of authority to object to policy measures they do not like and justify policies with which they agree. This suggests that citizens may not be effective in checking officials who flout constitutional requirements in our democratic system.

According to social contract theory, the ultimate repository of official authority is the people. In a system of limited government, citizens, at the very least, must be able to recognize, and correct for, gross encroachments of institutional authority. It seems our increasingly polarized climate may be creating an environment in which it is exceedingly difficult for citizens to agree on what those violations might look like. Findings also demonstrate it is less likely that individuals will heed the warnings of constitutional experts when those authorities express opinions that are incompatible with their own predispositions.

Summary of Findings on How People Think about Institutions and Fundamental Change

In chapter 5 we explored how citizens come to value democratic institutions such as the US Supreme Court in terms of perceived benefits. There are several advantages to exploring how people think about governing bodies in this manner. First, it comes closer to approximating how people actually think about democratic structures when they are considering changes to those bodies than do extant measures of diffuse support. Moreover, various considerations are likely to come into play in such valuations, making them an excellent summary of citizens' subjective assessments of how they are faring with respect to those bodies. As such, subjective valuations are useful for making theoretically grounded predictions about how individuals will respond to calls for changes to governing bodies.

The experimental findings reported in chapter 5 reveal that how individuals assess retrospective benefits and prospective risks from the court's outputs is influenced in predictable ways by how their partisan identities interact with previous court legacies and different levels of uncertainty about the future. These assessments are distinct from political orientations, including ideology and partisanship; we observed a weak positive correlation between liberalism (and democratic partisanship) and retrospective benefits and a modest negative correlation between those orientations and the expectation of future gains from the court. Participants' assessments of retrospective and prospective gains, however, were positively correlated with one another. This suggests that some individuals are more likely to assess court outputs as beneficial, generally, than others.

The findings from part 3's exploration of support for institutional change reveal that citizens across parties are quite willing to agree that the United States is facing a "constitutional crisis." We also observed a surprising amount of latent support for strategies and measures that involve fundamental change to governing institutions despite conventional wisdom suggesting that citizens are resistant to making essential alterations in our democratic system.

Moreover, we saw that individuals' feelings about fundamental change are influenced by perceptions of whether they stand to gain or lose from government and its institutions. In chapter 6 we observed that, as prospect theory predicts, survey participants who expected their party to lose ground in national elections were more likely to support strategies embracing fundamental institutional change, including amending the Constitution and holding a constitutional convention to rethink the political system. The findings revealed that electoral prospects are particularly important for explaining support for fundamental changes involving the presidency, a unitary institution where the results of democratic contests clearly reflect the goals of incoming officeholders.

Employing an alternative operationalization of institutional prospects in chapter 7, we observed that the expectation of future gains significantly influences citizens' support for measures involving change to the Supreme Court, consistent with prediction from prospect theory. Specifically, survey respondents who expected gains from future decisions of the court were less likely to support changing the institution in fundamental ways that could put those victories in jeopardy. Conversely, respondents who expected losses were more likely to accept the risk inherent in changing the way the court functioned, to avoid personal and societal harms they anticipated from the court's judgments.

Interdisciplinary Give-and-Take

As someone who is committed to interdisciplinary research, I think it is also important to point out what investigating these phenomena in political science may contribute to knowledge in other disciplines. Political science is often characterized as a "borrowing" discipline because we commonly employ theory from other fields to study phenomena we are interested in understanding (McGraw 2000). As such, it seems important to consider how knowledge of the political phenomena investigated here can contribute to thinking and theory building across disciplinary lines.

First, the findings reported here demonstrate that legitimacy is fundamentally a compound concept and that conceptualizations from law (legitimacy as rule compliance) and political science (legitimacy as public support) should be integrated into research and theorizing. In showing that institutional rules and aspects of the political environment are important in how individuals asses the appropriateness of particular actions, I hope I have made a strong case for this proposition. That both normative and political considerations operate in the minds of citizens when they make simple assessments of the appropriateness of official action should make researchers across disciplines more mindful of the operation of each in people's thinking about government authority.

In terms of what the findings reported here add to our understanding of psychological processes, I point primarily to findings about the consideration of expertise from chapters 3 and 4. Distinguishing between people's motivations for crediting expert assessments that they agree with (because it serves self-esteem interests) and the motivations they may have for viewing experts in ways that are similar to partisan groups with which they are aligned (to feel close to relevant others) seems like an important effort worth exploring in other decisional context. Moreover, the evidence in chapter 3 suggesting that experimental participants may have misreported (or misperceived) the influence of expert consensus on their judgments to achieve some independent "value-expressive" goal is an intriguing notion that merits further investigation. Finally, the disconnect between the observed influence of expertise on citizens' assessments of appropriate authority (in chapter 2) and the extent to which survey respondents mentioned experts in justifying their evaluations (in chapter 4) is another part of a larger empirical puzzle about how people use and acknowledge expertise suggested by this inquiry.

To my knowledge, this is the first study that uses perceived interests to explore how people value the Supreme Court, and the first study that explicitly draws on insights from prospect theory to explore individuals' support for change to national institutions. I hope it is not the last. Demonstrating how insights from prospect theory can apply to individual thinking about the value of institutions and fundamental government change raises the possibility of new, interesting inquiries about political transition in other domains.

As with all empirical studies, in conducting the investigation as I have, I made theoretical choices and decisions about operationalizations that other researchers may have employed differently. At the very least, I hope this research illustrates how insights from prospect theory apply intuitively to understanding how people think about government institutions. I sincerely hope others will take up the challenge of testing these ideas in different contexts and using alternative evidence and methods. Only time and further research will reveal how useful the framework is for explaining how people come to value institutions and for predicting support for institutional change.

Lingering Questions and Limitations of the Inquiry

Like most empirical studies, this inquiry has raised as many questions for scholars of law and courts as it has answered. First among these may be how individuals' perceptions of government action, explored in part 2, combine to form larger orientations toward institutions. Future research can and should focus on whether people keep a running tally about institutions, including the court and Congress, that gets updated as they hear about outputs they favor or disfavor (Lodge et al. 1989), or whether evaluations of institutions involve more of a random memory–based survey of considerations that re-volve around some central tendency (Zaller and Feldman 1992). Indeed, the process may vary across citizens depending on the extent they are inclined to have ready impressions of different kinds of governing institutions (Mc-Graw 2000).

Moreover, findings concerning the evaluations of benefits from the court indicate that most individuals think about personal and societal benefits in similar ways. But it is certainly plausible that there are distinct types of people who weigh personal benefits more heavily and others who may emphasize benefits to society. Or as research by Zilis (2021) suggests, one might posit that there are individuals who are particularly mindful of social "group prospects," in line with the thinking I propose here. It would certainly be interesting to see whether there are gendered differences in valuations of benefits from the court after the recent *Dobbs* decision.[3] Moreover, one might be able to create experimental treatments to see whether it is possible to elevate so-ciotropic interests over personal interests, or vice versa, in the valuations of democratic institutions.

This leads to another aspect of the inquiry that could provide grounds for further investigation. Some may be concerned that in demonstrating fram-ing effects for the valuations of the court as I do by calling people's attention to particular court legacies and degrees of uncertainty that those valuations are ephemeral or unstable because they are subject to change. I have been careful to make it clear that I am talking about individuals' *subjective percep-tions* of benefits; as such, it is not surprising that such assessments can change when their attention is directed to different features of the court's decision-making. It does not mean that those valuations are not real or that they are inconsequential.

Moreover, the fact that it is possible to influence citizens' thinking about government outputs in this manner is important to understand. Clearly, thinking about benefits and losses can influence citizens' thinking about governing institutions in consequential ways. Such tactics can be used by political elites to different ends. For example, those seeking to promote fundamental government change might use this knowledge strategically to convince citizens to change democratic institutions to make them work more efficiently; but politicians are certainly capable of employing the logic in ways that are more self-serving. One could posit, for instance, that one reason former President Trump was so successful with White working-class voters in 2016 was that he was able to exploit their sense of impending loss in such a way as to persuade them to support his risky "outsider" candidacy.

Keeping in mind that the kind of thinking I explore here can be used to advance different goals, it is important to acknowledge that a primary objective of this inquiry was to investigate why people support or oppose institutional change. The chapters here do not say anything about what those measures should look like. I am mainly interested in understanding *how people think about change* rather than making arguments about *what specific changes should be adopted.* I leave that hard discussion to others. Clearly, there are obstacles to fundamental change in the United States other than public support; Levinson (1988) and Lazare (1996) both mention malapportionment in the United States Senate that has become increasingly problematic with migration patterns over the nation's history. That malapportionment gets reproduced in the Electoral College and our amendment process, giving smaller states with a minority of the population disproportionate leverage in those outcomes.

Moreover, as we have seen so recently in Chile, broad support for change does not necessarily translate into backing specific measures with concrete winners and losers. In that nation, 78 percent of voters supported constitutional revision in 2020, but just two years later, in September 2022, 62 percent of the population voted to reject the proposed constitution resulting from that effort. Most recently Chile's Congress empaneled a Council of Experts in January 2023 to revisit the constitutional revision process.

Similarly, we should not let the fact that it may be difficult prevent us from considering institutional change, especially where there are so many individuals who are expressing frustration with how things are currently working.

There are intelligent people with excellent ideas about how our government could work better. Obviously, those ideas will need to be vetted and discussed broadly before they are implemented. Asking individuals to consider how they think government institutions should operate, *assuming their preferred leaders are not in power,* might be a way to foster a sort of cautious consensus that we can build on. The research reported here suggests we should not let the idea that citizens are fundamentally opposed to institutional change stop us from having these difficult conversations. Indeed, it may be an opportune time to do just that.

A Way Forward

I conclude by discussing the potential implications of findings regarding support for fundamental change because I think they may provide a bright spot in what appears for many to be a dark time where citizens are increasingly frustrated with our government and how its institutions operate. The findings reported in part 3 demonstrate both a considerable amount of latent support for change to governing institutions and that citizens' feelings about fundamental change are influenced by their perceived prospects. Rather than resisting fundamental government change as a knee-jerk reaction because it is "too hard" or "too unsettling," perhaps we can channel the frustration and sense of relative loss that individuals feel in the current moment into support for a meaningful conversation about how to make our system work better. It is entirely possible that by renewing citizens' investment in how government bodies function, individuals will be more attentive to those considerations in making simple judgments about authority than we observed in chapter 2. Newly adopted institutional constraints may do more to temper the influence of politics in citizens' assessments of official action than rules the framers implemented over two centuries ago.

As with the formation of interest groups around unorganized identities that exist in different segments of society, putting constitutional change into motion requires the effort of political entrepreneurs who know how to navigate the political system (Olsen 1965). Recently, we have seen elites trying to move against long-standing constitutional inertia by suggesting how things might be different, with respect not just to the court but to other democratic institutions. The success Democratic primary candidates had in putting institutional change to the Supreme Court on the political agenda during the 2020 primary season is evidence that people are at least open to such arguments.

Moreover, the fact that Republican officials were championing similar arguments not too long ago demonstrates that there may be potential entrepreneurs interested in exploring fundamental institutional change on both sides of the political aisle. *Or perhaps sustained calls for institutional change will come from somewhere else.* It may not be reasonable to expect those seeking office to effectively push for institutional change. As with the proposals for term limits discussed in chapter 6, once individuals win office, their incentives to revise the governing system they have joined are very likely diminished.

The findings reported here suggest that entrepreneurs who try to implement systemic alterations to the American system should be strategic in whom they attempt to sway and how they construct their arguments. Perhaps they should consider how to use citizens' frustrations with the current system to foster support for fundamental government change. It seems there is a good deal of frustration to go around. This inquiry reveals most citizens seem to agree that in the current political moment, Congress is afflicted with partisanship and gridlock that prevent it from working efficiently. The analyses in chapter 6 indicate there is significant bipartisan support for measures that make it more difficult for parties in Congress to change the rules to their advantage. Moreover, it is not just Democrats who want to change the Supreme Court. The survey findings in chapter 7 reveal that even though Democratic candidates were championing proposals to change the court in the 2020 election cycle, some of those ideas garnered widespread democratic support from over 70 percent of survey respondents. Perhaps these represent good places to begin a conversation about meaningful changes to our governing institutions. These incremental measures could lead to broader thinking about systemic change.

Even a vision to implement more drastic change may not be completely out of reach if constitutional entrepreneurs are thoughtful in the way they go about achieving that goal. That 44 percent of citizens said it would be a good or excellent idea to hold a constitutional convention to "rethink our system" demonstrates there may be substantial latent support for such efforts. If advocates choose to take this route, they can certainly learn some important lessons from the framers when they proposed the Constitution to replace the Articles of Confederation so long ago. First, we do not have to lose our fundamental freedoms to implement change. We can keep the parts of the Constitution that work in a new government framework *at the same time* that we address the parts that need changing. If individuals understand that they can retain the protections that so many of us agree are essential to our rights as citizens, they should be more likely to consider fundamental changes to governing bodies.

Second, the alternative to constitutional change is not anarchy. It is important to remember that when the Constitution was enacted, the existing government system remained intact until the necessary number of states ratified the document. We can make it clear that a similar strategy can be adopted for current times so that altering government institutions is not equated with a state of lawlessness. Perhaps the most strategic thing that the framers did was change the manner in which change could be implemented. Under the Articles of Confederation, important changes required unanimous agreement from all the states of our young republic. Article VII of the Constitution, however, states that nine states needed to ratify the document for it to go into effect.[4] Applying the framers' thinking to our current predicament would mean that a new government framework could define its own terms for enactment as long as that procedure appealed to current sensibilities. As such, this new framework may not require the approval of two-thirds of both houses of Congress and three-fourths of the states, a procedure that so many have argued gives undue power to voters in sparsely populated rural states. The framework could include its own terms for ratification, just as our Constitution did so long ago.

Admittedly, having a conversation about meaningful change to our governing institutions will be difficult, but it may also be our best hope to protect our system from less desirable antidemocratic measures championed by segments of the population that are frustrated with the current situation. Of course, we should not be under the illusion that such discussions will be easy or free from individuals seeking to gain partisan (or other types of) advantage, but it is certainly possible that smart individuals thinking creatively can come up with solutions that may better serve our democracy, in light of modern issues and changing demographics. It seems a risk worth considering, and one that, ironically, citizens who feel they are losing ground may be particularly willing to take.

Experimental Scenarios Used in CCES and TESS Administrations

JUDICIAL AUTHORITY ARTICLE (CCES ADMINISTRATION)

Participants were presented with differing versions of the following article. The article was manipulated to vary the reason for the judge's ruling (a bribe, a political contribution, political beliefs, or a legal justification); the direction of the ruling; and the direction of popular majority support. The possible versions for each variation are presented in brackets.

The Final Frontier? Immigration Cases in the "Third Branch"
of Government

AP—The controversy surrounding immigration has expanded to our legal system in recent years. More cases involving the restriction of benefits to undocumented immigrants are being filed in state and local courts. In one particularly high profile example, it was reported that Steven Coggins, a county court judge in Indiana, decided a case the way he did because [*bribe:* he accepted a bribe from Immigration Access Inc., a party interested in the outcome of the litigation / *contribution:* he accepted a substantial political contribution from Immigration Access Inc., an interest group interested in the outcome of the litigation / *political beliefs:* of his political views about immigration / *legal justification:* of his interpretation of the Constitution].

The case, *Abbrara v. Ball State University,* concerned whether Indiana could legally deny in-state tuition benefits to undocumented students. Judge Coggins ruled that a new state law limiting benefits to US citizens and legal residents [*for immigration rights:* violates the equal protection clause of the Constitution. As a result, John Marcus Abbrara, an undocumented student who has lived in Indiana all his life, will be able to finish his senior year in college / *against immigration rights:* does not violate the equal protection clause of the Constitution. As a result, John Marcus Abbrara, an undocumented student who has lived in Indiana all his life, will have to leave college in this, his senior, year].

Many similar issues related to immigration continue to be litigated in America's courts. A recent opinion poll indicates that over 85 percent of the public in Indiana support the idea that in-state tuition benefits should be [*popular majority support for immigration rights:* extended to undocumented students / *popular majority support against immigration rights:* limited to citizens and legal residents of the United States]. Judge Coggins's decision and his behavior in this case could have long-standing implications for citizens' confidence in the legal system to deal with such controversial policy issues.

LEGISLATIVE AUTHORITY ARTICLE
(TESS ADMINISTRATION)

Participants were presented with different versions of the following articles. The articles were manipulated to vary the level of public support and the opinion of legal experts on Congress's authority. The possible versions for each variation are presented in brackets.

Tuition Benefits Scenario

New Federal Law Regarding Tuition Benefits Raises
Constitutional Concerns

(AP—12/7/14) Federal lawmakers may make it significantly harder for undocumented college students to get the same tuition benefits as classmates they have grown up with. Congress is considering a bill providing that no school that receives federal funding may allow undocumented students to receive in-state tuition benefits; any school that makes this sort of allowance will immediately lose all federal money that it receives.

Schools use federal dollars for everything from building research facilities to funding student scholarships. "This is a hit that no state university can afford to take," said Matthew Lorne, president of Irving State University in Rhode Island. "It effectively forces state schools to punish undocumented students, and there is nothing we can do about it." James Lott, the congressman from Virginia who is sponsoring the bill, was quick to point out "the law does not prevent anyone from attending college, it just requires undocumented students to pay the same as out-of-state students. It stops those here illegally from getting the special treatment rightfully reserved for legal state residents."

Currently it is up each state to decide whether undocumented students can receive in-state tuition. Eighteen states allow such benefits for undocumented students, while three states specifically prohibit undocumented students from receiving in-state tuition. A recent public opinion poll indicates that [over 85 percent / under 15 percent] of Americans support congressional action that restricts tuition benefits to undocumented students as a matter of national policy.

[*Clear congressional authority:* Legal experts overwhelmingly agree that Congress has the constitutional authority to enact such legislation in our federal system. "The Supreme Court would surely uphold this statute," said Robert Farber, a constitutional law professor at George Washington University. "Article I gives Congress broad discretion in saying how federal funds should be spent and making laws pertaining to immigration. While it is true states are independent entities under the Tenth Amendment, this is not an unfair intrusion on each state's ability to decide how to allocate their own tuition benefits."]

[*Unclear congressional authority:* Legal experts are currently divided about whether or not Congress would be overstepping its constitutional authority by enacting such legislation in our federal system. "It is hard to say how the Supreme Court would rule on this issue," said Robert Farber, a constitutional law professor at George Washington University. "Article I gives Congress broad discretion in saying how federal funds should be spent and making laws pertaining to immigration, but states are independent entities under the Tenth Amendment. It is unclear whether this legislation is an unfair intrusion on each state's ability to decide how to allocate their own tuition benefits."]

[*Clearly no congressional authority:* Legal experts overwhelmingly agree that Congress does not have the constitutional authority to enact such legislation in our federal system. "The Supreme Court would surely strike down this statute," said Robert Farber, a constitutional law professor at George Washington University. "Article I gives Congress broad discretion in saying how federal funds should be spent and making laws pertaining to immigration, but states are independent entities under the Tenth Amendment. This is clearly an unfair intrusion on each state's ability to decide how to allocate their own tuition benefits."]

Gun Control Scenario

New Federal Gun Regulations Raise Constitutional Concerns

(AP—12/1/14) Congress is considering federal legislation that would require background checks for all gun buyers, including those who purchase from private sellers, currently exempt from such regulations. The proposed legislation would also limit the sale and manufacture of ammunition in automatic magazines to ten rounds. A recent public opinion poll indicates [over 85 percent / under 15 percent] of Americans support federal legislation addressing gun violence in these specific respects.

Gun rights advocates say that the proposed legislation is a violation of their Second Amendment rights. They also argue that the federal law infringes on states' police powers to regulate for the health, safety, and morals of local citizens. James Lott, a representative from the National Rifle Association, says, "This is just another example of Congress trying to impose its will on the citizens of the several states." Matthew Lorne, a gun control advocate, is quick to point out that "the bill only fills loopholes in current laws and bans extremely dangerous weapons. No sportsman needs more than ten rounds to kill a deer."

[*Clear congressional authority:* Legal experts overwhelmingly agree that Congress has the constitutional authority to enact such legislation in our federal system. "The Supreme Court would surely uphold this statute," said Robert Farber, a constitutional law scholar at George Washington University. "Article I gives Congress broad discretion to regulate goods shipped through interstate commerce, including firearms. While it is true that most gun safety regulations are passed as a matter of state authority under the Tenth Amendment, this law does not represent an impermissible intrusion on state police powers."]

[*Unclear congressional authority:* Legal experts are currently divided about whether or not Congress would be overstepping its constitutional authority by enacting such legislation in our federal system. "It is hard to say how the Supreme Court would rule on this issue," said Robert Farber, a constitutional law scholar at George Washington University. "Article I gives Congress broad discretion to regulate goods shipped through interstate commerce, including firearms. But most gun safety regulations are passed as a matter of state authority under the Tenth

Amendment. It is unclear whether this law represents an impermissible intrusion on state police powers."]

[*Clearly no congressional authority:* Legal experts overwhelmingly agree that Congress does not have the constitutional authority to enact such legislation in our federal system. "The Supreme Court would surely strike down this statute," said Robert Farber, a constitutional law scholar at George Washington University. "Article I gives Congress broad discretion to regulate goods shipped through interstate commerce, including firearms. But since most gun safety regulations are passed as a matter of state authority under the Tenth Amendment, this law clearly represents an impermissible intrusion on state police powers."]

EXECUTIVE AUTHORITY ARTICLE (CCES ADMINISTRATION)

Participants were presented with different versions of the following article. The article was manipulated to the consensus opinion of legal experts on Congress's authority and the level of public support. The possible versions for each variation are presented in brackets.

Sanctuary Cities Raise Debate about Executive Authority

AP—Earlier this year President Trump issued an executive order that would take away federal funds from police departments in cities that refuse to fully comply with immigration laws by reporting undocumented individuals to federal immigration authorities. There is some controversy about whether the President can do so, or whether it should be Congress that takes this action. The administration cites the President's constitutional authority as "Chief Executive" in Article II and the wide discretion presidents are generally given over budgetary issues as sufficient authority for this action.

[*Clear authority consensus:* Several cases are working their way up the federal legal system, but the Supreme Court has yet to rule on this issue. Most constitutional law scholars agree that the President has clear authority to deny funds to sanctuary cities without consulting Congress. Professor Andrew Holmes, a noted authority on government powers, says, "It is clear the Supreme Court will uphold this exercise of unilateral executive authority."]

[*Unclear consensus:* Several cases are working their way up the federal legal system, but the Supreme Court has yet to rule on this issue. Constitutional law scholars are currently divided about whether the President has the authority to deny funds to sanctuary cities without consulting Congress. Professor Andrew Holmes, a noted authority on government powers, says, "It is unclear whether the Supreme Court would uphold or strike down this exercise of unilateral executive authority."]

[*No authority consensus:* Several cases are working their way up the federal legal system, but the Supreme Court has yet to rule on this issue. Most constitutional law scholars agree that the President does not have the authority to deny funds to sanctuary cities without consulting Congress. Professor Andrew Holmes, a noted authority on government powers, says, "It is clear the Supreme Court would strike down this exercise of unilateral executive authority."]

Our immigration problem is not going away any time soon. A recent opinion poll indicates that [over 85 percent / under 15 percent] of Americans agree that sanctuary cities should lose money for failing to report individuals to federal authorities. It is sure to be an important issue in the coming months, raising questions about the means available to the President to deal with such problems.

Question Wording

Participants were asked to answer the following questions relevant to the analyses in chapter 2. Policy opinions were uniformly asked before participants were exposed to hypothetical articles. The variable measured by each question and the scenario to which that variable is relevant follow the question text in brackets.

CCES ADMINISTRATION QUESTIONS

Some people believe that government should limit benefits like emergency health care and public education to people who are legally in this country; others believe that the denial of basic services and benefits to undocumented immigrants and their children is wrong. To what extent do you agree with the following statement, or haven't you thought about it much?

The government should strictly limit basic services and benefits to citizens and legal residents of the United States. [Support for restrictions for undocumented individuals; judicial scenario]

> 1—strongly disagree / 2—somewhat disagree / 3—slightly disagree / 4—slightly agree / 5—somewhat agree / 6—strongly agree / 9—haven't thought about it

How important is this issue to you? [Immigration salience]

> 1—very important / 2—somewhat important / 3—slightly important / 4—not at all important / 9—no answer

How much do you agree with the following statement?

Judge Coggins's behavior in this case represents a legitimate (or appropriate) exercise of judicial authority. [Appropriateness; judicial scenario]

> 1—strongly disagree / 2—somewhat disagree / 3—slightly disagree / 4—neutral / 5—slightly agree / 6—somewhat agree / 7—strongly agree

Some people believe that because undocumented individuals are likely to commit serious crimes, municipal law enforcement agencies have an obligation to report them to federal immigration authorities. Others think these individuals are not more likely to commit crimes, so it is not up to local law enforcement to report undocumented individuals to immigration authorities. To what extent do you agree with the following statement, or haven't you thought about it much?

Local law enforcement agencies should report undocumented individuals to federal immigration authorities. [Opinion on sanctuary cities; executive scenario]

> 1—strongly disagree / 2—somewhat disagree / 3—slightly disagree / 4—slightly agree / 5—somewhat agree / 6—strongly agree / 9—haven't thought about it

How important is this issue to you? [Sanctuary city salience]

> 1—very important / 2—somewhat important / 3—slightly important / 4—not at all important / 9—no answer

Do you think that constitutional law scholars are credible experts with regard to this issue of executive authority? [Credible experts; executive scenario]
  1—yes / 2—no / 3—don't know

Do you agree that the President should take the action described the article? [Desirability]
  1—strongly disagree / 2—somewhat disagree / 3—slightly disagree / 4—slightly agree / 5—somewhat agree / 6—strongly agree

Do you think the President's action described in the article represents a legitimate (or appropriate) exercise of executive authority? [Appropriateness]
  1—clearly not legitimate / 2—probably not legitimate / 3—perhaps not legitimate / 4—neutral / 5—perhaps legitimate / 6—probably legitimate / 7—clearly legitimate

How much do you approve of the job each of the following is doing? [Satisfaction with Trump, Congress, and state governor]

President Donald Trump
  1—strongly approve / 2—somewhat approve / 3—somewhat disapprove / 4—strongly disapprove

The United States House of Representatives?
  1—strongly approve / 2—somewhat approve / 3—somewhat disapprove / 4—strongly disapprove

The United States Senate?
  1—strongly approve / 2—somewhat approve / 3—somewhat disapprove / 4—strongly disapprove

[Relevant state governor]?
  1—strongly approve / 2—somewhat approve / 3—somewhat disapprove / 4—strongly disapprove

What is your political party affiliation? [Asked with follow-up to leaners in CCES sample]

1—strong Democrat / 2—not so strong Democrat / 3—leans
Democrat / 4—independent / 5—leans Republican / 6—not
so strong Republican / 7—strong Republican / 8—don't know /
9—no answer

What is your political ideology?
1—very liberal / 2—liberal / 3—neutral / 4—conservative / 5—
very conservative / 8—don't know / 9—no answer

TESS Administration Questions

Some people believe that government should limit benefits like welfare and
public education to people who are legally in this country, others believe that
the denial of basic services to undocumented immigrants and their children
is wrong.

To what extent do you agree with the following statement?

The government should limit basic services to United States citizens and legal
aliens. [Policy view: immigration reform]
1—strongly disagree / 2—disagree/ 3—slightly disagree /
4—slightly agree /5—agree / 6—strongly agree

Some people think guns are dangerous weapons that should be strictly regulated by the government, others believe guns are not inherently dangerous
and it is up to individuals to control their own actions.

To what extent to do you agree with the following statement?

Guns should be strictly regulated by the government. [Policy view: gun
control]
1—strongly disagree / 2—disagree/ 3—slightly disagree /
4—slightly agree /5—agree / 6—strongly agree

Some people believe the federal government is taking too much authority from
states to deal with important political issues, others think that solutions to complex problems often require a coordinated national response to be successful.

Please indicate the extent to which you agree with the following statement.

The federal government is taking too much authority from the states to deal with important issues. [Federal authority]
>   1—strongly disagree / 2—disagree / 3—slightly disagree /
>   4—slightly agree / 5—agree / 6—strongly agree

Do you think that constitutional law scholars are credible experts with regard to this issue of congressional authority? [Expert credibility; legislative scenarios]
>   1—yes / 2—no / 3—don't know

Do you agree that Congress should take the action described in the article? [Legislative desirability]
>   1—strongly agree / 2—agree / 3—slightly agree / 4—slightly
>   disagree / 5—disagree / 6—strongly disagree

Can you please briefly explain your answer to the last question in as sentence or two?

Which of the following reflects your views about whether it would be a legitimate (or appropriate) exercise of authority for Congress to pass this legislation? [Legislative appropriateness]
>   1—clearly legitimate / 2—probably legitimate / 3—perhaps
>   legitimate / 4—neutral / 5—perhaps not legitimate / 6—probably
>   not legitimate / 7—clearly not legitimate

Can you please briefly explain your response to the last question in a sentence or two?

How would you describe your ideology?
>   1—very conservative / 2—conservative / 3—slightly
>   conservative / 4—moderate / 5—slightly liberal / 6—liberal /
>   7—very liberal

What about your political party affiliation? [Asked with follow-up to leaners in TESS sample]

1—strongly Republican / 2—Republican / 3—lean
Republican / 4—independent / 5—lean Democrat /
6—Democrat / 7—strongly Democrat

How much do you approve of the job Congress is doing? [Approval Congress]
1—strongly approve / 2—somewhat approve / 3—slightly
approve / 4—neutral / 5—slightly disapprove / 6—somewhat
disapprove / 7—strongly disapprove

How much do you approve of the job your state legislature is doing? [Approval
state legislature]
1—strongly approve / 2—somewhat approve / 3—slightly
approve / 4—neutral / 5—slightly disapprove / 6—somewhat
disapprove / 7—strongly disapprove

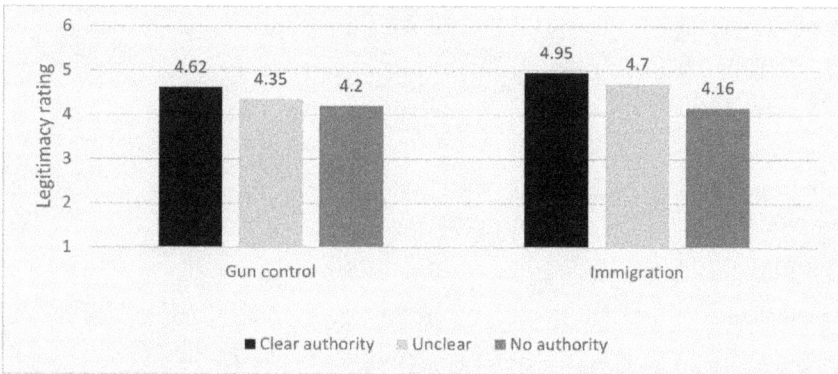

FIGURE A.1. Marginal means for expert consensus conditions across issues in legislative authority experiment

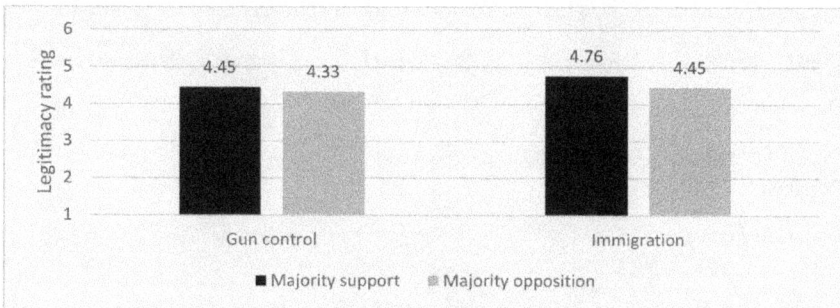

FIGURE A.2. Marginal means for support conditions across issues in legislative authority experiment

TABLE A.1. Legislative authority experiment: Confirmatory analyses of results from administration with Mechanical Turk sample

		Authority consensus conditions		
	Full model	Clear authority	Divided consensus	Clearly no authority
Manipulations				
Authority consensus	−.42** (.14)	—	—	—
Majority opposition	−.07 (.43)	.16 (.30)	.33 (.34)	.51 (.28)
Issue	.58 (.47)	.37 (.32)	.06 (.32)	.01 (.30)
Issue × Majority opposition	−.46 (.65)	−.38 (.45)	−.67 (.47)	−.56 (.42)
Authority × Majority opposition	.23 (.19)	—	—	—
Authority × Issue	−.20 (.21)	—	—	—
Authority × Majority opposition × Issue	−.06 (.29)	—	—	—
Preferences				
Policy question	.31*** (.04)	.35*** (.07)	.40*** (.07)	.25*** (.07)
"Too much" federal authority	−.09+ (.04)	−.11 (.08)	−.18+ (.07)	−.03 (.08)
Controls				
Female	−.09 (.13)	−.04 (.22)	.22 (.27)	−.29 (.21)
Conservative	−.16* (.07)	−.25* (.12)	.00 (.15)	−.15 (10)
Democrat	.13+ (.07)	−.17 (.12)	−.07 (.17)	−.12 (.11)
Dissatisfied with Congress	−.09+ (.05)	.00 (.09)	−.06 (.10)	−14 (.09)
Dissatisfied with state institutions	.01 (.02)	.00 (.01)	.03 (.04)	.02 (.04)
N	299	102	89	108
Likelihood ratio	105.80***	39.18***	40.61***	21.19**

+$p < .10$, *$p < .05$, **$p < .01$, ***$p < .001$ (two-tailed test). Standard errors in parentheses.

Percentages of Credibility Ratings by Partisanship and Agreement Condition

TABLE A.2. Expert credibility responses by partisanship across administrations (%)

	TESS 2016			CCES 2017		
	Expert credible	Not credible	Don't know	Expert credible	Not credible	Don't know
Democrat (n = 401, 227)	47	15	37	55	15	28
Republican (n = 372, 154)	38	26	34	37	31	32

TABLE A.3. Expert credibility responses by condition agreement across administrations (%)

	TESS 2016			CCES 2017		
	Expert credible	Not credible	Don't know	Expert credible	Not credible	Don't know
Consistent (n = 267, 156)	46	17	35	53	14	32
Inconsistent (n = 273, 156)	37	23	39	44	23	32
Unclear (n = 254, 164) (divided consensus)	45	22	34	41	29	29

Supplemental Regression Analyses

Here I code "consistency" as an ordinal variable. It is coded 1 if the expert consensus about government authority is inconsistent with a participant's policy views, 2 for participants in the divided authority conditions, and 3 if the expert consensus cited is consistent with the respondent's policy views about the relevant measure. All other variables are identical to analyses in the main text. Table A.4 shows that as expert consensus becomes more consistent with participants' expressed views, participants demonstrate less skepticism about the credibility of experts.

TABLE A.4. Ordered probit skepticism across administrations (consistency measure)

Variable	TESS 2016	CCES 2017
Consistency	−.13** (.05)	−.16* (.07)
Republican	.11*** (.02)	.09*** (.03)
White	−.35*** (.10)	−.27* (.12)
Female	.03 (.08)	.01 (.11)
Birth year (younger)	.00 (.002)	−.01⁺ (.003)
Education	−.24*** (.04)	−.23*** (.04)
Majority opposition	.01 (.08)	.05 (.11)
Issue	−.13 (.08)	—
N	792	450
LR χ²	76.39***	58.27***

⁺p < .10, *p < .05, **p < .01, ***p < .001 (two-tailed test). Standard errors in parentheses.

TABLE A.5. Probit "credible" response across administrations (consistency measure)

Variable	TESS 2016	CCES 2017
Consistency	-13^{**} (.06)	$.17^{*}$ (.08)
Republican	$-.10^{***}$ (.02)	$-.08^{**}$ (.03)
White	$.37^{***}$ (.11)	$.24^{+}$ (.14)
Female	$-.15$ (.09)	$-.16$ (.13)
Birth year (younger)	.00 (.002)	.00 (.004)
Education	$.26^{***}$ (.05)	$.24^{***}$ (.04)
Majority opposition	.01 (.09)	$-.02$ (.12)
Issue	$-.13$ (.09)	—
Constant	-1.58 (.32)	-9.39 (7.00)
N	792	451
LR χ^2	64.73^{***}	50.92^{***}

$^{+}p < .10$, $^{*}p < .05$, $^{**}p < .01$, $^{***}p < .001$ (two-tailed test). Standard errors in parentheses.

TABLE A.6. Probit "not credible" responses across administrations (consistency measure)

Variable	TESS 2016	CCES 2017
Consistency	$-.11^+$ (.06)	$-.16^+$ (.09)
Republican	$.12^{***}$ (.03)	$.09^{**}$ (.03)
White	$-.30^*$ (.12)	$-.29^+$ (.16)
Female	$-.14$ (.11)	$-.21$ (.14)
Birth year	.00 (.003)	$-.01^+$ (.004)
Education	$-.22^{***}$ (.05)	$-.19^{***}$ (.05)
Majority opposition	.00 (.10)	.08 (.14)
Issue	$-.13$ (.10)	—
Constant	1.01 (.37)	14.69 (8.00)
N	792	451
LR χ^2	47.42^{***}	38.34^{***}

$^+p < .10, ^*p < .05, ^{**}p < .01, ^{***}p < .001$ (two-tailed test). Standard errors in parentheses.

TABLE A.7. Probit "don't know" responses across administrations (consistency measure)

Variable	TESS 2016	CCES 2017
Consistency	−.05 (.06)	−.04 (.08)
Republican	.01 (.02)	.03 (.03)
White	−.18[+] (.11)	−.06 (.14)
Female	.24[**] (.09)	.35[**] (.13)
Birth year	.00 (.003)	−.00 (.004)
Education	−.11[*] (.05)	−.11[**] (.04)
Majority opposition	.01 (.09)	−.02 (.12)
Issue	−.03 (.09)	—
Constant	−.27 (.32)	−4.01 (7.19)
N	792	451
LR χ^2	17.39[*]	15.21[*]

[+]$p < .10$, [*]$p < .05$, [**]$p < .01$, [***]$p < .001$ (two-tailed test). Standard errors in parentheses.

CCES 2019: Team Module Question Wording Regarding Risks and Benefits from Supreme Court Decision-Making

Judging by its recent decisions, do you think the Supreme Court is generally liberal, generally conservative, or is it making decisions more on a case-by-case basis? [Supreme Court—subjective perception; from Bartels and Johnson [2013], used to code subjective agreement with a five-point measure of respondent's ideology.]

    1—generally liberal / 2—generally conservative / 3—case-by-case basis

Many people talk about the US Supreme Court in terms of specific decision-making eras. Since [1945 / 2005], the Supreme Court has made many decisions about individual rights, civil liberties, economic issues, and politics.

In general, how do you think SOCIETY has been influenced by decisions of the Supreme Court in the past [75 / 15] years? [Supreme Court retrospective—society]

    1—benefited a great deal / 2—benefited somewhat / 3—benefited slightly / 4—not really influenced / 5—been hurt slightly / 6—been hurt somewhat / 7—been hurt a great deal

Specifically, how do you think PEOPLE LIKE YOU have been influenced by decisions of the US Supreme Court over the past [75 / 15] years? [Supreme Court retrospective—PLY]

    1—benefited a great deal / 2—benefited somewhat / 3—benefited slightly / 4—not really influenced / 5—been hurt slightly / 6—been hurt somewhat / 7—been hurt a great deal

How much do you think SOCIETY is likely to [benefit from / be hurt by / be influenced by] decisions of the Supreme Court in the NEXT [75 / 15] years? [Supreme Court prospective—society; the order of responses was reversed for the "hurt by" conditions.]

    1—likely to be substantially better off / 2—likely to be somewhat better off / 3—likely to be slightly better off / 4—likely to be

slightly worse off / 5—likely to be somewhat worse off / 6—likely
to be substantially worse off

How much do you think PEOPLE LIKE YOU are likely to [benefit from /
be hurt by / be influenced by] decisions of the Supreme Court in the NEXT
[75 / 15] years? [Supreme Court prospective—PLY; the order of responses
was reversed for the "be hurt by" conditions.]

1—likely to be substantially better off / 2—likely to be somewhat
better off / 3—likely to be slightly better off / 4—likely to be
slightly worse off / 5—likely to be somewhat worse off / 6—likely
to be substantially worse off

Survey Wording 2020 CCES

Some see the current situation in Washington, D.C., including congressional gridlock and events surrounding investigations into the President's conduct, as "politics as usual," but an increasing number of [legal experts / Democratic officials / Republican officials] are arguing that we are in the middle of a *constitutional crisis* that needs to be addressed as soon as possible.

Do you agree that we are currently in a constitutional crisis?
  1—strongly disagree / 2—somewhat disagree / 3—slightly disagree / 4—neutral / 5—slightly agree / 6—somewhat agree / 7—strongly agree

To what extent do you see the following as responsible for the current difficulties in Washington, D.C.?

The President?
  1—not at all responsible / 2—slightly responsible / 3—somewhat responsible / 4—very responsible

Congress?
  1—not at all responsible / 2—slightly responsible / 3—somewhat responsible / 4—very responsible

Democratic officeholders like Nancy Pelosi?
  1—not at all responsible / 2—slightly responsible / 3—somewhat responsible / 4—very responsible

Republican officeholders like Mitch McConnell?
  1—not at all responsible / 2—slightly responsible / 3—somewhat responsible / 4—very responsible

A flawed government system?
  1—not at all responsible / 2—slightly responsible / 3—somewhat responsible / 4—very responsible

To what extent do you believe we should use the following tactics to address the current situation?

Mobilize voters to change officeholders.
> 1—terrible idea / 2—bad idea / 3—neutral / 4—good idea / 5—excellent idea

Amend the Constitution to make specific changes.
> 1—terrible idea / 2—bad idea / 3—neutral / 4—good idea / 5—excellent idea

Call for a constitutional convention to rethink how our system works.
> 1—terrible idea / 2—bad idea / 3—neutral / 4—good idea / 5—excellent idea

How likely do you think it is that the Democratic Party will win the following in the 2020 election?

The presidency?
> 1—very likely / 2—likely / 3—election could go either way / 4—unlikely / 5—very unlikely

A majority in the House of Representatives?
> 1—very likely / 2—likely / 3—election could go either way / 4—unlikely / 5—very unlikely

A majority in the Senate?
> 1—very likely / 2—likely / 3—election could go either way / 4—unlikely / 5—very unlikely

How likely are you to support measures that take the following actions to address current inefficiencies in how our federal government operates?

Alter the powers of the president.
> 1—very likely to oppose / 2—likely to oppose / 3—neutral / 4—likely to support / 5—very likely to support

Alter the powers of Congress.

    1—very likely to oppose / 2—likely to oppose / 3—neutral /
    4—likely to support / 5—very likely to support

Alter the powers of the Supreme Court.

    1—very likely to oppose / 2—likely to oppose / 3—neutral /
    4—likely to support / 5—very likely to support

Make it more difficult for parties in Congress to change the rules to their advantage.

    1—very likely to oppose / 2—likely to oppose / 3—neutral /
    4—likely to support / 5—very likely to support

Change the authority of specific officeholders with respect to foreign affairs.

    1—very likely to oppose / 2—likely to oppose / 3—neutral /
    4—likely to support / 5—very likely to support

Change the Electoral College rules about how the President is elected.

    1—very likely to oppose / 2—likely to oppose / 3—neutral /
    4—likely to support / 5—very likely to support

Change provisions regarding salary and/or benefits for officeholders.

    1—very likely to oppose / 2—likely to oppose / 3—neutral /
    4—likely to support / 5—very likely to support

TABLE A.8. Ordered probit support for changes to presidential powers (no prediction/other excluded category)

	Alter presidential powers	Changes to Electoral College
Expects party to win presidential election	.01 (.08)	.07 (.08)
Expects party to lose presidential election	.45*** (.14)	.33* (.14)
Trump approval	−.41*** (.06)	−.49*** (.05)
Flawed system	.22*** (.04)	.19*** (.04)
Conservative	−.15*** (.05)	−.31*** (.05)
Republican	−.09*** (.03)	−.10*** (.03)
Younger	.00 (.002)	.00 (.004)
Female	.03 (.07)	.34*** (.08)
Education	.01 (.02)	.01 (.03)
White	.18* (.08)	.12 (.08)
N	899	900
Pseudo-R^2	.13***	.21***

*$p < .05$, **$p < .01$, ***$p < .001$ (two-tailed test). Standard errors in parentheses.

2019 CCES Team Module Question Wording Regarding Support for Changes to the Supreme Court

Judging by its recent decisions, do you think the Supreme Court is generally liberal, generally conservative, or is it making decisions more on a case-by-case basis? [Supreme Court—subjective perception; from Bartels and Johnson [2002], used to code subjective agreement with five-point measure of respondent's ideology.]

> 1—generally liberal / 2—generally conservative / 3—case-by-case basis

In the past several years there has been some discussion about making changes to the US Supreme Court. Do you support or oppose making changes to the Supreme Court? [Supreme Court—general change]

> 1—strongly support / 2—somewhat support / 3—slightly support / 4—slightly oppose / 5—somewhat oppose / 6—strongly oppose

I am going to ask you about how much you would support or oppose specific proposals that have been discussed to change the US supreme Court. [Supreme Court–specific changes]

Changing the lifetime term of membership on the Supreme Court to a period of eighteen years. [Term limits]

> 1—strongly support / 2—somewhat support / 3—slightly support / 4—slightly oppose / 5—somewhat oppose / 6—strongly oppose

Electing Supreme Court justices rather than having them appointed by the President. [Electing justices]

> 1—strongly support / 2—somewhat support / 3—slightly support / 4—slightly oppose / 5—somewhat oppose / 6—strongly oppose

Adding several justices to the Supreme Court above its current level of nine.

1—strongly support / 2—somewhat support / 3—slightly support / 4—slightly oppose / 5—somewhat oppose / 6—strongly oppose

Introduction

1. A You Gov/CBS News Poll (June 24–25, 2022) showed 60 percent of Americans disapproved of the court's decision in *Dobbs*.
2. Levinson and Lazare also raise extremely important arguments about how the US Senate has become increasingly malapportioned owing to migration patterns over the nation's history and how that malapportionment gets replicated in both the Electoral College and our amendment processes. In this book I primarily address public support for institutional change, fully acknowledging that other barriers to such change might need to be addressed.

1. Conceptualizing and Studying Perceptions of Appropriate Government Authority and Support for Institutional Change

1. Specifically, Fuller argued laws must be general, widely promulgated, prospective, clear, noncontradictory, reasonable, constant, and enforced consistently to be moral. (See Murphy 2005 for a review of the impact of his arguments.)
2. For instance, one question that has consistently been used to measure diffuse support is: "If the Supreme Court started making a lot of decisions that most people disagree with, it might be better to do away with the Court altogether." Survey respondents who agree with this statement are coded as manifesting lower levels of diffuse support for the court than respondents who disagree with it. A similar question on the scale rather vaguely asks individuals whether they agree with limiting the court's jurisdiction: "The right of the Supreme Court to hear certain types of controversial issues should be reduced."
3. A Pew poll from June 2020 indicates that 74 percent of individuals support the program, and a Vox/Data for Progress poll (conducted in February 2021) indicates 72 percent support for the program (Krogstad 2020; Narea 2021).

2. Exploring How People Think about Government

1. Additionally, prior to securing the national sample used to test assessments of legislative authority, a pilot study using the same experimental manipulations was conducted with a sample using Mechanical Turk workers in Mach 2015. I include results from that experimental administration in the appendix to chapter 2 as further evidence of the replicability of results presented here.
2. Admittedly, bribes and contributions are not commonly attributed as the cause of judicial pronouncements. Both do, however, occur in the US system and can have implications for how people think about the legitimacy of judicial pronouncements. For instance, in 2019 a state court judge in Texas was convicted for taking bribes, which were hidden in in six packs of beer (Karimi 2019). An example of a contribution affecting perceptions is the famous Supreme Court case *Caperton v. A.T. Massey Coal Company* (2009), involving judicial recusals.

3. Using bribes at one end of the continuum and legal criteria at the other specifically allows me to see how individuals react to motives that are clearly illegitimate or legitimate in judicial decision-making. This allows for comparison of how people think about the influence of ideology and contributions with clearly appropriate and inappropriate influences on judgments.

4. I include policy views as a dichotomous factor because I am interested in how such views interact with the direction of the judicial decision. One hundred eighty-four participants indicated support for restricting tuition benefits, 324 did not.

5. Sixty-six percent of participants indicated that the issue of limiting benefits for undocumented individuals was somewhat or very important to them.

6. Although congressional authority to legislate regarding particular matters of public concern has certainly expanded over the past century, cases such as *United States v. Lopez* (1995) and *Morrison v. United States* (2000) illustrate that congressional authority is not limitless.

7. Additionally, to obtain the national TESS sample, a pilot study with the same manipulations was conducted with MTurk participants in March 2015. The ordered probit regression results from that sample are included in the appendix to chapter 2. They serve as evidence of replicability of results as the findings largely confirm the results presented in this chapter.

8. Exploring the predictors of skepticism about constitutional expertise is the subject of the analyses in the following chapter. In the national sample, 43 percent of respondents replied that constitutional law scholars were credible experts, 36 percent were not sure, and another 20 percent expressed the opinion that they were not credible. At any rate, the article for each scenario presents a realistic approximation of how citizens learn about constitutional rules in light of proposed government action.

9. Moreover, for the MTurk sample who received the legislative authority scenarios on gun control and tuition benefits reported in the appendix, correlations between desirability and appropriateness are .76 and .56, respectively.

10. Appendix 2 figures A.1 and A.2 demonstrate the expert consensus and public support variables act in a similar fashion across issue contexts.

11. The proportion of participants expressing support for this proposition was similar to that in the legislative authority study. Here 46 percent of participants indicated they believed experts cited in the article were credible on the issue of executive authority, 33 percent said they did not think so, and 21 percent were not sure. Once more, the responses of all participants are included in the analyses to reflect the fact that such differences of opinion exist in the general population.

12. Sixty-four percent of participants in the sample indicated that the issue of limiting funds to sanctuary cities was somewhat or very important to them.

3. Assessing the Credibility of Constitutional Experts

1. All responses in this book are the complete, verbatim answers of participants explaining either their desirability or legitimacy assessments of actions concerning gun control or immigration. I note which question and which scenario is relevant in the response after each answer.

2. Additionally, Koehler (2016) finds that "balanced" reporting of expert opinion can create a false perception that there is division among experts when there is widespread consensus.

3. The three cases Simon and Scurich (2011) investigate do not involve government powers; moreover, as these authors are primarily interested in experimental treatment effects, they do not control for demographic factors like partisanship or education in their analyses of the credibility afforded to experts.

4. I would love to be able to parse the distinct effects of partisanship, ideology, and feelings about President Trump in this inquiry. As one might expect, measures of presidential approval are highly correlated with both partisanship ($r = .71$ and $.68$) and ideology ($r = .61$ and $.68$) in both experimental administrations. Moreover, the partisanship and ideology are correlated with one another ($r = .61$ and $.66$) such that it precludes their inclusion in the same model. Indeed, if I run separate models using each as an independent variable, they are all significant in credibility assessments, but if I include them together the effects of one (or two) of these closely related variables tend to "wash out" in the in presence of the others. I choose to focus on partisanship, which to some extent reflects, both affinity toward political actors and views of government, but acknowledge that these three concepts are theoretically distinct.

5. To do this the investigation involves both experimental and observational hypotheses. As set forth below, participants were randomly assigned to conditions where expert opinion was divided, or where participants agreed, or disagreed, with consensus expressed by constitutional experts. Thus, controlling for partisanship and the other relevant demographic factors mentioned here is not strictly necessary to test experimental treatment effects. Still, as these demographic variables were measured in both survey instruments and they are *theoretically relevant to this specific inquiry,* including them in my models allows me to observe their influence on credibility assessments as well. This is quite common in experimental research in political science (see, e.g., Nelson, Clawson, and Oxley 1997; Gerber and Green 2000).

6. Arguably, participants might find constitutional experts more credible if a high-prestige law school like Harvard or Yale were invoked. Journalists might not always have access to experts from the most prestigious echelons of academia. Although it is not generally considered one of the nation's top ten, George Washington University has a law school that is nationally recognized; moreover, owing to its location in the nation's capital, its professors are commonly cited in the media. At any rate, this is a constant for all participants across conditions in the experiment involving legislative action.

7. While there not much reason to think majority support will influence assessments of expert credibility, I control for its influence in the analyses.

8. Appendix tables A.3.1 and A.3.2 demonstrate that this is also true across partisanship and agreement conditions in both samples.

9. The appendix to this chapter includes supplementary regression models using a three-level "consistency" measure to reflect agreement with expert consensus for each of the regression models presented here. Results are entirely consistent across both operationalizations.

10. I choose to do separate probit models for each response rather than a multinomial probit of the three-level variable because the analyses are more closely related to my theoretical question. Because I am fundamentally interested in *how people think about credibility,* I am interested in which factors are important in each individual response (yes, no, don't know) rather than the relative risk ratio of a certain type of respondent answering one way or another.

11. This is also true for the consistency variable in the supplemental regressions (tables A.3.3 and A.3.4) in the appendix. It achieves conventional levels of statistical significance in the analyses of credible responses across both experiments, but not in the analyses of "not credible" responses (where it is marginally significant across samples).

4. Examining Justifications for Citizens' Evaluations of Legislative Action on Gun Control and Immigration

1. I only analyze open-ended responses for assessments about legislative authority for this reason. The 2016 TESS survey included prompts asking participants to explain their assessments of authority; the 2017 CCES survey did not.

2. There was some attrition in responses to the legitimacy question because it came in close succession in the survey to the open-ended question asking people to justify their assessment of the desirability of the legislative action. Several of the answers deemed "not responsive" for the legitimacy justification referred to the previous response about desirability.

3. The χ^2 tests in this chapter indicate whether the frequencies observed across comparison groups are significantly different from those that would be expected if the variable was equally distributed across those groups. I do not use statistical tests to compare respondents' desirability and legitimacy responses, as answers were not strictly independent. The two probes came in close succession. Moreover, respondents responding to the desirability question may not have been aware they would have the opportunity to answer and explain questions about the appropriateness of the proposal. I use them here to get an idea of gross differences in responses.

4. The small number of participants who mentioned experts in the immigration scenario makes it difficult to make similar comparisons in that scenario.

5. Valuing Institutions

1. In their 1992 article, Caldeira and Gibson define specific support as "*a set of attitudes toward an institution based on fulfillment of demands for particular policies or action*" (637, emphasis added). While it may be that they were referring to attitudes based on agreement with individual decisional outputs, my point here is that there are *other attitudes* toward an institution that may be relevant in citizens' reactions to court outputs.

2. Three hundred sixty-seven respondents identified as Republicans, 455 identified as Democrats. The traditional seven-point party identification was used to code this variable; party leaners are included as identifying with the relevant party. The confirmatory regression analysis that follows allows us to observe the influence of partisanship along its entire seven-point range.

3. The measure is created by using a cross tab of the respondents' own ideology (rated on a five-point scale) and a three-point measure their subjective perception of the court's decision making that was asked on the team module well before questions about retrospective and prospective benefits.

4. The survey took place in 2019, before the replacement of Ruth Bader Ginsburg on the court or the *Dobbs* decision.

6. Electoral Expectations and Support for Constitutional Change

1. Constitutional reverence is operationalized by agreeing the Constitution "works well today and does not need to be changed" (as contrasted with responding that it needs minor or major revision) in Dawes and Zink (2016, 2022). Brown and Pope (2019) use the seven-point scale measuring respect for the Constitution.

2. Brown and Pope (2019) investigate whether providing information (e.g., amendment rates, word count) about federal and state constitutions can improve citizens' evaluations of these documents on their seven-point battery. Dawes and Zink (2022) borrow this measure to demonstrate that people who exhibit higher level of veneration are more likely to prefer implementing change through statutory means as opposed to constitutional amendments.

3. In this scenario the authors ask people about their preferences over two solutions for addressing a disease in Asia where the problem and solutions are alternatively phrased as saving people versus allowing them to die. Where options are phrased as the number of lives saved, participants tend to pick the sure thing from statistically equivalent outcomes because they are thinking in terms of gains. When phrased as the number of lives lost participants are more likely to choose the risky option because they are thinking in terms of losses.

4. Electoral time horizons differ, of course. An advantage of this study is that it examines electoral prospects in a presidential election year when control of the executive branch and both houses of Congress were to be determined. It is difficult to say how citizens may see their prospects at the next midterm or whether any particular time frame (e.g., two versus four years or even longer) is brought to mind in defining the duration of expected gains versus losses for any individual respondent. Expressed expectations should, however, reflect respondents' risk domain (whether they are in the domain of gains v. losses) at the time of the survey. This is ultimately what is important in assessing how it impacts support for risky strategies and solutions.

5. As with the attributions for responsibility, there are partisan differences in the extent to which citizens are willing to employ these tactics. Democrats expressed a greater willingness to engage in all three strategies than Republican respondents ($p < .001$).

6. In all other instances Democrats expressed more support than Republicans for the proffered change ($p < .001$).

7. Democrats (including leaners) who said Democrats would win are coded as expecting wins, Republicans (including leaners) who said Democrats would win are coded as expecting losses. The opposite is true for Democrats who said their party would lose and Republicans who said the Democrats would win. Independents are coded as "unclear," along with respondents who indicated the race "could go either way"

and people who identified with other political parties, because their preferences for winners between the major parties for president and congressional majorities are unknown.

8. This scheme does not differentiate between people who expect to win both houses and those who expect to win one house and the presidency. Although one could argue there is a difference between the two, I am not able to make such fine distinctions with these data. The basic logic is that people who expect more wins will be more resistant to strategies that involve fundamental change.

9. All predicted probabilities are from the model with both perspectives, all other independent variables held at their mean values.

7. Institutional Prospects

1. In what is commonly referred to as Roosevelt's "court packing plan," the president proposed adding a justice to the Supreme Court for every justice over seventy years. Many have characterized this as an attempt to retaliate for a predominantly conservative court striking down several of his New Deal policies. At the time there were six justices over seventy, which would have resulted in fifteen seats on the court. Ultimately, Roosevelt's plan was not successful.

2. See Macooey and Turner (2019).

3. In retention elections Supreme Court justices could be subject to being voted off the bench after a term of years (Zezima 2015).

4. Amber Phillips, "What Is Court Packing and Why Are Some Democrats Seriously Considering It?," *Washington Post*, October 8, 2020.

5. For instance, given generational differences that have been identified in support for such values (Claassen and Magalhães 2022), one may posit this sort of rebound may work better for older individuals than younger citizens.

6. Caldeira and Gibson have demonstrated that knowledge of the court is related to diffuse support. Those who are more educated should have more knowledge of the court and thus should be more resistant to change.

7. Marquette Law School Supreme Court Poll, conducted September 1–15, 2020 (https://law.marquette.edu/poll/wp-content/uploads/2020/09/MLSPSCOTUS02Toplines.html), accessed October 10, 2020.

8. Following Bartels and Johnston (2013), the measure is created by using a cross tab of the respondents' own ideology (rated on a five-point scale) and a three-point measure of their subjective perception of the court's decision-making that was asked on the team module significantly before questions about retrospective and prospective benefits.

9. Thanks to the anonymous reader who suggested looking at the influence of assessments in support for change across party lines.

Conclusion

1. Admittedly, this same characteristic decreases the ability to generalize from the undergraduate sample to a population of citizens who are more skeptical about accepting the opinion of constitutional authorities. As long as researchers are careful

to acknowledge such limitations, however, I think this speaks to the usefulness of using different types of samples (including undergraduates) to test certain kinds of theoretical expectations.

2. Further testing can help us to determine whether it was the particular policy domain, presidential personality, or an erosion in the importance of rules generally that seemed to magnify the significance of political factors in assessments of unilateral executive action that was evident across experimental administrations.

3. The data in chapter 5 predate *Dobbs*, but some have speculated that the decision will have a strong influence on how women in particular see the court. Thinking about the subjective valuations for the institution by members of different groups might be an interesting way to get at such questions.

4. Of course, all states eventually ratified the document, but unanimity was not a precondition to its authorization.

REFERENCES

Abramowitz, Alan I., and Steven Webster. 2016. "The Rise of Negative Partisanship and The Nationalization of US Elections in the 21st Century." *Electoral Studies* 41: 12–22.

Ackerman, Bruce. 1991. *We the People.* Cambridge, MA: Harvard University Press.

Anderson, Ashley, Dietram A. Scheufele, Dominique Brossard, and Elizabeth A. Corley. 2012. "The Role of Media and Deference to Scientific Authority in Cultivating Trust in Sources of Information about Emerging Technologies." *International Journal of Public Opinion Research* 24(2): 225–37.

Arceneaux, Kevin. 2012. "Cognitive Biases and the Strength of Political Arguments." *American Journal of Political Science* 56(2): 271–85.

Badas, Alex. 2019a. "The Applied Legitimacy Index: A New Approach to Measuring Judicial Legitimacy." *Social Science Quarterly* 100(5): 1848–61.

———. 2019b. "Policy Disagreement and Judicial Legitimacy: Evidence from the 1937 Court-Packing Plan." *Journal of Legal Studies* 48(2): 377–408.

———. 2016. "The Public's Motivated Response to Supreme Court Decision-Making." *Justice System Journal* 37(4): 318–30.

Bartels, Brandon L., and Christopher D. Johnston. 2020. *Curbing the Court: Why the Public Constrains Judicial Independence.* New York: Cambridge University Press.

———. 2013. "On the Ideological Foundations of Supreme Court Legitimacy in the American Public." *American Journal of Political Science* 57(1): 184–99.

Bartels, Brandon L., and Eric Kramon. 2021. "All the President's Justices? The Impact of Presidential Co-Partisanship on Supreme Court Job Approval." *American Journal of Political Science* 66: 171–86.

Bartels, Larry M. 2020. "Ethnic Antagonism Erodes Republicans' Commitment to Democracy." *Proceedings of the National Academy of Sciences* 117(37): 22752–759.

Baum, Lawrence. 2021. *The Supreme Court,* 14th ed. Washington, DC: CQ Press.

Berejikian, Jeffrey D. 2002. "A Cognitive Theory of Deterrence." *Journal of Peace Research* 39(2): 165–83.

Blake, William D., and Ian G. Anson. 2020. "Risk and Reform: Explaining Support for Constitutional Convention Referendums." *State Politics & Policy Quarterly* 20(3): 330–55.

Blake, William D., and Sanford V. Levinson. 2016. "The Limits of Veneration: Public Support for a New Constitutional Convention." *Constitutional Studies* 2: 1–22.

Blank, Joshua M., and Daron Shaw. 2015. "Does Partisanship Shape Attitudes toward Science and Public Policy? The Case for Ideology and Religion." *Annals of the American Academy of Political and Social Science* 658(1): 18–35.

Bolsen, Toby, and James N. Druckman. 2018. "Do Partisanship and Politicization Undermine the Impact of a Scientific Consensus Message about Climate Change?" *Group Processes & Intergroup Relations* 21(3): 389–402.

Braman, Eileen. 2021. "Thinking about Government Authority: Constitutional Considerations and Political Context in Citizens' Assessments of Judicial, Legislative, and Executive Action." *American Journal of Political Science* 65(2): 389–404.

———. 2016. "Exploring Citizen Assessments of Unilateral Executive Authority." *Law and Society Review* 50(1): 189–223.

———. 2009. *Law, Politics and Perception: How Policy Preferences Influence Legal Reasoning.* Charlottesville: University of Virginia Press.

Braman, Eileen, and Beth Easter. 2014. "Normative Legitimacy: Rules of Appropriateness in Citizens' Assessments of Individual Judicial Decisions." *Justice System Journal* 35(3): 239–68.

Braman, Eileen, and J. Mitchell Pickerill. 2011. "Path Dependence in Studies of Legal Decision Making." In *What's Law Got to Do with It? What Judges Do, Why They Do It and What's at Stake,* ed. Charles Gardner Geyh. Stanford, CA: Stanford University Press.

Brown, Adam R., and Jeremy C. Pope. 2019. "Measuring and Manipulating Constitutional Evaluations in the States: Legitimacy versus Veneration." *American Politics Research* 47(5): 1135–61.

Brewer, Marilynn B. 2007. "The Importance of Being We: Human Nature and Intergroup Relations." *American Psychologist* 62(8): 728.

Bybee, Keith J. 2010. *All Judges Are Political Except When They Are Not: Acceptable Hypocrisies and the Rule of Law.* Stanford: Stanford University Press.

Caldeira, Gregory A., and James L. Gibson. 1992. "The Etiology of Public Support for the Supreme Court." *American Journal of Political Science* 36(3): 635–64.

Cann, Damon M., and Jeff Yates. 2016. *These Estimable Courts: Understanding Public Perceptions of State Judicial Institutions and Legal Policymaking.* New York: Oxford University Press.

Carmines, Edward G., and Michael Fowler. 2017. "The Temptation of Executive Authority: How Increased Polarization and the Decline in Legislative Capacity Have Contributed to the Expansion of Presidential Power." *Indiana Journal of Global Legal Studies* 24(2): 369–98.

Carrington, Paul D., and Roger C. Cramton. 2008. "Judicial Independence in Excess: Reviving the Judicial Duty of the Supreme Court." *Cornell Law Review* 94: 587.

Chong, Dennis. 1993. "How People Think, Reason, and Feel about Rights and Liberties." *American Journal of Political Science* 37(3): 867–99.

Christenson, Dino, and David Glick. 2015. "Roberts' Health Care Decision Disrobed: The Micro-Foundations of the Court's Legitimacy." *American Journal of Political Science* 59(2): 403–18.

Christenson, Dino P., and Douglas L. Kriner. 2020. *The Myth of the Imperial Presidency: How Public Opinion Checks the Unilateral Executive.* Chicago: University of Chicago Press.

———. 2017. "Constitutional Qualms or Politics as Usual: The Factors Shaping Support for Unilateral Action." *American Journal of Political Science* 61(2): 335–49.

Claassen, Christopher, and Pedro C. Magalhães. 2022. "Effective Government and Evaluations of Democracy." *Comparative Political Studies* 55(5): 869–94.

Clark, Jason K., and Abigail T. Evans. 2014. "Source Credibility and Persuasion: The Role of Message Position in Self-Validation." *Personality and Social Psychology Bulletin* 40(8): 1024–36.

Cole, Richard L., and John Kincaid. 2006. "Public Opinion on US Federal and Intergovernmental Issues in 2006: Continuity and Change." *Publius: The Journal of Federalism* 36(3): 443–59.

Cole, Richard L., and John Kincaid. 2000. "Public Opinion and American Federalism: Perspectives on Taxes, Spending and Trust." *Publius: The Journal of Federalism* 30: 189–201.

Cole, Richard L., John Kincaid, and Alejandro Rodriguez. 2004. "Public Opinion on Federalism and Federal Political Culture in Canada, Mexico, and the United States, 2004." *Publius: The Journal of Federalism* 34(3): 201–21.

Cramton, Roger C. 2007. "Reforming The Supreme Court." *California Law Review* 95: 1313–34.

Dahl, Robert A. 1957. "Decision-Making in a Democracy: The Supreme Court as a National Policy-Maker." *Journal of Public Law* 6: 279.

Dawes, Christopher T., and James R. Zink. 2022. "Is 'Constitutional Veneration' an Obstacle to Constitutional Amendment?" *Journal of Experimental Political Science* 9(3): 395–406.

Dixon, Richard D., Roger C. Lowery, Diane E. Levy, and Kenneth F. Ferraro. 1991. "Self Interest and Public Opinion toward Smoking Policies: A Replication and Extension." *Public Opinion Quarterly* 55: 241–54.

Doherty, David, and Jennifer Wolack. 2012. "When Do Ends Justify the Means? Evaluating Procedural Fairness." *Political Behavior* 34: 301–23.

Druckman, James N. 2004. "Political Preference Formation: Competition, Deliberation, and the (Ir)Relevance of Framing Effects." *American Political Science Review* 8(4): 671–86.

Druckman, James N., and Mary C. McGrath. 2019. "The Evidence for Motivated Reasoning in Climate Change Preference Formation." *Nature Climate Change* 9(2): 111–19.

Easton, David. 1965. *A Systems Analysis of Political Life.* New York: Wiley.

Eckles, David L., Cindy D. Kam, Cherie L. Maestas, and Brian F. Schaffner. 2014. "Risk Attitudes and the Incumbency Advantage." *Political Behavior* 36(4): 731–49.

Epstein, Lee. and Jack Knight. 1997. *The Choices Justices Make.* Washington, DC: CQ Press.

Epstein, Lee, Andrew D. Martin, Kevin M. Quinn, and Jeffrey A. Segal. 2007. "Ideological Drift among Supreme Court Justices: Who, When, and How Important." *Northwestern University Law Review* 101: 1483.

Epps, Daniel, and Ganesh Sitaraman. 2019. "How to Save the Supreme Court." *Yale Law Journal* 129: 148–206.

Fallon, Richard H. Jr. 2017. "Arguing in Good Faith about the Constitution: Ideology, Methodology, and Reflective Equilibrium." *University of Chicago Law Review* 84: 123–45.

Feldman, Stanley, and Marco R. Steenbergen. 2001. "The Humanitarian Foundation of Public Support for Social Welfare." *American Journal of Political Science* 45(3): 658–67.

Feldman, Stanley, and John Zaller. 1992. "The Political Culture of Ambivalence: Ideological Responses to the Welfare State." *American Journal of Political Science* 36(1): 268–307.

Friedman, Lawrence Meir, and Grant M. Hayden. 2017. *American Law: An Introduction.* New York: Oxford University Press.

Fuller, Lon. 1964. *The Morality of Law.* New Haven: Yale University Press.

Funk, Carolyn L. 2000. "The Dual Influence of Self-Interest and Societal Interest in Public Opinion." *Political Research Quarterly* 53(1): 37–62.

Gangl, Amy. 2003. "Procedural Justice and Evaluations of the Law-Making Process." *Political Behavior* 25: 119–49.

Gauchat, Gordan. 2012. "Politicization of Science in the Public Sphere: A Study of Public Trust in the United States, 1974 to 2010." *American Sociological Review* 77(2): 167–87.

Gerber, Alan S., and Donald P. Green. 2000. "The Effects of Canvassing, Telephone Calls, and Direct Mail on Voter Turnout: A Field Experiment." *American Political Science Review* 94(3): 653–63.

Gerring, John. 2012. "Mere Description." *British Journal of Political Science* 42(4): 721–46.

Gibson, James L. 2015. "Legitimacy Is for Losers: The Interconnections of Institutional Legitimacy, Performance Evaluations, and the Symbols of Judicial Authority." In *Motivating Cooperation and Compliance with Authority,* ed. Brian H. Bornstein and Alan J. Tomkins. Nebraska Symposium on Motivation 62. New York: Springer.

———. 1989. "Understandings of Justice: Institutional Legitimacy, Procedural Justice, and Political Tolerance." *Law and Society Review* 58(2): 469–96.

Gibson, James L., and Gregory A. Caldeira. 2009. *Citizens, Courts, and Confirmations: Positivity Theory and the Judgments of the American People.* Princeton, NJ: Princeton University Press.

Gibson, James L., Gregory A. Caldeira, and Lester Kenyatta Spence. 2003. "The Supreme Court and the US Presidential Election of 2000: Wounds, Self-Inflicted or Otherwise?" *British Journal of Political Science* 33(4): 535–56.

Gibson, James L., Milton Lodge, and Benjamin Woodson. 2014 "Losing, but Accepting: Legitimacy, Positivity Theory, and the Symbols of Judicial Authority." *Law and Society Review* 48(4): 837–66.

Gibson, James L., and Michael J. Nelson, 2016. "Change in Institutional Support for the US Supreme Court: Is the Court's Legitimacy Imperiled by the Decisions It Makes?" *Public Opinion Quarterly* 80(3): 622–41.

———. 2015. "Is the US Supreme Court's Legitimacy Grounded in Performance Satisfaction and Ideology?" *American Journal of Political Science* 59(1): 162–74.

Graham, Matthew H., and Milan W. Svolik. 2020. "Democracy in America? Partisanship, Polarization, and the Robustness of Support for Democracy in the United States." *American Political Science Review* 114(2): 392–409.

Green, Donald Philip, and Ann Elizabeth Gerken. 1989. "Self Interest and Public Opinion toward Smoking Restrictions and Cigarette Taxes." *Public Opinion Quarterly* 53: 1–16.

Haas, Mark L. 2001. "Prospect Theory and the Cuban Missile Crisis." *International Studies Quarterly* 45(2): 241–70.

Hibbing, John R., and Elizabeth Theiss-Morse. 2002. *Stealth Democracy: Americans' Beliefs about How Government Should Work.* New York: Cambridge University Press.

Hodson, Gordon, John F. Dividio, and Samuel L. Gaertner. 2002. "Process in Racial Discrimination: Differential Weighting of Conflicting Information." *Personality and Social Psychology Bulletin* 28(4): 460–71.

Hornsey, Matthew J., and Kelly S. Fielding. 2017. "Attitude Roots and Jiu Jitsu Persuasion: Understanding and Overcoming the Motivated Rejection of Science." *American Psychologist* 72(5): 459–73.

Hornsey, Matthew J., Emily A. Harris, Paul G. Bain, and Kelly S. Fielding. 2016. "Meta-Analyses of the Determinants and Outcomes of Belief in Climate Change." *Nature Climate Change* 6(6): 622–26.

Hovland, Carl Iver, Irving Lester Janis, and Harold H. Kelley. 1953. *Communication and Persuasion.* New Haven, CT: Yale University Press.

Howell, William G., and Terry M. Moe. 2020. *Presidents, Populism, and the Crisis of Democracy.* Chicago: University of Chicago Press.

Huddy, Leonie, Lilliana Mason, and Lene Aarøe. 2015. "Expressive Partisanship: Campaign Involvement, Political Emotion, and Partisan Identity." *American Political Science Review* 109(1): 1–17.

Hurwitz, Leon. 1973. "Contemporary Approaches to Political Stability." *Comparative Politics* 5(3): 449–63.

Hurwitz, Mark S., and Drew Nobel Lanier. 2008. "Diversity in State and Federal Appellate Courts: Change and Continuity across 20 Years." *Justice System Journal* 29(1): 47–70.

Iyengar, Shanto, Yphtach Lelkes, Matthew Levendusky, Neil Malhotra, and Sean J. Westwood. 2019. "The Origins and Consequences of Affective Polarization in the United States." *Annual Review of Political Science* 22: 129–46.

James, Scott C. 2009. "Historical Institutionalism, Political Development and the Presidency." In *The Oxford Handbook of the American Presidency,* ed. George C. Edwards and William G. Howell. Oxford: Oxford University Press.

Johnson, Dawn E. 2004. "Functional Departmentalism and Non-Judicial Interpretation: Who Determines Constitutional Meaning?" *Law and Contemporary Social Problems* 67: 105–47.

Johnston, Christopher D., and Andrew O. Ballard. 2016. "Economists and Public Opinion: Expert Consensus and Economic Policy Judgments." *Journal of Politics* 78(2): 443–56.

Jolley, Daniel, and Karen M. Douglas. 2017. "Prevention Is Better Than Cure: Addressing Anti-Vaccine Conspiracy Theories." *Journal of Applied Social Psychology* 47(8): 459–69.

Kahan, Dan M., Hank Jenkins-Smith, and Donald Braman. 2011. "Cultural Cognition of Scientific Consensus." *Journal of Risk Research* 14(2): 147–74.

Kahneman, Daniel, Jack L. Knetsch, and Richard H. Thaler. 1990. "Experimental Tests of the Endowment Effect and the Coase Theorem." *Journal of Political Economy* 98(6): 1325–48.

Kam, Cindy D. 2012. "Risk Attitudes and Political Participation." *American Journal of Political Science* 56(4): 817–36.

Kam, Cindy D., and E. N. Simas. 2012. "Risk Attitudes, Candidate Characteristics, and Vote Choice." *Public Opinion Quarterly* 76(4): 747–60.

Karimi, Faith. 2019. "A Former Texas Judge Is Convicted for Accepting Cash Bribes Stashed in Beer Boxes." CNN, September 26, 2019.

Kay, Herma Hill. 1991. "The Future of Women Law Professors." *Iowa Law Review* 77: 5.

Kincaid, John, and Richard L. Cole. 2008. "Public Opinion on Issues of Federalism in 2007: A Bush Plus?" *Publius: The Journal of Federalism* 31(3): 469–87.

———. 2001. "Changing Public Attitudes on Power and Taxation in the American Federal System." *Publius: The Journal of Federalism* 31(3): 205–14.

Kinder, Donald R., and D. Roderick Kiewiet. 1981. "Sociotropic Politics: The American Case." *British Journal of Political Science* 11(2): 129–61.

Kinder, Donald R., and Thomas R. Palfrey, eds. 1993. *Experimental Foundations of Political Science.* Ann Arbor: University of Michigan Press.

Koehler, Derek J. 2016. "Can Journalistic 'False Balance' Distort Public Perception of Consensus in Expert Opinion?" *Journal of Experimental Psychology: Applied* 22(1): 24.

Kraft, Patrick W., Milton Lodge, and Charles S. Taber. 2015. "Why People 'Don't Trust the Evidence': Motivated Reasoning and Scientific Beliefs." *Annals of the American Academy of Political and Social Science* 658(1): 121–33.

Krewson, Christopher N., and Jean R. Schroedel. 2020. "Public Views of the US Supreme Court in the Aftermath of the Kavanaugh Confirmation." *Social Science Quarterly* 101(4): 1430–41.

Krogstad, Jens Manuel. 2020. "Americans Broadly Support Legal Status for Immigrants Brought to the U.S. Illegally as Children." Pew Research Center, June 17.

Kunda, Ziva. 1990. "The Case for Motivated Reasoning." *Psychological Bulletin* 108(3): 480–98.

Lasswell, Harold D. 1936 "The *Encyclopedia of the Social Sciences* in Review: *Encyclopedia of the Social Sciences.*" *International Journal of Ethics* 46(3): 388–96.

Lau, Richard R., and David P. Redlawsk. 2006. *How Voters Decide: Information Processing during Election Campaigns.* New York: Cambridge University Press.

Lazare, Daniel. 1996. *The Frozen Republic: How the Constitution Is Paralyzing Democracy.* New York: Harcourt.

Levinson, Sanford. 1988. *Constitutional Faith.* Princeton, NJ: Princeton University Press.

Levinson, Sanford, and William D. Blake. 2016. "When Americans Think about Constitutional Reform: Some Data and Reflections." *Ohio State Law Journal* 77: 211–36.

Levitsky, Steven, and Daniel Ziblatt. 2018. *How Democracies Die.* New York: Broadway Books.

Lipset, Seymor Martin. 1983. *Political Man: The Social Basis of Politics,* 2nd ed. London: Heineman Press.

Lodge, Milton, Kathleen M. McGraw, and Patrick Stroh. 1989. "An Impression-Driven Model of Candidate Evaluation." *American Political Science Review* 83(2): 399–419.

Lodge, Milton, and Charles Taber. 2013. *The Rationalizing Voter.* New York: Cambridge University Press.

Lord, Charles G., Lee Ross, and Mark R. Lepper. 1979. "Biased Assimilation and Attitude Polarization: The Effects of Prior Theories on Subsequently Considered Evidence." *Journal of Personality and Social Psychology* 37(11): 2098–121.

Lowande, Kenneth, and Jon Rogowski. 2021. "Executive Power in Crisis." *American Political Science Review* 115(4): 1406–23.

Maccoey, Skakel, and Samuel Turner. "Former AG Holder Advocates for Court Packing at YLS Event." *Yale Daily News,* March 8, 2019.

MacCoun, Robert J. 1998. "Biases in the Interpretation and Use of Research Results." *Annual Review of Psychology* 49(1): 259–87.

Malhotra, Neil. 2008. "Partisan Polarization and Blame Attribution in a Federal System: The Case of Hurricane Katrina." *Publius: The Journal of Federalism* 38(4): 651–70.

Marshall, William P. 2008. "Eleven Reasons Why Presidential Power Inevitably Expands and Why It Matters." *Boston University Law Review* 88: 505–22.

Masters, Daniel. 2004. "Support and Nonsupport for Nationalist Rebellion: A Prospect Theory Approach." *Political Psychology* 25(5): 703–26.

McDermott, Rose. 2001. *Risk-Taking in International Politics: Prospect Theory in American Foreign Policy.* Ann Arbor: University of Michigan Press.

McGraw, Kathleen M. 2000. "Contributions of the Cognitive Approach to Political Psychology." *Political Psychology* 21(2): 805–32.

McMahon, Kevin J. 2011. *Nixon's Court: His Challenge to Judicial Liberalism and Its Political Consequences.* Chicago: University of Chicago Press.

Mercer, Jonathan. 2005. "Prospect Theory and Political Science." *Annual Review of Political Science* 8: 1–21.

Merkley, Eric. 2020a. "Are Experts (News)Worthy? Balance, Conflict, and Mass Media Coverage of Expert Consensus." *Political Communication* 34(4): 1–20.

———. 2020b. "Anti-Intellectualism, Populism, and Motivated Resistance to Expert Consensus." *Public Opinion Quarterly* 84(1): 24–48.

Milosh, Maria, Marcus Painter, Konstantin Sonin, David Van Dijcke, and Austin L. Wright. 2021. "Unmasking Partisanship: Polarization Undermines Public Response to Collective Risk." *Journal of Public Economics* 204, art. 104538.

Moe, Terry M., and William G. Howell. 1999. "The Presidential Power of Unilateral Action." *Journal of Law Economics and Organization* 15(1): 132.

Mondak, Jeffery J., and Shannon Ishiyama Smithey. 1997. "The Dynamics of Public Support for the Supreme Court." *Journal of Politics* 59(4): 1114–42.

Murphy, Colleen. 2005. "Lon Fuller and the Moral Value of the Rule of Law." *Law & Philosophy* 24: 239–62.

Murphy, Sean D. 1999. "Democratic Legitimacy and the Recognition of States and Governments." *International & Comparative Law Quarterly* 48(3): 545–81.

Murphy, Walter F., and Joseph Tanenhaus. 1973. "Explaining Diffuse Support for the United States Supreme Court: An Assessment of Four Models." *Notre Dame Law Review* 49: 1037.

Mutz, Diana C. 2011. *Population-Based Survey Experiments.* Princeton, NJ: Princeton University Press.

Narea, Nicole. 2021. "Poll: Most Americans Support a Path to Citizenship for Undocumented Immigrants." *Vox*, February 4, 2021.

Nelson, Thomas E., Rosalee A. Clawson, and Zoe M. Oxley. 1997. "Media Framing of a Civil Liberties Conflict and Its Effect on Tolerance." *American Political Science Review* 91(3): 567–83.

Nichols, Tom. 2017. *The Death of Expertise: The Campaign against Established Knowledge and Why It Matters*. New York: Oxford University Press.

Nicholson, Stephen P., and Thomas G. Hansford. 2014. "Partisans in Robes: Party Cues and Public Acceptance of Supreme Court Decisions." *American Journal of Political Science* 58(3): 620–36.

Nisbet, Erik C., Kathryn E. Cooper, and R. Kelly Garrett. 2015. "The Partisan Brain: How Dissonant Science Messages Lead Conservatives and Liberals to (Dis)trust Science." *Annals of the American Academy of Political and Social Science* 658(1): 36–66.

Niv-Solomon, Anat. 2016. "When Risky Decisions Are Not Surprising: An Application of Prospect Theory to the Israeli War Decision in 2006." *Cooperation and Conflict* 51(4): 484–503.

Olson, Mancur. 1965. *Logic of Collective Action: Public Goods and the Theory of Groups*. Cambridge, MA: Harvard University Press.

Petty, Richard E., and John T. Cacioppo. 1986. "The Elaboration Likelihood Model of Persuasion." In *Communication and Persuasion*. New York: Springer, 123–205.

Phillips, Amber. 2020. "What Is Court Packing and Why Are Some Democrats Seriously Considering It?" *Washington Post*, October 8, 2020.

Pornpitakpan, Chanthika. 2004. "The Persuasiveness of Source Credibility: A Critical Review of Five Decades' Evidence." *Journal of Applied Social Psychology* 34(2): 243–81.

Pritchett, C. Herman. 1948. "The Roosevelt Court: Votes and Values." *American Political Science Review* 42(1): 53–67.

Quattrone, George A., and Amos Tversky. 1988. "Contrasting Rational and Psychological Analyses of Political Choice." *American Political Science Review* 82(3): 719–36.

Reeves, Andrew, and Jon C. Rogowski. 2022. *No Blank Check: The Origins and Consequences of Public Antipathy towards Presidential Power*. New York: Cambridge University Press.

Rudolph, Thomas J. 2003. "Who's Responsible for the Economy? The Formation and Consequences of Responsibility Attributions." *American Journal of Political Science* 47(4): 698–713.

Salgado, Sinué, and Dorthe Berntsen. 2019. "My Future Is Brighter Than Yours: The Positivity Bias in Episodic Future Thinking and Future Self-Images." *Psychological Research* 84(7): 1829–45.

Schneider, Saundra K., William G. Jacoby and Daniel C. Lewis. 2010. "Policy Opinion toward Intergovernmental Policy Responsibilities." *Publius: The Journal of Federalism* 41: 1–30.

Schubert, Glendon. 1962. "The 1960 Term of the Supreme Court: A Psychological Analysis." *American Political Science Review* 56(1): 90–107.

Schumacher, Gijs, Marc van de Wardt, Barbara Vis, and Michael Baggesen Klitgaard. 2015. "How Aspiration to Office Conditions the Impact of Government Participation on Party Platform Change." *American Journal of Political Science* 59(4): 1040–54.

Segal, Jeffrey A., and Harold J. Spaeth. 2002. *The Supreme Court and the Attitudinal Model Revisited.* New York: Cambridge University Press.

———. 1993. *The Supreme Court and the Attitudinal Model.* New York: Cambridge University Press.

Shapiro, Robert Y., and John M. Gilroy. 1984 "The Polls: Regulation—Part I." *Public Opinion Quarterly* 48(2): 531–42.

Shen, Francis X., and Dena M. Gromet. 2015. "Red States, Blue States, and Brain States: Issue Framing, Partisanship, and the Future of Neurolaw in the United States." *Annals of the American Academy of Political and Social Science* 658(1): 86–101.

Shepsle, Kenneth A. 2006. "Rational Choice Institutionalism." *The Oxford Handbook of Political Institutions,* ed. R. A. W. Rhodes, Sarah A. Binder, and Bert A. Rockman. Oxford: Oxford University Press, 23–38.

Simon, Dan, and Nicholas Scurich. 2013. "The Effect of Legal Expert Commentary on Lay Judgments of Judicial Decision Making." *Journal of Empirical Legal Studies* 10(4): 797–814.

———. 2011. "Lay Judgments of Judicial Decision Making." *Journal of Empirical Legal Studies* 8(4): 709–27.

Skowronek, Stephen. 1996. *The Politics Presidents Make: Leadership from John Adams to Bill Clinton.* Cambridge, MA: Harvard University Press.

Solum, Lawrence B. 2010. "The Interpretation-Construction Distinction." *Constitutional Commentary* 27: 95.

Stephanopoulos, Nicolas O., and Mila Versteeg. 2016. "The Contours of Constitutional Support." *Washington University Law Review* 94(1): 113–90.

Strother, Logan, and Shana Kushner Gadarian. 2022. "Public Perceptions of the Supreme Court: How Policy Disagreement Affects Legitimacy." *Forum* 20(1): 87–134.

Suhay, Elizabeth. 2017. "The Politics of Scientific Knowledge." In *Oxford Research Encyclopedia of Communication,* ed. Jon Nussbaum. New York: Oxford University Press.

Suhay, Elizabeth, and James N. Druckman. 2015. "The Politics of Science: Political Values and the Production, Communication, and Reception of Scientific Knowledge." *Annals of the American Academy of Political and Social Science* 658(1): 6–15.

Tversky, Amos, and Daniel Kahneman. 1987. "Rational Choice and the Framing of Decisions." In *Rational Choice: The Contrast between Economics and Psychology,* ed. Robin M. Hogarth and Melvin W. Reder. Chicago: University of Chicago Press.

———. 1981. "The Framing of Decisions and the Psychology of Choice." *Science* 211(4481): 453–58.

Tyler, Tom R. 2006. "Psychological Perspectives on Legitimacy and Legitimation." *Annual Review of Psychology* 57: 375–400.

———. 1994. "Governing amid Diversity: The Effect of Fair Decision-Making Procedures on the Legitimacy of Government." *Law & Society Review* 28: 809–32.

———. 1990. *Why People Follow the Law: Procedural Justice, Legitimacy and Compliance*. New Haven: Yale University Press.

———. 1982. "Personalization in Attributing Responsibility for National Problems to the President." *Political Behavior* 4: 379–99.

Tyler, Tom R., and Kenneth Rasinski. 1991. "Procedural Justice, Institutional Legitimacy, and the Acceptance of Unpopular US Supreme Court Decisions: A Reply to Gibson." *Law and Society Review* 25(3): 621–30.

Vis, Barbara. 2011. "Prospect Theory and Political Decision Making." *Political Studies Review* 9(3): 334–43.

———. 2010. *The Politics of Risk: Welfare State Reform in Advanced Democracy*. Amsterdam: Amsterdam University Press.

Von Billerbeck, Sarah, and Birte Julia Gippert. 2017. "Legitimacy in Conflict: Concepts, Practices, Challenges." *Journal of Intervention and Statebuilding* 11(3): 273–85

West, Emily A., and Shanto Iyengar. 2022. "Partisanship as a Social Identity: Implications for Polarization." *Political Behavior* 44(2): 807–38.

Whitehead, Jack L. Jr. 1968. "Factors of Source Credibility." *Quarterly Journal of Speech* 54(1): 59–63.

Whittington, Keith E. 1999. *Constitutional Construction: Divided Powers and Constitutional Meaning*. Cambridge MA: Harvard University Press.

Whittington, Keith E., and Daniel P. Carpenter. 2003. "Executive Power in American Institutional Development." *Perspectives on Politics* 1(3): 495–513.

Zaller, John, and Stanley Feldman. 1992. "A Simple Theory of the Survey Response: Answering Questions versus Revealing Preferences." *American Journal of Political Science* 36(3): 579–616.

Zeisberg, Mariah. 2013. *War Powers: The Politics of Constitutional Authority*. Princeton, NJ: Princeton University Press.

Zezima, Kate. 2015. "Ted Cruz Calls for Retention Elections of Supreme Court Justices." *Washington Post,* June 27.

Zilis, Michael A. 2021. *The Rights Paradox: How Group Attitudes Shape US Supreme Court Legitimacy*. New York: Cambridge University Press.

Zink, James R., and Christopher T. Dawes. 2016. "The Dead Hand of the Past? Toward an Understanding of 'Constitutional Veneration.'" *Political Behavior* 38(3): 535–60.

Zink, James R., James F. Spriggs II, and John T. Scott. 2009. "Courting the Public: The Influence of Decision Attributes on Individuals' Views of Court Opinions." *Journal of Politics* 71(3): 909–92.

INDEX

www.ingramcontent.com/pod-product-compliance
Lightning Source LLC
Chambersburg PA
CBHW030358270326
41926CB00009B/1167